PHILOSOPHY AND ART

**STUDIES IN PHILOSOPHY
AND THE HISTORY OF PHILOSOPHY**

General editor: Jude P. Dougherty

Studies in Philosophy
and the History of Philosophy   Volume 23

Philosophy and Art

edited by Daniel O. Dahlstrom

THE CATHOLIC UNIVERSITY OF AMERICA PRESS
Washington, D.C.

The paper used in this publication meets the minimum
requirements of American National Standards for Information
Science—Permanence of Paper for Printed Library Materials,
ANSI Z39.48-1984.
∞

LIBRARY OF CONGRESS CATALOGING-IN-PUBLICATION DATA
Philosophy and art / edited by Daniel O. Dahlstrom.
      p.   cm. —(Studies in philosophy and the history of
philosophy ; v. 23)
    1. Arts—Philosophy.   2. Aesthetics.   I. Dahlstrom, Daniel O.
II. Series.
BH39.P474   1991
700'.1—dc20
ISBN 978-0-8132-3070-2 (pbk.)
89-77750

Contents

Introduction

The essays in the following collection are marked by a diversity of philosophical styles and perspectives on art. While some authors focus on specific forms of art, others are more concerned with the interpretation given to art by past and contemporary philosophers and artists. In some essays nothing less than the outline of a systematic account of the arts is ventured, even as other authors raise the question of the very possibility of such interpretations or argue for the conditions that must be met by an adequate account or evaluation of the arts. Yet, in one way or another, all the essays address the question of specifying the distinctiveness of artworks or art itself.

Each of the essays in the first group takes a specific genus or object—e.g., theater, television, or painting—as its point of departure, but in each case not without important implications for the way arts in general are to be approached, appreciated, and understood. The second group of essays is a series of challenges to contemporary philosophy of art, mounted from several points of view, though all linked by a concern for the ontological identity of an artwork. In the final group of essays the perspectives of key figures in the history of the modern philosophy of art are traced and brought to bear on contemporary approaches to art.

I

The difference between the story of Oedipus and the work *Oedipus* is the point of departure for *Thomas Prufer*'s explication of the bearing Aristotle's understanding of being, especially in the most privileged sense (*nous*), has on his account of tragedy in the *Poetics* and its relation to the possibilities of understanding human affairs. By excluding what is indeterminate in the events of a story, the maker of the work provides an order where there is none, at least none for Aristotle in contrast to the theodicies of modern philosophies of history. At the same time, the work embellishes the story, giving intelligible point to it, thereby transforming even a terrible event into something for us to see (*eidos*) and contemplate with delight.

Paul Woodruff's essay is a response to the sceptical challenge that it does not make good sense to speak of "understanding theater." Understanding in the proper sense, the sceptic insists, admits a consensus painfully absent among critics and audiences, and real-life understanding does not involve merely playful emotions aroused within the sphere of a few acts. Woodruff argues, to the contrary, that understanding theater is being appropriately moved by the events it represents, events that, whether historical or fictional, objectively have certain emotion-engaging properties. There is, moreover, a web of understanding such that the ability to appreciate events represented on stage is enhanced by the capacity to understand events offstage *and vice versa.* Being appropriately moved, whether by events depicted in the theater or by the events of our own lives, can take a lifetime.

Just as baseball is often considered boring by a baseball ignoramus or a movie is often panned according to standards of the theater, so television is often construed as something unworthy of serious consideration or as chamber cinema. Challenging these prejudices, *Ted Cohen* contends that viewing television need be no more passive than reading or listening to music, and that television is no more affected than any art by commercialism, the limitation of a medium, or the use to which it might be put. Nevertheless, those prejudices do point to the need to raise the question what television is, specifically, what sort of object of appreciation it is, before convincing ourselves that it is good, bad, or indifferent. Cohen suggests that, at least at the present stage of its history, television affords a special capacity for the development and delineation of character, neatly exemplified by the series *Colombo.*

"Does art have its origin in love?" With this question in mind, *Karsten Harries* turns to the roles played by the tales of Narcissus and Pygmalion in attempts to understand art. Alberti's remark, in *On Painting,* that Narcissus is the inventor of painting suggests that at least the origin of Renaissance and post-Renaissance art is indeed the very inversion of love, a pride that, moreover, like the metamorphosis of Narcissus into the perennial, allows the artist to overcome mortality. In other readings, the narcissistic ideal of integral satisfaction leads to a concept of art as a figure of paradise (Marcuse), by way of a necessary, contemplative flight from time and reality (Gide). The story of Pygmalion, Harries contends, provides the necessary corrective to the narcissistic conception of art. The artwork holds a promise of not utopian, but really possible and procreative happiness, and its metamorphosis into a reality is, like Pygmalion's statue, not a work of art.

II

The failure, among philosophers of art, to give accounts of what it is to identify something as an artwork or even what it is to function as an artwork, together with the postmodernist challenge to the very possibility of such accounts, forms the point of departure for *Joseph Margolis's* essay on the nature of art's nature. Certain minima of discourse (reference and predication), Margolis argues, make possible theorizing about art, within and across historical horizons, without privileging any particular account as to art's nature. Multiple, even mutually inconsistent ontologies are advantageous, so long as they contribute to the pursuit of a more adequate model of what we altogether empirically (historically and contingently) take artworks to be. Given the untenability of both reductive and nonreductive physicalisms, Margolis argues for the necessity of countenancing culturally emergent, indissolubly complex, and physically embodied entities, among which are artworks.

Contemporary aestheticians are often reluctant to attempt to define and systematically classify works of art or to determine their objective properties and distinctive modes of being. Relying on principles of Aristotelian-Thomistic metaphysics, *Francis J. Kovach* sets for himself precisely these tasks. After singling out the purpose (beauty) distinguishing works of fine art from other artworks, Kovach argues that each work of fine art falls into one of only four possible genera, yielded by the dichotomies of being either physical or mental and either creative or reproductive. Whereas all physical works of art (visual artworks and artistic performances) are singular, original compositions and their interpretations (the two mental genera) have the character of genus and species respectively. Objectively, Kovach argues further, physical works of fine art have a completeness and immultiplicability absent in even the greatest mental artworks. In conclusion Kovach addresses the question of the mode of being proper to artworks in each genus.

Contemporary thinkers have been scrambling to find a theoretical framework to accommodate Marcel Duchamp's readymades within a philosophy of art. That this effort has had mischievous consequences for the philosophy of art and, not least, for the distinction between philosophy and art, is the thesis of *John Brough's* essay. While agreeing with George Dickie's contention that artworks must be made, Brough argues that Dickie's attempts to countenance readymades as artworks confuses artifactuality and utensility. Brough then turns to Arthur Danto for whom, again under the influence of readymades, what singles something out as an artwork is, not an appropriately intended making, but rather a relation to an interpretation. Danto's account of interpretation, Brough contends, is notoriously vague. The idea that interpretation confers the status of art on an object is, moreover, at odds with the normal sense of 'interpretation,' the object of which is already presumed to be an artwork. At the cost of readymades, Brough argues that the appropriate criterion of an artwork is that something be *made* with the *intention* that it be art. In conclusion Brough suggests that such a criterion, belonging to the philosophy of art, preserves the integrity of both art and philosophy.

Taking his cues from what is meant to be noticed but overlooked in artworks, *Kenneth Schmitz* argues for the essential significance of artistic boundaries in the constitution of artworks. Like any boundary, an artwork's boundaries both separate it from and join it to the rest of the world. Yet artistic boundaries, Schmitz contends, are neither simply physical nor imaginary, neither static nor characteristic of everything that calls itself 'art.' Artistic boundaries define alone those artifacts that have culturally gained a certain density of form, content, and meaning. Thus, Schmitz concludes, various kinds of institutions— playwrights, actors, audiences, and critics—are part of the boundaries that mediate between artworks and others (including other artworks).

That works of art are one sort of creation and that the beauty pertinent to them is one of many prospective excellences capable of guiding and controlling a creative process is the starting point of *Paul Weiss's* reflections on beauty in art. After differentiating natural beauties from the beauty of artworks, Weiss argues that the tight unity of the latter distinguishes them from copies and forgeries. The significance of this unity for the novelty, boundaries, and materials of artworks is also elaborated. In conclusion Weiss explicates the delicate relation obtaining between the created beauties of artworks and their creators and appreciators.

III

Kant's mature aesthetics is elaborated as part of a critique of teleological as well as aesthetic reflective judgments, a critique that also addresses unfinished business and unresolved issues at various junctures of his theoretical and practical philosophy. The first step in *Robert Wood's* study of aesthetics in the Kantian project is to identify this systematic context by way of introducing the notion of purposiveness as the organizing principle of the *Critique of Judgment*. The stage is then set for unpacking Kant's treatments of beauty, sublimity, and the relations obtaining between art and nature and between aesthetic and moral sensibilities. Wood concludes by linking two notions he considers pivotal, not only to the *Critique of Judgment,* but to the whole Kantian enterprise: nature as the creation of divine art and sublimity as the emotional ground of the critical project.

As suggested by his own attempts to combine scientific and popular styles in a "beautiful literary manner," Friedrich Schiller subscribes to the aesthetic ideal of the unity of reason and imagination, to a kind of human self-conception by means of art. *Walter Hinderer* demonstrates that this ideal, under one formulation or another, was in fact a constant preoccupation for Schiller, from his youthful writings to his major philosophical works, most notably, *On Naive and Sentimental Poetry.* In Hinderer's account, this 'anthropological aesthetics,' as he aptly dubs it, not only embraces an ideal fundamental to the educational program of the eighteenth century, but also entails a utopian method for criticism of social and physical realities.

In a sketch of the metaphysical character of the issue of aesthetic origins, *William Desmond* notes the troubling questions about the status of otherness raised by the modern turn to the consciousness of artist and aesthete. That turn is both radicalized and reformed by Hegel, for whom art is a process of self-mediation in which the spirit comes through otherness to knowledge of itself. This process, Desmond shows, is elaborated by Hegel both at the level of the individual and at the level of the historical world as a whole in the development from Symbolic to Classical and Classical to Romantic art. Paradoxically, Hegel would have this development demonstrate precisely the aesthetic limits to overcoming otherness and consequently the need to move beyond art to religion and philosophy. Desmond, however, suggests that a quite different inference can be drawn from this development, namely, the existence of a radical sort of otherness, ultimately recalcitrant to the absolute claims of dialectical self-mediation and Hegelian self-knowledge to comprehend completely all otherness.

My own essay begins with a consideration of the extent to which art appears increasingly to take the place of religion, beyond the limits of science, in the contemporary world. The emergence of the relative autonomy of the arts is something that contemporary philosophers too often have ignored in their efforts to explicate the distinctive identity of art and artworks. Only by explaining the religion of art, I argue, can the identity of art be explained. In conclusion one mode of such an explanation is sketched on the basis of remarks made in the early phases of German idealism.

***

Most of the essays in this collection were delivered in the lecture series *Philosophy and Art,* sponsored by the Matchette Foundation at The Catholic University of America, Fall 1988. In addition, William Desmond, Francis J. Kovach, and Paul Weiss were invited to write original compositions for this collection. The completion of my essay, *The Religion of Art,* was made possible by the support of the Humboldt Foundation (Bonn). I would also like to thank Ms. Susan Needham for her fine work as copyeditor of this volume.

D.O.D.

PHILOSOPHY AND ART

1   Providence and Imitation: Sophocles's *Oedipus* and Aristotle's *Poetics*

THOMAS PRUFER

I

King Laius and Queen Jocasta of Thebes have a son, Oedipus. The oracle of Apollo foretells that the son will kill his father. In order to prevent the fulfillment of the oracle, the infant's two feet are pierced and bound together, and he is given to a shepherd to be left on Mount Cithaeron to die. Out of pity the shepherd does not leave the child to die but gives him to a fellow shepherd, who in turn gives him to childless King Polybus and Queen Merope of Corinth.

Years pass.

A man who had too much to drink tells Oedipus that he is not the son of Polybus and Merope. Oedipus asks the oracle of Apollo at Delphi whose son he is. The oracle does not answer his question but says that he will kill his father and marry his mother. Oedipus, in order to prevent the fulfillment of the oracle, does not return to Corinth. Measuring the way by the stars, he goes to Thebes, where he cleverly solves the riddle of the Sphinx, saving the city from the Strangler, the One Who Binds. (The answer to the riddle is "man.") Oedipus is made king of Thebes, in place of King Laius, who, on his way to the oracle of Apollo at Delphi, had been killed at a place where one road becomes two (or two roads become one), killed together with all those with him except one, a slave who escaped.

Oedipus marries Jocasta, Laius's widow and the queen of Thebes.

A plague is destroying Thebes. Oedipus sends Creon, Jocasta's brother, to the oracle of Apollo. The oracle says that in order to save the city the murderer of Laius must be discovered. Oedipus calls down a curse on the one who has stained the city. Tiresias, a blind seer of Apollo, discloses to Oedipus that Oedipus himself is the murderer of the king and the polluter of the city. Oedipus suspects Tiresias of being used by Creon in a plot to overthrow him. Oedipus and Tiresias taunt each other's blindness with angry words. Tiresias calls the origin of Oedipus into question. Oedipus angrily accuses Creon of undermining him by false oracles in order to gain the city.

In deprecation of all oracles, Jocasta tells Oedipus that the oracle foretelling the death of Laius was false because Laius was killed not by his own son but by foreign robbers at a place where two roads become one (or one road becomes two). Oedipus remembers that on his way from Delphi to Thebes he killed in anger with a staff at just such a place. The slave who escaped is sent for; he is to say whether many or only one killed.

A messenger comes from Corinth to tell Oedipus that King Polybus is dead (and so the oracle of parricide seems false) and that Oedipus will be king of Corinth. But Oedipus fears returning to Corinth because of the oracle of incest. In order to quiet this fear, the messenger tells Oedipus that he is not the son of Polybus and Merope: many years ago the messenger himself gave them the child Oedipus. While shepherding on Mount Cithaeron he in turn had been given the child by another shepherd. The Theban slave who escaped the killing is that very same shepherd. The slave says that he in turn had been given the child by Jocasta, who wished it killed in order to prevent the fulfillment of the oracle. The outsider become king is shown to be born to the throne and to be the source of the stain by uniting with his origin.

Jocasta hangs herself.

Oedipus blinds himself. He still wishes to be touched and to touch. He goes with a staff, leaning and probing.

Creon will ask the oracle of Apollo if Oedipus is to be banished from the city of Thebes.

Thebes is cleansed. Both oracles are shown to have been true. The prophet Tiresias and the ruler Creon are vindicated.

II

What is the difference between the story of Oedipus and the work *Oedipus*? In the tragedy the events are not narrated, they are presented; more exactly, they are represented; they are not spoken about, but displayed; more exactly, they are played. The players who display the action, the actors who act out the action, are transformed and embellished by mask and costume; their words and gestures are transformed and embellished by meter, music, and dance. But it is the plot which is the soul and perfection (*telos*)[1] of the work. The action dis-

1. 50a22–23, 38–39 = *Poetics* 1450 Kassel.

played in and through the plot is embedded in a matrix of antecedent and concurrent and consequent events which are not displayed; these events are either narrated or simply left out. The plot has a beginning, a moment artificially without antecedents, and an end, a moment artificially without consequents. Not everything that happens to someone or during a time is displayed; and nothing is displayed that happens merely after something: in the display what happens happens because of what has happened before. In the work nothing is left to chance, although in the story, in the matter of the artifice by which the poet constructs the work, a great deal happens by chance.

The work is an imitation of action. As an imitation of action, it limits the indefinite context of antecedent and concurrent and consequent actions, and it tightens the episodic sequence of actions to a pattern, a "syntax" (*systasis, synthesis*), an orderedness. The result is a completeness to which nothing can be added and from which nothing can be taken away, an articulated whole, neither too large nor too small to be well taken in all together by a gaze or a look (*eusynopton*). This completeness is a likeness of organic wholeness and necessity, a likeness of the wholeness and necessity in the relations of the parts of animals to one another. The limiting and tightening by means of the imitating work fit the action imitated in and through the work for contemplation which delights. This contemplation is not reducible to constating the verisimilitude of the work; much less is it for the sake of exhortation to virtuous action.[2] In what then do we take delight when we contemplate this imitation of action, this display of events in and through a work constructed by the artifice of the poet?

"Why should we honor the gods in song and dance (*choreuein*)?

"Why should we go to Delphi, the center of the world, . . . if concord between oracle and event be not displayed for all to see?"[3]

"It is rightly (*orthōs*) done when the poet misrepresents the way things are by presenting the impossible—if this happens because of the purpose and perfection (*telos*) of the work. . . . But not rightly, if not. . . ."[4]

The first quotation is from Sophocles's *Oedipus*; the second quotation is from Aristotle's *Poetics*. In the first quotation the chorus breaks out of the role it plays as the Elders of Thebes and speaks as itself, the means for representing or imitating the Elders of Thebes. (There is a moment in Aristophanes's *Clouds* that startles in a comparable way: the leader of the chorus steps out of the role he plays as Cloud

2. 60b13–15.
3. *OT* 896, 901–2 = *Oedipus Tyrannus*; cf. *OT* 1086, 1094.
4. 60b23–28; cf. 33.

and speaks as Aristophanes, the author—or as a facsimile of the author.) In the second quotation Aristotle is concerned with the casuistry of verisimilitude, with how we are to judge cases in which the imitation misrepresents the way things are. Comparing tragedy and painting, he gives two examples: a painter paints a horse with both right legs lifted up and put forward;[5] a painter paints a doe or hind with horns.[6] (Both examples are examples of misrepresentation of the animal world.)

What is the relation between these two quotations, the one from *Oedipus* and the other from *Poetics*? In order to understand the relation between the two quotations, consider the first quotation in the light of another quotation from *Oedipus* and consider the second quotation in the light of another quotation from *Poetics*:

"Zeus and Apollo, minding (*xunetoi*)[7] and knowing (*eidotes*) human affairs. . . ."[8]

"Sweetening the work with other good things, the poet thereby covers over and keeps out of sight (*aphanizei*) the out-of-place (*atopon*) [whatever lacks *logos* (*alogon*)]."[9]

The themes of these two quotations are brought together by Aristotle in a single passage.[10] In discussing the use of "the machine," he speaks of events "outside the representation (*drama*), either having happened before, but being such that they could not be humanly known, or having not yet happened and being knowable only by prophecy. (For we hold that all things are seen by the gods.) There should be nothing *alogon* in the events, or if there be, let it be outside the representation (*tragōidia*), as in *Oedipus* of Sophocles. . . . It is necessary to imitate the skilled makers of likenesses: they reproduce the proper features or the look of the originals, at the same time making them look more beautiful."

To speak bluntly, there is no place in Aristotle's philosophy for the gods, although he recognizes and gives importance to the longstanding and widespread belief in the gods, and he calls excellent being and most excellent being "divine"; indeed, the most privileged sense of being he calls in an honorific way "god." But that most privileged sense of being has no knowledge of and no concern for anything lesser or lower than its own excellence; and a fortiori it has no knowledge

5. 6ob18–19.
6. 6ob31–32.
7. Cf. Heraclitus, fr. 114 Diels/Kranz.
8. *OT* 499–500; cf. 904: *mē lathoi*; 1191–92.
9. 6ob1–2.
10. 54b2–11.

of and no concern for the indeterminacy of choice and chance, the choice and chance which are so much a part of human affairs.

For Aristotle there is no truth about the future insofar as the future depends on choice and chance.[11] (It is not that the truth about the future is not known; there simply is no truth about the future to know.) The future is indeterminate and therefore unpredictable insofar as what will be depends on which of two alternatives, neither of which has yet been chosen, will indeed be chosen. And a chance event has no intelligibility of its own, but rather a borrowed intelligibility, an intelligibility borrowed from the intelligibility of the two teleological lines whose intersection results in the chance event. Virtue gives a kind of intelligibility to choice, and luck gives a kind of intelligibility to chance. We rightly expect the virtuous agent to choose in the future to do the virtuous deed, as he has done virtuous deeds in the past. This reliability of virtue lends intelligibility to the indeterminacy of choice, just as luck lends intelligibility to some chance events, insofar as a chance event is such that it could have been purposed, although it comes about by chance and not on purpose. Nevertheless, for Aristotle both choice and chance, and therefore the course of human affairs, lack intrinsic intelligibility.[12]

In *Oedipus,* on the other hand, an oracle has been spoken over future choice and chance; a word has been spoken, a *fatum,* a word that tells what the future will be. The action represented in *Oedipus* is the discovery that the oracle has indeed been fulfilled, that the word has been truly spoken. The discovery of the truth of the oracle vindicates the gods and cleanses the city. This prophetic word, which manifests the bond or nexus between past and future, comes from the gaze of the gods. There is a collecting look turned toward human affairs: there is a *xunon* and an *eidos* of human affairs. Providence,[13] foreseeing by a gaze or a look, makes possible prophecy or prediction, foretelling by a word. The gods "mind" human affairs: human affairs have the look of being looked at by the look of the gods.

In *Oedipus*[14] just before the reversal that comes about in the course

---

11. *On Interpretation* IX.

12. The intelligibility appropriate to (a) the artifact tragedy differs from the intelligibility exercised by (b) the virtuous agent (*phronimos, spoudaios*) and from the intelligibility thematized by Aristotle in (c) the book *Nichomachean Ethics* (1103b27–29). Each of these three intelligibilities is contrasted with its correlative lack of intelligibility: (a′) the indefinite and episodic sequence of actions, (b′) incontinent and vicious actions, (c′) false "theories" about actions; cf. Kant, *Foundation of the Metaphysics of Morals* 404ff. and *Nicomachean Ethics* 1105b12–14.

13. *OT* 978.

14. *OT* 977–78; cf. 709, 723–24, 857–58, 946–47, 953, 971–72.

of the announcement by the Corinthian messenger that the king of
Corinth, thought to be the father of Oedipus, is dead, just before the
discovery that what seemed to show the falsity of the oracle has led to
the discovery of the opposite, the truth of the oracle, just before Jocasta's recognition of the truth of the oracle, Jocasta, in order to quiet
Oedipus's fear that the oracle could be true, calls on the rule of
chance[15] and rejects providence (*pronoia*) together with the prophecy
it makes possible.

In *Poetics* Aristotle, after recalling the opinion that the gods see all
things, rejects the *alogon* in events insofar as they are represented in
the well-made tragedy,[16] just as he bans from representation in the
plot events related to one another by chance.[17]

It is wondrous, most wondrous, says Aristotle—and we delight in
the wondrous[18]—when what is at first displayed and shown as being
without *logos,* as happening merely by chance, turns out, against the
first display and show (*doxa*), to have come about because of something
else that happened before.

For Aristotle being is not episodic, like a poorly constructed tragedy;[19] being is not helter-skelter, not one thing after another without
being because of another; being is not a mere heap (*sōros*).[20] The
unifying plot of being, so to speak, is the eros[21] by which that which
is less than excellent or not most excellent is drawn toward the most
excellent. But the most excellent, because it is most excellent and
therefore ignorant of the lesser and the lower, is without knowledge
of human affairs in their indeterminacy. For Aristotle there is no
nonhuman gaze, no divine gaze, no gaze of the gods in and for and
through which the scatteredness and the indefiniteness and the for-
tuitousness, that is, the unintelligibility of human affairs, are drawn
into intelligibility, that display of unity and definition and necessity
for which there is no better word than *eidos*. For Aristotle the *eidos* of
human affairs is an artificial *eidos*, the artifact tragedy, the plot constructed by the artifice of the poet. The gaze of the gods, the collecting
gaze which binds together, the gaze which takes in what is past and
passing and to come,[22] has for Aristotle no philosophical equivalent.

15. Cf. the view rejected in *Physics* II, 8 & 9.
16. 54b5–7.
17. 59a24; 51b34–35; 50b32–33, 36.
18. 60a11–14, 17, 27–29; 52a4–7; 55a16–18.
19. *Metaphysics* 1076a1; 1090b19–20.
20. *Metaphysics* 1040b8–9; 1041b11–12; 1044a4–5; 1045a8–14.
21. *Metaphysics* 1072b3; 1075a18–19.
22. 59b19–20; cf. 59a32–33; 50b38–51a2, 4, 10–11; cf. *Politics* 1326b24; *Rhetoric*
1409a35–b4.

But it is the unity of this gaze which the tragedy *Oedipus* celebrates ("Why should we sing and dance if there is no providence of human affairs?"). For Aristotle the *eidos* of artifacts is in the soul of the artificer;[23] there is an *eidos* of human affairs, but it is not in the gaze of the gods; rather it is in the soul of the poet, the artificer of tragedy, tragedy whose plot adds necessities and sets boundaries and thereby excludes the too much and the too little, the indefinite. Aristotle says in speaking of "god," the most excellent and most privileged sense of being, that "there are some things it is better not to see;"[24] but tragedy displays for our eyes the obscene and speaks for our ears the nefarious.[25] Just as the indefinite is transformed by the limiting *eidos* of the constructed plot, and the fortuitous is transformed by the artificial "syntax" or orderedness according to which one represented event follows with necessity (or probability) what precedes it, so the obscene and the nefarious are transformed by the beauty[26] of the imitating medium. This transformation of the indefinite and the fortuitous and of the obscene and the nefarious is the Aristotelian equivalent of the "theodicies" of modern "philosophies of history." Plot is the artificial form of action: *mythos* is the artificial *eidos* of *praxis*. This is the Aristotelian equivalent of "philosophies of history," but it differs crucially from "philosophies of history" because this *eidos* of human affairs is artificial—and known to be artificial.

The plot constructed by the poet is neither a slavish copy of the action it imitates, nor an autonomous structure, a structure set up on its own as a law unto itself, a structure in its own right, freed from its model: plot is not "abstract" art. Aristotle understands imitation as something between these two extremes, copy or reproduction, on the one hand, and structure in its own right, on the other hand. Let us call that something between the extremes, for want of a better word, reflux.

The poet selects and organizes. The artifact he thus constructs gives unity and completeness, definition (*horos*)[27] and limitation (*peras*), necessity and orderedness to a scattered, indefinite, and loose "subject" matter. This selecting and organizing is the relation between the art of the poet and its matter, action. But because the constructed plot remains an imitation, an imitation of action, the artificial unity, definiteness, and necessity of the imitation reflux back on the imitated

23. *Metaphysics* 1032b1, 23; 1034a24.
24. *Metaphysics* 1074b32–33.
25. *OT* 1312; cf. 1224, 1334–39, 1430–31; cf. *Oedipus Coloneus* 1641–42.
26. 50b34ff.
27. 49b14; 51a6, 10, 15; 59b18.

action, thus unifying, defining, and ordering the action itself: the artificial imitation refluxes on the imitated action itself as imitated, as itself (re)presented in and through the unified, definite, and ordered imitation. The spectators gaze on action itself as (re)presented in and through the transforming and embellishing artifact constructed by the poet.

It is precisely because the discrimination of characteristics proper to the plot from the action imitated by and thus displayed in and through the plot is derivative and secondary that the artifice of the plot transforms the represented events themselves into an *eidos*. The action itself is displayed for us to see, but the action we see is heightened and sharpened by the means or medium in and through which it is there for us to see. The relation between the imitation and what it imitates is irreducible to verisimilitude, but this does not mean that the imitation is indifferent to the truth of what it imitates. The original is enriched, not distorted, by its image.[28] The imitated action is heightened and sharpened by the imitation into being more truly itself than it would be if it were not imitated and thus made available for contemplation in and through the transforming imitation.

What is displayed and that in and through which it is displayed are not split off from each other. Such a splitting off or amputation results in *membra disjecta*: "the aesthetic," on the one hand, and "the historical" or "the moral," on the other hand; but this modern opposition is foreign to Aristotelian imitation, which lives in the integrity of display and being displayed, show and being shown.

Tragedy displays the terrible, and this display of the terrible gives

---

28. For Aristotle the primary sense of *ousia*, the sense of *ousia* toward which all other senses tend, is *eidos*. Book Zeta of *Metaphysics* is the key to understanding *Poetics*. See *Metaphysics* 1030a6–9, b7–11; 1032a1–4; *sōros* ("heap"): 1040b8–9; 1041b11–12; 1044a4–5; 1045a8–14. What comes to be called "history" is a *sōros*; tragedy is an *eidos*. ". . . (things) drawn by art differ from true (things) by gathering together into one the scattered (things) (which are) separately. . . ." *Politics* 1281b12–13; cf. *Metaphysics* 1065a24–26: *atakta, apeira*.

The tension between the imitating plot and the actions that the plot imitates is like the tension in Book Zeta between (a) form as form itself and not *kat' allou* (1030a11), not *en allō* (1037b3–4), form as *tode ti* (form "in some important sense a this"—but not a particular), on the one hand, and (b) form as form in matter, form as form said of matter ("in some extended sense a predicate"—but not a predicate said of a particular), on the other hand. See John Driscoll, "EIΔH in Aristotle's Earlier and Later Theories of Substance," in *Studies in Aristotle*, ed. D. J. O'Meara, *Studies in Philosophy and the History of Philosophy*, 9 (Washington, D.C.: The Catholic University of America Press, 1981), 156.

As the subject matter action (*praxis*) is to the artifice plot (*mythos*), so *hypokeimenon* is to *eidos*. Cf. Pindar, *Nemea* VII 20–22: ". . . through sweet-speaking Homer the *logos* of Odysseus became more than what happened."

delight, the delight proper[29] to tragedy. How is it possible to delight in the terrible? The imitated terrible is *aufgehoben,* retained and transformed in and through the beauty of the imitating artifact which contains it, offering it as thus formed and transformed to a contemplation which delights in what it sees.

The expression "what it sees" is irreducibly ambiguous. It means as a unity both the moving and once-and-for-all-and-never-again action, the terrible action imitated, and the unchanging and repeatable imitation, the beautiful imitation in and through which the terrible action is imitated. Thus the delight proper to the contemplation of tragedy is delight in the terrible as displayed in and through a beautiful imitation.[30]

And just as delight is a kind of accompaniment of achieving (*energeia*), but sharpens what it accompanies and depends on,[31] so the artifact tragedy, the imitation of action, depends on its paradigm, action as lived, but this imitation adds a sharpness, a "point," to the imitated original which it thereby exceeds.[32]

Aristotle tells us that, because of an indefiniteness (*aoristia*)[33] of matter, natural processes lack teleological precision and that art sharpens (*epitelei*)[34] nature and brings it to completeness when nature itself fails to work through to its appropriate completeness.[35] Action too as lived lacks definiteness; but the art of tragedy heightens and sharpens action for display to mind avid for intelligibility, mind avid for unity and limitedness and connectedness.

Gazing on the artificial *eidos* of human affairs displayed in tragedy, this mind remembers the gaze of the gods, a gaze which has become for Aristotle only a longstanding and widespread opinion, a mere opinion shown up as such in the light of the rare knowledge of the most excellent and most privileged sense of being, separate mind unmindful of human affairs, separate mind knowing and enjoying its own excellence, that highest sense of being toward which human mind, which is somehow all things and not only the highest things, is turned in eros. It is this same eros which takes delight in the contemplation of the terrible in human affairs transformed by the form of tragedy.

29. 52b32–33; 53a35–36, b10–14; 59a21.
30. 48b10–11; 53b12.
31. *Nicomachean Ethics* 1174b31–33; 1175b13–14.
32. 61b13–14.
33. *On the Generation of Animals* 778a5–9; cf. *Metaphysics* 1037a27; 1065a24–26; *Rhetoric* 1409b2; cf. 51a17.
34. *Physics* 199a15–16.
35. *Protreptic,* fr. 11 Ross.

III

"What is drawn on a panel or incised on a tablet is both living (thing) [what-is-portrayed] and likeness: same-and-one and both [the two]; nevertheless the to-be is not the same to both, and there is gazing (*theōrein*) on [it/them] both as living (thing) and as likeness. . . ."[36]

All signs are irreducibly ambivalent; one sign is two: both signifier and signified. The sign (re)presents the signified in and through the signifier. Both words and pictures are signs; tragedy as an imitation of action is a sign that signifies action in a way that has something in common with the way words and pictures signify. Every signifier has characteristics of its own, characteristics proper to it, which are nevertheless in the service of signifying the signified.

The irreducible ambivalence of the sign consists in the polarity between "proper to . . . ," on the one hand, and "in the service of . . . ," on the other hand. The signifier is transparent in relation to its signified, but reflection can bring to the fore and discriminate the proper characteristics of the signifier, the structure it has in its own right.

To say that tragedy is an imitation of action is to say that tragedy is a sign whose signifiers are in the service of signifying the signified of tragedy, action. The proper characteristics of the most important signifier of tragedy, plot, are selection and organization, limiting and tightening, definition and necessity. Although reflection can bring to the fore and discriminate these proper characteristics for themselves, nevertheless, because they are first and primarily transparent in the service of (re)presenting action, they transform action itself as (re)presented.

36. *On Memory and Recollection* 450b21–23.

Understanding Theater

PAUL WOODRUFF

de te fabula narratur
    Horace

Tis a knavish piece of work, but what of that?
Your majesty, and we that have free souls,
it touches us not.
    Hamlet, III.ii

My question is why it makes sense to speak of understanding a particular work of theater, *Miss Julie*, for example, or *Chorus Line*. We do speak of understanding theater often enough: a teacher will wonder if her students understand *Antigone*; a critic will ask whether a director understands the plays he stages; and one day I hope to be able to say that I understand the first scene of *King Lear*. But a number of skeptical difficulties bristle around this way of talking. If a work of theater is to be understood, then, for example, understanding it ought to be the same for everyone and on all occasions. But understanding Euripides's *Bacchae* would seem to be different on different occasions, depending on how the play is produced, and different for different people, depending on what experiences they bring to the theater.

The skeptical difficulties I have in mind are not specific to theater, but are similar to general ones raised in the Ten Modes of Aenesidemus. Still, they are especially hard to answer in the case of theater. Here I am looking for answers not to global skepticism, but to skepticism about understanding theater. The skeptic to whom I wish to reply is a moderate one: he concedes that many things can be understood, but theater cannot. Similarly, he would say, many things can be heard, but colors cannot.

In this paper I try to show that if anything in life can be understood, then good theater can be understood as well. Being understandable is, at least in theater, a virtue.

1. UNDERSTANDING AND THE EMOTIONS

"Understanding" is not a technical word as I am using it, although I expect a sharper sense of what it is to understand will emerge from my discussion. Many different sorts of things are said to be understood—explanations, events, concepts, logical proofs, texts, foreign languages, paintings, and even persons are said to be understood. Plays represent events more than anything; the greater part of understanding a play is understanding the events in it.

A brief parenthesis is in order here concerning the mimetic transparency of theater. As a text, a playscript is as complicated as any other. Understanding a text may involve being sensitive to subtexts, to what is called intertextuality—allusions to other texts—and to all sorts of other complicating factors too tiresome to mention. From all of this, in the theater, we have a blessed release. Even the most avant-garde play is constituted by the events it shows; even the most elaborate allegorical drama grips us, if it grips us at all, by making us care about the events it represents. This is a fundamental law that any playwright knows. Writers who are not playwrights violate this law at their peril. When theater ceases to be transparent, i.e., when it directs attention away from what it represents and makes us look at the medium of theater itself, then it utterly fails; and the audience—if their emotions are not engaged—simply walk out.[1] Although in some sense there may be a play without an audience, there is not theater—no institution of watching—without an audience.

For our purposes, then, theater is a transparent medium for the representation of events. Events include actions as well as natural events; and actions include speaking, waiting, remembering, and the like. Although there is no significant action in *Waiting for Godot*—I mean there is no action that is significant for the characters in that play—there is action in my sense nonetheless, and there are events. Moreover, in most plays there are overarching events, such as the causing of this by that, that bind the play together. These too must be understood by anyone who is to understand the play.

What is it to understand an event? It is not the same as merely recognizing the event for what it is. We can recognize an event without beginning to understand it. "Yes," we say, "that is a love scene, but, no, that is not the hero; she is falling in love with the wrong man."

---

1. Brecht's alienation effects serve not to divert the audience's attention to the medium, but to distance the audience from the events represented. On this, see my "Engaging Emotion in Theater: A Brechtian Model in Theater History," *Monist* 71 (1988), 235–57.

That sort of response is usually easy for us, unless we are watching a play that is rich in ambiguity, like *Hamlet.* Recognizing a scene for what it is is a threshold for what I am calling understanding. The central process of understanding, and the factor that most provokes the skeptic, is emotion. Understanding consists largely in having certain emotions. Suppose I am being attacked by a fire-breathing dragon, and I recognize that this is happening to me. If I feel no fear, then I do not understand what is happening to me. If, on the other hand, I am frightened out of my wits, then again I do not understand what is happening to me. Failure to experience the proper emotion is a failure of understanding; while an excess of emotion, or an access of the wrong emotion, can cloud one's mind altogether.

⁕ Understanding a play ought to be like that; it should involve feeling appropriate emotions. If I feel nothing at all when I see Agave in the *Bacchae* proudly bearing the torn pieces of her son's body, then I have not understood the play; but if what I feel is amusement, and I laugh at the absurdity of the scene, then again I have not understood it. Understanding a play is mainly a matter of feeling what ought to be felt on viewing the scenes it represents.[2]

After this my skeptic would say that the analogy between theater and life breaks down in three crucial respects:

a. Emotions that go with understanding real events always entail dispositions to act; the emotions of theater, says my skeptic, do not. If I understand that a crazy mother is about to harm her child, I am upset and I call the police or the child welfare services. But in the theater, I may be equally upset if I understand what is happening in the *Bacchae,* but I do not rush to the lobby and telephone for help. Emotions in theater are playful, says the skeptic, and this seems to divide them from the serious emotions of real-life understanding. Understanding the events of your life threatens to change the way you live; understanding theater, apparently, does not.

b. Understanding events takes time, and this is not granted in the same way in theater as in life. Understanding theater, if by this we mean understanding a play in performance, ought to take place in the theater during the short course of the play itself. Life, fortunately, gives us more time. When a young student friend of mine heard his father had died, and made a joke about it, I knew he had not understood, except in a minimally cognitive sense, what had happened to

2. Martha Nussbaum writes of this as a kind of knowing that is not allowed in Plato's philosophy: "There is a kind of knowing that works by suffering because suffering is the appropriate acknowledgement of the way human life, in these cases, is." *The Fragility of Goodness* (Cambridge: Cambridge University Press, 1986), 45–46.

him. But when, after years of grieving, he was able to joke about this in a new way, then I knew he had understood the loss of his father. Only a few professional scholars and directors give the same time and attention to understanding *Hamlet* as this young man gave to understanding his father's death; but their understanding, since they are not in the audience, is not strictly theatrical. Understanding theater, if it happens at all, should happen to an audience during a play. So says the skeptic, reversing the cliche: life is long, art is short, and the experience of art is too brief for what could properly be called understanding.

c. The third point is the most important, but the most difficult to put sharply: understanding theater, if it is possible, is more heavily conditioned by the different experiences of different viewers than is understanding events in real life.

Suppose you and I, serving together in an infantry unit, drive the enemy from a neutral village after softening them up with artillery and rockets. As we enter the village we see a small child, soaked with blood, crying over the remains of her mother. If we understand what we see, we are shocked, upset, angry at the war and at ourselves, and overwhelmed with pity. It does not matter what experiences each of us brings to the event. If I am a father to a young child and you are not, my reaction may be more intense than yours. But insofar as we are understanding the scene in the village—and not some imagined catastrophe to our own children—we are coming to the same understanding.

(It is important to the example that you and I have played a similar role in the action we are coming to understand. If, by contrast, you and I are on different sides of the war, we will have different emotions; but this is not because we have had different past experiences; it is because the events to which we are responding are different. In that case, I would be understanding the outcome of *my own* attack on the village, while you would be understanding an enemy attack on the village. These are different things, owing to the intentionality of events.)

If we pull back from the event we witness, so that we are witnesses only, and no longer participants, then we are seeing the event as theater, and not as part of our lives. And in seeing it that way we open for ourselves a field of vision in which our own past experiences cast long shadows. The more theatrical our experience, the more it is subject to radical conditioning by our past lives. Suppose, now, that you and I see the same scene I described earlier, but this time in a movie theater. I am a war veteran, you are not. It is impossible for us to respond in the same way to the scene. I, for example, will remember what I have done in the war, and therefore I will feel a guilt that you cannot experience. I will say that you cannot understand the scene at all; you will say that you do understand it, but that we have different understandings of the scene. The skeptic will say that if different understandings are equally acceptable, neither counts as real understanding, for the process that gives them is not uniform and therefore not cognitively reliable. He—the skeptic—will go on to say that *if* you and I understand anything as we watch this scene, it is the different contents of our own lives, and not the scene itself, that we understand.

What *does* happen to an audience during a play? My skeptic will argue that if they understand anything, it is not the play.

2. WHAT WOULD IT BE LIKE TO UNDERSTAND THEATER?

I am not asking about fathoming a text, or about seeing through the style of a director, or even about mastering the art form known as theater. I am asking what happens when an audience in a theater understands the play they are watching.

We have a fairly clear sense of what happens when an audience fails to understand a play. It happens all too often. Any playwright knows that critics have a special talent for this. They laugh at the wrong lines, or perhaps they do not laugh at all. They get up and walk out in the middle of an exciting scene. In short, the critics do not respond to the events of the play with appropriate emotions. To give them their due, this is not always the fault of the critics: the playwright, or the director, or the actors, may have failed to represent the events of the play effectively. This, of course, is the art of the theater: to engage the emotions of an audience in such a way that they laugh at what is laughable, are shocked by what is horrible, and are gripped by what is gripping. It is not an easy thing to do for an audience who have different past experiences and therefore different emotional dispositions, or what the eighteenth century called different *humours*.

Suppose, however, that the artists have done their job well, and that a performance has the emotion-engaging properties it is supposed to have. Can a spectator misunderstand the play? Suppose I am in love with the actress playing Ophelia, and during her mad scene I can think of nothing but our last evening together; then I am suffused with warmth and love and longing, and the sorrow and the pity of the scene are quite lost on me. Or, to give a different sort of example, suppose I am a recently returned shell-shocked veteran; every scene with Fortinbras gives me the shakes, and I am unable to respond to him with the admiration that the play requires. Again, I have failed to understand the play because of an intrusion of my own emotional life.

A purist would say that I should have left my emotional life behind me as I entered the theater, checking it along with my hat and coat in the lobby, planning to pick up my own personal loves and fears again on the way out. But should I, in order to be an understanding theatergoer, allow myself only those emotions that are provoked by the play itself? I cannot imagine doing this. I cannot leave behind my emotional dispositions in this way. If I could, I do not think I would be able to have any emotions at all in the theater. If I left all my fears at the door, what in the theater could ever frighten me? Perhaps what the purist means is that I should leave behind all emotional dispositions that are peculiar to me, and bring to the theater only those dispositions that are universal and common to all of humanity.

Again, I do not think that this is possible; emotions and emotional dispositions are not like that. Each person's felt emotions, on the theory I am presupposing, have particular objects that are peculiar to those emotions. The object of an emotion is what differentiates it from every other emotion. There is no universal fear that any one person actually feels. True, we all fear death; but my fear of death is not the same as yours. For one thing, our different lives have given us different conceptions of death; and for another, my death is not the same as yours—it will bring grief or joy to different people, and these are the consequences I fear when I fear death. Each person's fears are peculiar to her because what she fears is peculiar to her. What is universal is that we all have people we love and things we fear; but there is no universal love or fear that we all feel or are disposed to feel.

No one can understand a play except with reference to his own emotional experience. Suppose, having survived a tempestuous romance in my teens, I later take my young daughter to a moving production of *Romeo and Juliet*; and suppose that my response is no different from that of the innocent ten-year-old child beside me. I think you would say that I have not fully understood the play. It *should* have brought back a flood of bittersweet memories, but it didn't. I blocked them out, and so I failed to understand the play.

Understanding theater lies somewhere in between two extremes. On the one hand, if you are overwhelmed by your personal emotions, as I was when I saw the love of my life playing Ophelia's part, you will not understand the play. On the other hand, if you shut down your personal emotional life entirely, as I did when I saw *Romeo* with my daughter, then you will not be able to respond emotionally to anything, least of all to a play. The problem is how to allow personal experience to impinge on one's understanding of a play without giving in to the skeptic.

One suggestion, due to Arthur Danto, is that the relation of fiction to personal experience is that of metaphor. I will examine this in more detail later. For now, let us see how brilliantly this proposal explains my two examples. If Danto is right, then understanding a scene would be seeing it as a metaphor for something in my own life. This is what I failed to do on both occasions. When I was in love with the actress playing Ophelia, I was not taking her scene as a metaphor for anything: it was only a chance to gaze at my girlfriend. Again, when I sat passively through *Romeo and Juliet*, I failed to take the scenes as metaphors, but responded to them abstractly without connecting them to my own life. This would explain, too, why not everyone can understand certain plays, and why different people seem to understand the same play differently. It leaves unanswered, however, my opening question: how should we answer the skeptic who says that this sort of attitude—each person's seeing a play as a metaphor for his own life— is not uniform enough to be a genuine case of understanding the play. Each of us no doubt understands the metaphor the play comes to be for his own life; but then each of us understands a different thing, a different metaphor. How is it possible for you and me to understand the same play?

3. DRAMA AS METAPHOR

According to Danto, each figure in literature, and each event, is an open metaphor—like an open sentence—that can be filled in by the reader with reference to himself:

The thought I want to advance is that literature is not universal in the sense of being about every possible world insofar as possible, as philosophy in its nonliterary dimension aspires to be, nor about what may happen to be the case in just this particular world, as history . . . aspires to be, but about each reader who experiences it . . . each work is about the "I" that reads the text, identifying himself not with the implied reader . . . but with the actual subject of the text in such a way that each work becomes a metaphor for each reader: perhaps the same metaphor for each.[3]

We are familiar with what is called the identification of spectator with character. But this is not what Danto had in mind. Identification

3. Arthur C. Danto, "Philosophy as/and/of Literature," from *The Philosophical Disenfranchisement of Art* (New York: Columbia University Press, 1986), 154–55.

is usually a fantasy, in which the spectator takes on the beauty, the strength, and the role of a lead character. But identification with a romantic hero feeds self-deception, whereas the self-referring interpretation Danto speaks of is one in which the reader sees his own life made clear by scenes he takes as metaphors.

Let us sharpen the point with a theatrical example, the most famous such example from fiction: when Claudius sees the play within *Hamlet* he is not confronted by a particular murder from history—not by the actual murder of Gonzago. Nor is he confronted by a universal murder—the murder in the heart of every Cain for his Abel. *What confronts Claudius, on this view, is a scene that is a metaphor for a particular event in his own life.*

When King Claudius understands Hamlet's production of *The Murther of Gonzago* he understands the mind of his nephew, and, if he did not do so before, he understands what he has done—his brother's murder, the rank offense "that smells to heaven." In understanding these things, besides, he is struck with emotions that take him out of his seat in the theater and bring him literally to his knees. And this appears to be what it is for Claudius to understand the play, for if he had not left his seat, not banished his nephew, and not fallen to his knees, desperate to pray but unable to do so—if he had not done all of that, we would not agree that he had understood the play. Somehow, we would say, he missed the point; perhaps he was distracted by a kiss from Gertrude, or perhaps he fell asleep or let his mind wander to affairs of state; perhaps he was watching Hamlet's crude behavior with Ophelia. But no, Claudius did not miss the point. It seems he understood the play.

Still, my skeptic will deny this: it is wrong, he will say, to call Claudius's experience "understanding the play." Perhaps, he concedes, Claudius has understood *something*: plainly he has responded with emotions that are appropriate. But appropriate to what? Not to the play. We—the audience outside the audience—saw the play also, and so did Hamlet; but it would not have been appropriate for us to rise from our seats flushed with guilt and anger, calling for lights to drown out the illumination of the stage, or later to fall into desperate prayer. What brought Claudius to his knees was not the play itself. It was Hamlet's special version of the play that did the job. And even this would not have succeeded without Claudius's guilt. A sense of his own guilt, more than anything, brought Claudius to his knees, and this was no part of the play or its production. Understanding no doubt happens in the theater, as Claudius's example shows; but what he understood was not a work of theater; Claudius has understood his own life as it was represented metaphorically on stage.

There are two further objections to saying that what Claudius has done is the same as understanding the play. Both lead to the same further question—what precisely it is that constitutes a play. The first objection is based on the special character of theatrical experience, the second on the requirement that cognitive attitudes be uniform.

a. *Theatrical Experience*

The core of the difficulty lies in the differences between life and theater. Theatrical experience, said the skeptic, is confined to the time between the rise and the fall of the curtains, and its effects on our active lives are minimal. Claudius did indeed come to an understanding in the theater, but this did not seem to be a theatrical experience. It was the stuff of real life. His understanding continued to grow after he had stopped the play, and no doubt it had been developing spontaneously for some time before the play began. Besides, his understanding involves a reaction so violent that he stops the play altogether: he shouts down the actors, he calls for lights, all to block out whatever further illumination the stage could offer him. This is the opposite of theatrical understanding, which keeps an audience's emotions engaged in the play until the final curtain. Theatrical understanding does not interrupt a play; its emotions have a limited effect on us, and this is what the skeptic meant by calling them *playful emotions*. Claudius's emotions brought him to his knees; our emotions in regard to the same scene have no such effect on us. Our response is contained in the closed world of the play, and its being contained is essential to its being a response *to theater* as opposed to a response *to real life*.

The objection is sound, I think: Claudius's experience is not an example of understanding theater. He does understand the play as an image of his own life, but that is an extraordinary way to understand a play, and it is not what we mean by "understanding theater." A play is rarely staged to catch the conscience of a king—or of any particular spectator, for that matter. Claudius's case is altogether the wrong sort of example. It belongs to the family of cases in which the spectator is so overwhelmingly involved in his own life that he is unable to respond to the play itself. But what *is* the play itself? Before I try to answer this, let me raise the same question from a different direction.

b. *Cognitive Uniformity*

Understanding is a cognitive process. That means that if understanding happens at all, it is something that can be shared. When we hope to understand something, we discuss it with the hope of reaching a consensus. If we fail to agree, then we can be sure that at least one of us has failed to understand. I shall say that this is the requirement that understanding be uniform. The requirement is general: whatever can be understood can be understood uniformly. Any process that cannot be uniform in the required way is not understanding. It follows that if a play can be understood, it can be understood in the same way by a number of people.

Claudius's experience—my skeptic will say—cannot be a model for understanding the play, because the emotions that constitute his understanding are entirely self-referring, and as such cannot in any way be shared by us. Arthur Danto valiantly speaks of literature offering "perhaps the same metaphor for each" reader, but it is hard to see what, except in a purely structural sense, would be the same in a set of different Claudius-type metaphors for different spectators. Such experiences cannot be uniform in different people.

On this point there is an easy answer we might give to the skeptic. The skeptic—the easy answer would say—should learn to see the difference between emotions and understanding. Of course, because different people have different dispositions, they will be moved differently by the same scene. But that does not mean that they cannot share, in an intellectual sense, an understanding of the scene. Getting the point of the play is the same for everyone who gets the point. Claudius and Hamlet got the point of the play, and so did all of us in the audience outside the audience. Claudius's mind was clouded with guilt, our minds were free; naturally the play touched him in a unique way. But he did not understand the play any better than we did. After all, we all got the point.

The easy answer does not solve the problem, however; it simply dismembers it. The only sort of understanding worth seeking does involve being touched and being affected and being moved. In this it depends on causal processes that operate differently on different cases, and so does not promise to be as uniform as we would like a cognitive process to be.

All the choices left us by this artificial debate seem unpalatable: if we follow the skeptic, we say that works of theater are not to be understood, and what passes for understanding theater is actually understanding real life. On the other hand, if we take the easy answer, and bleed all emotion out of understanding, we drain away its vital juices. Plainly, two people cannot share self-referring emotions. But can they share emotional attitudes that refer to scenes in which they do not see themselves? Unless we abandon our hope for cognitive uniformity, which I take to be fundamental, we need to develop a theory that explains how two people in the theater can share emotional attitudes to the same play.

But what is the same play? The debate has been naive on this point. Neither my skeptic nor his easy-minded opponent has examined what it is that Claudius and we are supposed to understand. We need to ask what a play is. If we find that there is no single entity that is *The Murther of Gonzago,* then the problem evaporates. But if there is, and we can say something about what kind of thing it is, we may hope to shed light on the problem.

4. WHAT IS A PLAY?

A play—a work of theater—can be produced in many different styles, and any one production can be performed differently on different occasions. *Hamlet* is put on in a variety of abridgements; it may be staged in English or German or Russian or French; it may be simplified in a version for children. In all this variety, there appears to be just one work of theater—*Hamlet*—which is repeated differently on different occasions. When I say that *Hamlet* defies my understanding, I mean that whenever I see the play, and in whatever fashion it is produced, it is beyond me. I do not mean that there is some particular production of *Hamlet* that defies my understanding. I am thinking of the play as what a philosopher would call a *repeatable* entity. Understanding a play, then, is like understanding a Platonic form. It is a case of understanding something that can have many instances.

On the other hand, what I see and hear in the theater is a particular performance, and the emotions that constitute my understanding of the play appear to have as their objects scenes and characters from this particular performance of the play. So it would seem that what I understand when I understand a play is not a work of theater, such as *Hamlet,* but a work-in-performance, such as West Lake High School's *Hamlet* last Friday evening. So now it appears that understanding a play is not like understanding a Platonic form; rather, it consists in understanding a particular event—this performance.

I think that both of these views are false. As we saw earlier, a play is transparently mimetic. This means that a play is identical neither to a repeatable universal nor to a particular performance. Anything that can be represented can be represented repeatedly. The events that comprise a play can be represented again and again, and this is what we mean when we say that a play is repeated. Theatrical representations, like photographs, can be reproduced in a variety of ways. Of course there are limits. If a children's play called *Hamlet* ends happily with the wedding of Hamlet and Ophelia, that is not the play we call *Hamlet*. I shall say that two performances are performances of the same play just if they are representations of roughly the same events.[4] This hypothesis does not give us criteria of identity for plays, as the criteria of identity for events are controversial; still, it tells us where to look. It tells us (if, as students of Aristotle, we did not already know) what sort of thing a play is.

Now I have already said that to understand a play is to understand the events it represents. Plays are almost perfectly transparent, and in this they differ from paintings and from works in other media. *The Bridge at Arles* is a representation of a certain bridge; but understanding this painting has very little to do with understanding the actual bridge at Arles. That, I think, is one reason we do not think that a reproduction of van Gogh's painting is at all the same thing as the original, nor is a photograph of the same bridge. On the other hand, unless we are unspeakably stuffy, we accept even a botched schoolboy production of a dumbed-down abridgement as the play we call *Hamlet*. That is because what counts in theater is the events it shows. Any performance of *Hamlet* represents roughly the same set of events; and in each case, understanding *Hamlet* is understanding these particular events. So understanding *Hamlet* is always roughly the same thing.

We are not moved emotionally by repeatable universals in the theater; we are moved by particular events, such as the slaying of Polonius. Although this event can be shown in many ways on many occasions, it is still roughly the same event,[5] and understanding it is still the same thing—it is having certain emotions of shock and surprise. For the same reason, when we are moved emotionally in the theater, what moves us is not the performance but what it represents. True, only a splendid performance can make me sorry for King Lear; but what I am then sorry for is an old man, King Lear. I am not sorry

4. There is no need to add "in a certain order" or "in certain relationships." The temporal sequence, I think, is not essential to a play; it is not uncommon for a play to be performed with a movable scene. What is essential to a play are the events—such as causal events—that connect one event with another. A play represents a set of events some of which serve as ordering relations among primary events. For example, the causal relationship between Hamlet's seeing his father's ghost and everything that follows is an event—it is the causing of these by that.

5. This is true for the most part, but not always. The killing of Polonius could be evidence for Hamlet's instability in one production; in another, it could be proof of his ruddy resolution to act vigorously. These cases show the killing in different positions in a causal nexus, and therefore may be thought to represent different events. Normally, such variations in interpretation can be accommodated by soggy formulation of my claim: two productions are of the same play if they represent roughly the same events. A radically new interpretive production of *Hamlet*, on the other hand, would be a new play altogether.

for the actor or for his performance—not, at any rate, unless the performance is a disaster.

ʌ Here, then, is the theory I propose: a play is a representation of events; these events, and the characters taking part in them, have certain emotion-engaging properties. By "emotion-engaging property" I mean such properties as being scary or amusing or boring or shocking (for events) or (for characters) being charming or hateful or admirable. It is crucial to see that these properties belong not to the play, but to the events and characters in the play. These properties belong to those events and characters whether we recognize them or not; I would say, to go out on a limb, that these properties belong to characters and events in a play whether or not the play represents them as having those properties. Playwrights and actors and directors, on my view, can simply make mistakes, as they would do if they represented a loathsome person as being admirable. The possibility that plays can be wrong in this way raises a special problem for the understanding of theater.

ι) Not every play can be understood. To be understandable, a play must show its events as having the emotion-engaging properties they actually have: a funny event must be funny, a pitiful one must be sad, and a frightening one must be scary. Many events have complex emotion-engaging properties, and these can be understood by those capable of complex responses. That is why there are such things as dramatic irony and black humor, and why these are not simply failures of consistency. Still, a playwright or director can, by mistake, give to his events the wrong properties, as did the director who made the gory scene from the *Bacchae* into a sick joke. In such a case, the play is simply not to be understood. To laugh at the scene is to miss the point of the event; not to laugh is to miss the director's point. Confronted with such a choice a wise audience should see that the play does not make sense, and not attempt to understand it as shown. Persons as well as scenes have emotion-engaging properties, and these may be misrepresented even by the person himself. Someone who seems a charming villain calls for a complex understanding; but someone who seems a genuinely *admirable* villain defies understanding. In real life, we demand to know him better before trying to understand him; in theater we simply reject him as badly drawn.

My theory of theater depends on two assumptions which I shall not attempt to defend in this paper: that there are events represented in theater, whether historical and fictional; and, second, that these objectively have emotion-engaging properties. Philosophically, both assumptions present us with great difficulties. I would argue, however, that only on such a basis can we hope to understand the actual practice of theater.

Now let me apply the theory to Claudius. By my hypothesis, Claudius and Hamlet, and we also, have seen the same scenes from *The Murther of Gonzago*, because we have all seen the same events as shown on the stage. *This means that the Claudius example is not an example of understanding theater.* The skeptic was right about that. Understanding theater is understanding the events that are represented on stage, and Claudius has, instead, understood his own life. What started out as a window was flooded with the light of Claudius's conscience, and so became a mirror. Claudius was luckier than most of us in this. We have all been brought up surrounded with theater, live, in movies, or on TV. Yet how many of us can say we have seen a play that brought us to our knees? I have scoured literature for another scene like this, but to no avail. We often hear of people being powerfully affected by music, or by music in musical theater, but almost never by theater alone. Only in the most extraordinary circumstances, when the currents of our lives are too strong to be diverted by theater, do we allow the window glass of a stage to turn opaque and reflect our images of ourselves.

Thomas Mann's *Blood of the Walsungs* comes powerfully to mind for a scene in which Wagner's overheated music, together with events on stage, bring a brother and sister to sense the underlying incest that is between them, and so to consummate it, like Siegmund and Sieglinde, on a bearskin rug. Like Claudius, they have understood themselves; but by no stretch of the imagination have they understood the scene they witnessed in the theater. They have taken it out of its myth and out of the framework of sin and retribution that make the scene what it is in Wagner's opera *Die Walküre*.[6]

But why not? The opera is fiction, not fact. I have been treating it as if it were the record of something real. What is there in fiction to understand, if there is nothing that it represents? History, as Aristotle famously told us, is a record of particulars, and these must be understood in their full particularity if they are to be understood at all. What then of fictional events? Aristotle would say that they are universal. It was to develop this insight that Danto made his proposal that the stuff of literature (as opposed to the stuff of history) is universal in that *any* reader can see it as a metaphor for himself or his life.

---

6. Flaubert shows a more complex response in *Madame Bovary*: the reawakening of erotic possibilities for Emma during a performance of *Lucia di Lamermoor*. Emma is excited by the tenor, loses interest in the opera, and leaves before it is over. She becomes aware again of stirrings in herself, but understands neither these nor the opera.

I want to ask whether this sort of distinction between history and fiction has any bearing on theater. Understanding events in history is not a matter of seeing Danto-metaphors. Should it be any different for understanding events in theater? In view of the way theater tends to represent its events as if they were history—as if they had happened—I would expect a negative answer.

5. UNDERSTANDING FICTIONAL EVENTS

I have been talking about such things as the slaying of Polonius as if they were events in good standing, for which criteria of identity would be forthcoming. But in fact Hamlet never did slay Polonius; this is only a play.

In passing, I should point out that theater does not need to be fictional. Plato's philosophical war against theater was not a war against fiction (how could the father of the good lie declare such a war?); Plato's war was a war against representation, not fiction, and especially against representations, such as theater, that engage the emotions. In fact, theater has from its beginnings shown history and fiction interchangeably. The defeat of the Persians, the founding of the Athenian legal system—these are historical events celebrated in very early plays. And of course no one needs to be reminded that Shakespeare wrote histories as well as comedies and tragedies. Understanding theater, then, has nothing to do with the special problem of understanding *fiction*. Understanding theater is understanding events represented on stage whether they are historical or not.

History and fiction may be different, but they do not require different kinds of understanding. Whether an event happened in real or fictional time, it should evoke the same response in an understanding audience. If it is in fact horrible, then you must be horrified by it if you are to understand it. Suppose I see a film about apartheid and take it to be historical. If, afterwards, I learn that I have been fooled, and that it was fiction all along, I would not retract my claim to have understood the film. What it depicted was horrible; I was properly horrified by it, and I went home to double my gift to Amnesty International, so vivid did it make the plight of political prisoners. Whether the events of a play are real or imagined makes no difference to the problem of understanding the events of a given play. Insofar as they engage our emotions at all, events in even the most avant garde theater seem real to us.

I do not mean to say, however, that fiction and history are indistinguishable, or that it does not matter which is which. It matters to a playwright whether her theater makes its events seem real to us in the manner of history. Bertolt Brecht wanted his audience to see his plays as representations of *history*, so as to engage their emotions in a particular way, and for this reason he called attention to the representing medium by means of alienation effects. What Brecht admired about historical theater is that, while it may remind us of us and of our times, it can never be mistaken for a mirror; it can never do to us what *The Murther of Gonzago* did to Claudius. Brecht preferred history over fiction not only because history is true, but because a historical style is less likely than a fictional one to invite us to thoughtless identification. We are more likely to watch and to respond directly to what we see as history and as therefore distinct from ourselves. Fantasy plots and characters, by contrast, tend to blur the theatrical relation between the watcher and the watched.

The difference between fiction and history matters to the historian because she wants to understand only certain events, namely historical ones. The difference might matter to ontologists, as well, if they care to mark off real from merely possible events. The difference matters also to philosophers of literature like Arthur Danto, who want to explain why, if literature is fiction, it is of any importance to us in the real world.

Nevertheless it seems to me that the real death of Anne Frank and the imagined death of Ophelia are important to me in exactly the same way and for the same reason. History, except to professional academic historians, is just another story, more convincing than fiction, perhaps, stranger, more gripping, and often harder to believe; but it is still a story that is contrived, and that matters to us because of the emotions that it engages. This is why Plato would have rejected history plays and even documentaries quite as firmly as he does anything else that is *theatrical.* They trifle with our emotions: they teach us to have emotions about trifles, about mere representations.

For our purposes, it makes no difference whether an event is historical or fictional. For one thing, the same skeptical problem arises for staged history as for staged fiction. For another, the value of understanding events has nothing to do with their ontological status. *I care to understand events because it is intrinsically worthwhile to do so, and because learning to understand one event enhances my capacity to understand another.* In that insight is the solution to the skeptical problem with which I began.

6. THE WEB OF UNDERSTANDING

Understanding an event, whether historical or fictional, whether present to us in life or *re*-presented to us on stage, is always the same thing, according to the theory that I am proposing: understanding an event is responding to it with appropriate emotions, and these emotions are intentionally linked to that particular event. That is why it was one thing to understand the scene in *The Murther of Gonzago*, and another for Claudius to understand his killing of his own brother: these are different events, and understanding them is constituted by different emotions. It does not follow, however, that the two understandings are not linked. Claudius's understanding the scene *does* lead to his understanding of his life, and, no doubt, if his life had not been overwhelming, his self-understanding would have contributed to his understanding of the play. I suspect that all of our understandings are woven together in a web of capacities for emotion and that this is why we set a high value on understanding even fictional events. When I understand the death of Ophelia I gain, not because this is exactly the same thing as understanding some event in my own life, but because a growing power to respond to the plight of frightened and abused women enhances my ability to understand both the play and the events of my life. Understanding an event is good in itself, but it is good also as evidence of an enhanced capacity to understand other events.

Here is a personal example of how this works. I have seen Shakespeare's *Henry V* on more occasions than I can specifically remember, and I have read it and studied the text. For years I felt anglophilic pride in the events of the play, as would befit a celebration of the conversion of naughty Prince Hal into a noble warrior king. This pride was so strong in me that I overlooked the seamy side of English Tudor jingoism, and felt no whit of horror at Henry's threatened massacre at Harflew. Shakespeare's bloodthirstier contemporaries probably felt less horror than I do now at such scenes; still, this speech of Henry's is remarkable even in Shakespeare. Sweet young Prince Hal would never have given it; nor would his foil, the intemperate Hotspur. Here is how Henry V threatens the burghers of Harflew:

> If not—why in a moment look to see
> The blind and bloody soldier with foul hand
> Defile the locks of your shrill-shrieking daughters,
> Your fathers taken by their silver beards
> And their most reverend heads dashed to the walls;
> Your naked infants spitted upon pikes

> Whiles the mad mothers with their howls confus'd
> Do break the clouds . . .
> What say you? Will you yield and this avoid?
>   ACT III, SCENE III

How could I have heard this with pride and excitement, as just another episode in the life of a warrior prince? But I did. In fact, I was so swept up in the mood of Henry's heroism that I felt the wooing of Katherine by Henry at the end of the play to be delightfully romantic. I was so proud of Henry, and I felt she was so lucky to have him, that I felt none of the shock I now feel at witnessing what now strikes me as a rape scene, and a symbol for the brutal conquest of France by England. I did not misinterpret the scene; I knew he was forcing himself on the young woman. But I did not respond as one should to such a scene. And when I heard the St. Crispin's Day speech—you know the one, it disgraces every anthology of heroic rhetoric—I was enthralled and inspired. Here is how Henry encourages his captains when they feel their numbers are too few to face the French:

> If we are marked to die, we are enow
> To do our country loss; and if to live,
> The fewer men, the greater share of honor.
> God's will, I pray thee wish not one man more.
>   .   .   .
> This story shall the good man teach his son;
> And Crispin Crispian shall ne'er go by,
> From this day to the ending of the world,
> But we in it shall be rememb'red—
> We few, we happy few, we band of brothers . . .
>   ACT IV, SCENE III

When I hear that speech, now, twenty-five years and a nasty little war later, I am angry and dismayed at seeing a shallow and violent young man manipulate his elders.[7] I still hear the ring of heroism, too, and I am excited by it as I always was; but I smell Evil in this plausible prince.

I think that now, at last, I understand the play. It is not, as I used to think, a simple celebration of English patriotism, to which the appropriate response is enthusiastic pride. Nor is it, as Sam Johnson saw it, an inconsistent rendering of a half-converted prince, sometimes sweet Hal and sometimes sour. Instead, the play represents the defeat

---

7. Kenneth Branagh's film version of *Henry V,* which presents the play much as I understand it, came to this country long after I wrote these lines.

of France by an irresponsible boy-king, an event that is stirring, exciting, and terrible all at once. The appropriate response is complex and disturbing.

I am able to respond in this way now because of my experience. It is not that I identify with Henry, or even see him as a metaphor for myself. I never did anything remotely like sending troops once more into the breach. But in attempting to understand what happened to me I have learned to feel emotions as complex as those required for an understanding of *Henry V.* I *might* say, "War is like this, war is a universal, the same for me and for Shakespeare." But this is to miss the point. My understanding *is not* of war in general. I am coming to understand *my own war,* and in doing so I am developing the capacity to understand Shakespeare's war as well. It is equally true the other way around: when I first heard the St. Crispin's day speech the way I do now it took my breath away, and I felt in the same moment both the enthusiasm of my joining the army and my horror at that enthusiasm. These were different understandings, my understandings of the play and of my life. But each strengthened the other.

An historicist would point out that I have not been alone in this. Our culture generally took pride in Prince Hal from the nineteen-forties to the late nineteen-sixties, and soured on him after Vietnam. My changing response reflects a changing culture. Perhaps there are many plays called *Henry V,* one for each period in the history of the interpretation of the play. But this does not explain my sense that I now have the experience I needed in order to understand more of the play than I did before. My earlier understanding of the play was forced; it made me overlook much of what went on. Now I can take all of this into account.

Of course I was not alone in this. As it is with individuals, so with those who share a culture. We should not be afraid to say that an entire culture misunderstands a play, if it is denied the experience it would need to support that understanding. If people are generally shocked by Restoration Comedy, for example, then they will not understand it. Those plays are funny, not shocking.

The historicist is right, however, to insist that those who saw Prince Hal with pride in their hearts were not making a mistake. There is nothing they could have done that they failed to do. They felt for Hal just what their history had prepared them to feel. So did I. But history can serve us well or badly in preparing us to understand. There is an element of luck in understanding: there are many things I would never have understood if I had not had children. So it is with theater: the more you have lived, the more you will understand. Perhaps no one will live through enough to understand any great and complex play completely.

7. REPLY TO THE SKEPTIC

The skeptic was wrong on all points. First, you remember, he urged us to confine understanding to the events of real life. In theater, he thought, there was not time for understanding to develop, nor scope for the active effect of understanding on our lives. But it turns out that theater is not so restrictive. Understanding events in theater *is* much the same as understanding past events in life. We were wrong to concede to him that understanding theater must happen in the brief time between curtains. Understanding *Henry V* has taken me twenty-five years, and so has understanding the parallel material in my own life. We were wrong also to concede to him that understanding theater is playful, that its emotions do not entail dispositions to act. My understanding of *Henry V* is like my understanding of any other event that is not present to me: it gives play to a capacity for emotions that do show themselves in action whenever possible. Understanding theater is no more playful than understanding history: when your emotions are engaged in an event that is not present to you, they cannot lead to direct action in regard to those events. The best they can do is to prepare the way for understanding events that do present opportunities for action.

You will remember the second objection also—that understanding theater, on the Claudius model, is hopelessly non-uniform. On that model, each person's individual experience determines what it is for him to understand a given play. But we have seen that the Claudius model is not a model for understanding theater. It is true that only spectators burdened (as I am) with sad experience, or blessed (as I am not) with unusual insight, will understand *Henry V.* Perhaps we never will fully understand the play. But if you and I do come to understand *Henry V,* the play we understand is the same for both of us, and no matter how different the experiences that have given us the depth to understand this play, our understanding of it will be the same.[8]

8. This essay is part of a larger work in progress in which I attempt to develop a poetics of theater in terms of a cognitivist theory of emotion. I owe a huge debt to F. M. Berenson's paper "Understanding Music," which started me on the reflections that led to this essay; to recent work in aesthetics by Arthur Danto; and also to recent work on the emotions by Robert Solomon, Ronald de Sousa, and F. M. Berenson. I am also grateful for advice to friends who work in theater, especially Michael Holden and James Loehlin.

Objects of Appreciation: Early Reflections on Television, with Further Remarks on Baseball[1]

TED COHEN

During the past few years I have been speaking and writing about a variety of things outside the canonical budget typically assigned to the philosophy of art. Among the things that have engaged me are figurative language, photography, the movies, jokes, and sports. Here I will persist in this eccentricity, but with a more reflective eye toward what it means to be taken with these presumably marginal topics. And I think I should begin with some turgid remarks of dialectical self-justification.

Some of my friends and colleagues, including some who have a good opinion of my philosophical sense and capacities, have wondered about my *seriousness,* and they have worried that I have become less *philosophical.* Those with a deep interest in the history of philosophy had expected more work on Kant's aesthetics, a monograph on Hume's marvelous essay on taste, and perhaps a new study of the argument of Aristotle's *Poetics.* The less historically minded expected a theory of art or a theory of beauty, or perhaps a sketch of the logic of fictional speech acts. A dozen years ago I wrote a couple of pieces about metaphor, and they seemed peculiar at the time, although the topic has since become relatively common. And my work on photography has seemed not so odd, I suppose, as a few other philosophers have been attracted to the topic. But I had moved off, meanwhile,

1. After delivering a version of this paper in The Catholic University of America's 1988–1989 Matchette series, I was able to try the topic again when I was invited to The Center for Philosophic Exchange at the State University of New York College at Brockport. I received considerable help in both places, and I would like to thank especially Daniel Dahlstrom in Washington, and Jack Glickman in Brockport. It is not easy to find a philosopher who is willing to sponsor a lecture on television, and it is even harder to find one who is also a generous host and a stimulating philosophical conversationalist. I found two.

producing remarks on Hitchcock's movies, jokes, and baseball. All this has made me dubious in the regard of both philosophers of art and philosophers in general. Many philosophers already regard the philosophy of art as a relatively unserious kind of philosophy, and philosophers of art are apt to suppose that the serious part of their study concerns (1) the understanding of art as a general philosophical problem, and (2) the specific study of the abstract characteristics of painting, literature, and music. When I moved, seemingly, to the periphery of even the philosophy of art, I wandered to the circumference of one of philosophy's more distant epicycles. Well, I am enjoying myself there, very much, and I would comfortably just stay there and leave it at that, but for two things I feel a need to say to those who are losing sight of me and worry over me on that account.

1. I am learning a great deal out here. The air is fresh. The view is not cluttered with moribund theories, and the terrain is not littered with monuments of Great Historical Importance.

2. I would like to ask, Who is being serious and philosophical, and who is not? My critics, friendly and otherwise, are sure that when I collaborated on a paper about Velazquez' painting *Las Meninas*, I was being more serious and more intellectually respectable than when I wrote a piece on baseball. Why do they think that? What makes them so sure? Is it obvious that the paintings of the Spanish Renaissance are more important, culturally and philosophically, than American baseball? I am a philosopher, after all, at least I have the customary credentials, and I should like to observe that declaring something *obvious* is one of the most anti-philosophical maneuvers I am aware of. It is a device that smells bad, like its companion declaration that something is *natural*. When someone tells us that something is obvious (and therefore true), or that something is natural (and therefore good), if we have any drop of true philosophical blood in us, we will demand a general account, a theory in fact, of obviousness and naturalness. There has to be some non-question-begging way of telling the obvious from the unobvious, the natural from the unnatural, besides simply accepting the pronouncement of a self-appointed judge. I know of no tenable theory along these lines. If the critic has no theory, and he has nothing to rest on except his conviction that this is the way things have always been done, or that these are the things that have always been believed, then he has no claim worthy of a philosophical response. The claim is all the less worthy if it rests upon nothing more than the fact that its proponent and his circle share certain preferences. We should remind him, gently if he or she is young, not so gently if he is as old as Allan Bloom, that instead of doing philosophy

he is just singing an old song; and then we might note that if an American has any birthright at all, it is one which releases him from the need to dance to the tunes of others.

I have not said that baseball is more noble than Spanish painting. I have not said that it is as noble. I have not said anything. I have the supremely good luck to be able to work on what interests me—if I did not have the luck I hope I would have the courage to do it anyway—and so it is not incumbent upon me, politically, to obtain a license for what I do; nor do I require, philosophically, an a priori apology for the value of the topics I address. As I see it, those who question the seriousness, the philosophical merit, or the value of these topics are the ones in need of justifications, a priori or otherwise. When they produce these arguments, I will attempt to answer them. Until then I will press on (maybe I will discover America), and it will do nicely to start with baseball.

Not everyone cares for baseball (in fact, among my colleagues in the Department of Philosophy at the University of Chicago I think there is only one baseball fan). Suppose a friend says that he does not care for baseball. He finds it boring. In fact he says it *is* boring. Could he be wrong about this? Can I argue with him about this? There are things I can say, although they may not be an argument, but it matters considerably whether he is speaking against baseball specifically, because if he isn't, then I will need to say other things. I will suppose for a moment that he is, and that he is not expressing a disdain for all spectator sports. Then I will ask him just what he means by saying that baseball is boring, or—better—just what is boring about baseball. Imagine that he tells us that baseball is not exciting, or that it is seldom exciting. Now he may mean by this that he himself does not often become excited when watching baseball, but we will already have known that, for that seems to be another way of saying (almost) what he had in mind when he made his first and unforgivable remark about baseball, calling it boring. When he elaborates he is likely to insist that the game itself is not exciting, and in particular he is likely to assert that in baseball not much happens.

And now we will ask, What counts as something happening? When this friend goes for a drive in the country, a stroll in the woods, a hike in the hills, nothing much happens, nor does it, as a matter of fact, when he visits an art museum. Is he bored then? Oh, but those outings are different, he says. The art museum example is simply irrelevant, because that concerns the experience of art and baseball is not art. Baseball is a sport, like football and soccer and tennis. But who says that baseball is *like* football and soccer and tennis? If you go to a baseball game looking for the kinds of things that happen in football, you won't find many. But why do you go to a baseball game looking for things like that? When you read a novel you note things happening, and things happen when you listen to music; but if you look for things like that when you are looking at paintings, you won't find any.

Suppose someone tells us that Bach's music is boring, and when we press him in the way we press the baseball ignoramus, he says that Bach's music leaves him flat because it doesn't lead him to clap his hands and dance. What will we say about that? And what will we say about someone who loves Bach's music just because whenever he hears it he does set his feet a-tapping and soon begin to dance?

It is not so easy to imagine someone who says these things about Bach and is telling the truth about his reactions, although it is considerably easier to imagine the one who finds the music boring than it is to imagine the one who likes getting down with the *St. Matthew Passion*. But let us try to imagine, just to begin to discover what we might say. Would you agree to something like this—that these responses to Bach's music are possible only in a listener who does not hear the music for what it is, who does not respond in terms of the kind of thing this music is? I am willing to say that, although I am not near being ready to say that a listener has an obligation to listen to music in terms of the kind of music it is, and so I am not in a good position to say that the listener has made an error.

I say the same thing about the benighted soul who is bored by baseball. When a spectator is bored by baseball (I mean bored in general, not just bored by a specific item), then he likely does not see baseball in terms of the kind of thing it is. This skewed view, I suspect, most often results from a mistaken sense of the units of possible interest. This brings me as close as I will get to the ostensible topic of this essay (although I will come this close more than once). What *thing* is it that is being appreciated (or not) when one appreciates baseball? What is the *object*? I have nothing especially metaphysical in mind. I am not interested in distinctions between physical and mental things, nor do I have an eye out for distinctions between the general and the particular, or the abstract and the concrete. I am after something more simple, although it is complex enough. If a spectator understands himself to have seen something happen in baseball only when a batter strikes out or walks, or a ball is hit out of the park or into the glove of a fielder or on the ground past the infielder, et cetera, or a batter-become-runner has either beaten or been beaten by a fielder's throw to first base, then that spectator has far too meagre a purview. What do you focus on when you watch baseball? A single pitch? A time at bat? A half-inning? The four-and-a-half innings that beat the rain? A whole, complete game? A weekend series, say, between the Cardinals and the Dodgers? How about a whole season? What does it mean to watch Sandy Koufax pitch? To see him throw one fastball to Willie McCovey? To see him work on McCovey throughout one time at bat? Through one whole game? How about through a whole season? How about through a whole career? When you sit in the stands and watch Koufax throw a high, inside fastball to McCovey, you have seen something that is somehow a part of all the things just enumerated. What did you see happen? (By the way, what do you hear happen when you are listening to one variation on a theme, when the whole theme-and-variations is itself set into one of the four movements of a classical symphony?)

Well, I do not mean to talk about baseball here, although it is always a welcome topic. I have mentioned it as a familiar example of misapprehension, as a context of possible appreciation in which it is not obvious what is the focal object. (I have my doubts that it is ever obvious what is the salient object: in some cases it has a traditional or habitual position.) I will spend most of my time with another object, one more likely to be thought of in connection with Art, although it is almost always assessed as being either not art or very, very inferior art: television. My aim in speaking about television is certainly not to settle any significant questions: I intend to raise questions and I hope to persuade you of the urgency of some of these questions and I will urge you that none of us is entitled to any firm convictions about the artistic, aesthetic, or cultural value of television.

We have no idea how good or bad or indifferent television is because we have no reliable idea of what television is. Those who hold firm opinions about the quality of television typically are in no doubt about just what kind of thing television is, and they see no reason to wonder about what it is because they implicitly think they know what it is. They have made an error, I think—I certainly made it—and it is an ironic replay of an earlier error made in the apprehension of movies.

Until after World War II, and well after the war for many of us, movies were seen as if they were theater. A movie was taken to be a visual recording of a play, with perhaps a few jumps in space and time thrown in. The appraisal of movies, accordingly, was carried out essentially in the idiom of dramatic criticism. (Many critics still carry on in this way; Siskel and Ebert, for example, and a number of *New Yorker* reviewers of recent years, but not Pauline Kael.) It is, therefore, not surprising that for a generation of movie viewers it was Ingmar Bergman who first made them believe that a movie might be Art. In *The*

Seventh Seal, Wild Strawberries, The Magician, for instance, one found just what one expected of good, serious drama. There were real acting, the kind associated with closely coached repertory theater, careful story composition, and even set design. Some people have stayed with movies like this, grouping them with what are called 'art films,' and I believe that those people have continued to see movies as derived forms of theater or painting. Others, including me, have come to a point at which it seems that the best movies of Bergman are no better, and certainly no more art, than many movies by John Ford, Howard Hawks, and Alfred Hitchcock. In fact I think that there are at least a half dozen movies by Hitchcock significantly better than any movie by Bergman. A good friend of mine, Alexander Sesonske, whose opinions about movies deserve more attention than almost anyone else's and certainly more than almost any other philosopher's, has argued to me that for a significant group of people the discovery of what movies are was made a generation earlier and centered around some Italian and Japanese movies that appeared in America almost immediately after World War II. The specifics of this history are not important. Nor does it matter whether you have a better opinion of Bergman than I do, or a lower opinion of Hitchcock. All that matters is that you agree with this: as long as movies are seen essentially as theater, they will always seem inferior. One might prefer a movie version of *King Lear* to a performance in the "legitimate theatre," but only because of something inherently irrelevant, say the fact that it is only in the film version that some particular actor plays Lear.

I would like to be untendentious in this little sketch of what I think of as the development of a sensibility adequate to movies, but I will have to be at least a little more concrete, and these specifics may be controversial. For those of us breaking away from seeing movies as theater and developing an appreciation of movies as movies, it was necessary to learn to do new things and to undo some old ones: to see John Wayne, or perhaps, that is, to see the Ringo Kid, but it is not to see John Wayne enact the role of the Ringo Kid; to move with the movie instead of the story, to accept the camera's delineations and innuendoes instead of only those of dialogue and plot. It was relatively easy for literary types to feel the force of Bergman's telling us of a man who is a magician precisely because he knows that he has no magic; it was harder—and certainly different—to come to feel the moral judgment Hitchcock passes in *Rear Window,* for Hitchcock uses the movie itself to do this, to trap us, to make us watch a watcher and feel for him.

We are now, I think, in a position to respond to movies, at least some of us are, and we are capable of complex responses and assessments. We can connect Hitchcock's *North by Northwest* with Shakespeare's *Hamlet,* and wonder whether Hitchcock can really be that good. We can connect *Apocalypse Now* with *Heart of Darkness* and see that Conrad's novel is better and that its point escapes Francis Ford Coppola.

What about television? The irony at work is that we see television as if we were seeing movies. If movies once went unappreciated because they were seen as ersatz theater, now it is our consciousness of movies, and the subtle habits that go with that sensibility, that stand between us and a rich appreciation of television. We see television, as an old school friend of mine once called it, as chamber cinema. Who is it who sees television as if he or she were watching a movie? I suppose that I have in mind mostly critics and academic intellectuals, although I think it is also true of many general viewers, especially those who are old enough to have had the habit of movie viewing before television appeared. Professor Daniel Brudney, my much-younger colleague, has pointed out to me that he and his coevals grew up watching television and consequently have television-watching habits at least as well entrenched as their movie-watching habits. Astonishingly, for all his youth, Professor Brudney is my one colleague, the one I mentioned earlier, who is a sophisticated baseball fan. He is a remarkable man.

As long as television seems to you to be a movie, it is almost certainly going to seem to be a bad movie. The screen isn't large enough for certain kinds of dynamism, the focus isn't sharp, the colors are neither accurate nor rich.

If watching television isn't roughly the same as seeing a movie, then what is it? Is television, properly appraised, better than most cultural critics say? Is television capable of art? No one can tell these things a priori. They cannot be told in advance and we are in advance as long as we haven't got a proper fix on television. Then what is television? I don't know. Maybe we can find an answer together. All I can do for now is clear some ground. My main goal is to begin to figure out what the object is, and it is almost time to get to that.

POLEMICAL INTERLUDE

For those with a need, or an interest, it may be useful for me to help us get past some common denigrations of television. It is not uncommon for us to criticize ourselves, or at least to express disappointment in ourselves for watching "too much" television, and there seems to be a general opinion to the effect that many American children watch too much television. Too much for what? A common enough sentiment seems to be that it would be better, especially for our children, to read, to read a book, than to watch television. This is surely a witless assertion. Surely it matters, for instance, *what* book one might be reading instead of watching television. What if one were reading *TV Guide*? Would it be better to read a novel by Dorothy Sayers or Sara Paretsky than to watch some *Cagney and Lacey*? Surely that is not obvious. Would it be better to read *Anna Karenina* than to watch *Dallas*? How about *Upstairs, Downstairs*? This is not obvious either, for it might be that one's powers of concentration or, if one is a child, even one's reading abilities are not up to *Anna Karenina*. Well, one might say, "all things being equal, it is better to read than to watch television." Even if we could agree with that, we would be agreeing to very little, for all things never are equal. And really, could it *always* be better to read than to watch television?

What if one read all the time? What if one spent so much time reading that one never listened to music? Never looked at paintings? Or what if it were not quite so extreme, and one did occasionally listen to music or look at an architectural work but never with the concentration and attention given to reading? Would that be acceptable: serious reading but no serious attention to other arts? To some, I suppose that seems better than committing everything to television, because television is already assumed not to be the equal of serious arts. But that is just an assumption. And anyway, I do not mean to be talking about someone who spends all his time watching television, for the assertion I am questioning is the one which says that it is never as good to watch television as to read a book. Rubbish.

Another common complaint is that watching television is just too "passive" an experience to be as valuable as the experience of genuine art. Television can be passive, certainly, and maybe it is more likely to be an unengaged activity than some others, but it is not only television that produces couch potatoes. After all, I know plenty of very passive listeners to music, lookers at paintings and movies, and readers. (Indeed I have been all those things myself.) You *can* just sit there from 7 till 10 p.m. (in the east it is 8 till 11 p.m.), letting the television pull you into its wash. But you can watch Hitchcock's *North by Northwest* and never even wonder where Cary Grant is going when he travels north by northwest, much less figure out where he is going, really see where he is going. You can read *Anna Karenina* and never wonder why the book is named for Anna and not for Levin. You can read *Lolita* and never notice the fun that is being made of T. S. Eliot. You can listen to Beethoven's Opus 131 and not hear the hocketing. When subscribers to our major symphony orchestras object to programming outside the usual repertoire of eighteenth-, nineteenth-, and early twentieth-century pieces, I would make the guess that they are asking for a relatively "passive" experience when they attend concerts. If there is no way to watch television except passively, that remains to be shown.

The commercialism of television distresses many critics, for they assume that the constraints of commerce are a bar to any significant artistic achievement in television. But why should this be an insuperable barrier only in television? Wonderful short stories by Hemingway, Fitzgerald, Mavis Gallant, John Updike, and countless others were first read by significant audiences in the pages of magazines like *Esquire* and *The New Yorker.* Those stories were flanked by and even interrupted by advertisements. One either overlooked that advertising or took time out to look it over, and I see no reason whatever why the same thing should not be done by a television watcher.

A comparable objection has been made in terms of the presumed need for television to appeal to such a large audience that it must, to succeed, subject itself to the constraints of vulgar taste and the political requirements of the day. And, of course, television has to fit itself into thirty- and sixty-minute segments. Similar objections were once leveled at the movies (and still are, by some critics), and if one thing has become clear it is this: artists face a variety of constraints, ranging from the intractability of the French horn through the optical chemistry of pigments and dyes and on to the linguistic and mnemonic capacities of audiences. Commercial constraints are different from those, no doubt, but they are still constraints that can be overcome or even exploited. I know of no argument to show there is a kind of constraint that can be overcome only at the cost of art.

It is a common idea that there are certain requirements that are a bar to the making of art. But it is difficult to credit this idea, because when it is explicated it always seems to be either senseless or false. The idea leads to pronouncements like these: you could not make a work of art if you had to make an object according to certain commercial specifications; you could not make a work of art if you had to make an object that would serve some mundane utilitarian purpose; you could not make a work of art if you had to make an object that would appeal to very many people. Why should we believe any of those things? Perhaps a proponent would say that the artist must be absolutely and entirely free if he or she is to be able to make real art. What does it mean to be absolutely and entirely free? Suppose a composer is writing a piece for piano. If he would like to construct a harmonic sequence in which e-sharp and f are two different pitches, he cannot do it: at least he is not free to do this when composing for a standardly tuned piano. Of course he might choose then not to compose for such a piano. But he has to compose for something, and whatever that instrument is, it is guaranteed to restrict the possibilities available to the composer.

No medium is indefinitely tractable. So what? Not just *anything* can be done with wood, or with ceramic materials, or with clarinets. It is surely correct to regard these mediums as coming with limitations, but it is exceedingly strange to think that these limitations are inimical to the creation of art.

It ought to be similarly strange to think that the possible uses of objects are barriers to art. A potter makes a cup, a woodworker makes a chair, a designer makes wallpaper. What difference does it make that the cup is to be drunk from, the chair sat in, and the paper pasted on walls?

My first acquaintance with the National Council on Education for the Ceramic Arts was in 1988, at the annual meeting of this wonderful group of ceramic artists, teachers, and critics. I had time to stop in some of the sessions, and one was devoted to a discussion of art and craft. Early on, one of the speakers asked the question "What is the difference between a pot and a vessel?" and someone in the audience immediately called out, "About $4,000." That answer is worth more than volumes of aesthetics and philosophy. It may register all the truth we need to know.

There is, perhaps, one distinction to be made and looked into. Suppose you are a talented ceramist. You decide to make a cup. Your intention is to make a work of art (whatever exactly it means to set out to do that), and your expectation is that it will become part of the permanent collection of a museum and that it will spend its time resting untouched on a pedestal. On the other hand, suppose that you are the same talented ceramist and that I come to you and commission a cup. Furthermore, as I make clear to you, I intend to use this cup daily for my morning coffee. Now what? The question is not whether you go about your cup making differently. You may, of course, depending upon your desire for fame, your opinion of me and my taste, your need for money, et cetera. The question is whether you *have to* go about your cup making differently. The distinction I have in mind is this: you might make the cup just as you would make it if you were going to keep it yourself, or place it in a museum, but then add in whatever is necessary to render the piece durable enough for the use I will make of it; or you might make this durability requirement itself more integral to the task. Do you see the difference? It is rather like the difference between creating a television program in such a way that it will not be damaged by being interrupted every fifteen minutes by a commercial, and creating it in such a way that its very own, internal rhythm requires these interruptions. Either way, there is nothing in the nature of things to prevent the cup or the television program from being a successful work of art, but my guess is that it will succeed more thoroughly or deeply if this additional (seemingly extrinsic) constraint is accepted as one that comes with the medium.

This distinction may also be introduced into the appreciation of objects. We can see the cup as if its utility were an incidental feature, entirely independent of the cup's artistry, or we can see it as an essential aspect of the medium in which the potter was working. I think that the latter is likely to be the better way to see the cup, but what I wish to note here is that these two ways of looking are virtually ways of looking at two different objects. What is the object of appreciation?

It is a persistent idea that television is irretrievably vulgar because it needs to appeal to such a wide audience. This idea is tied to the conviction that nothing very good can have such a wide appeal, I suppose because only a relatively few auditors can appreciate the truly good. What reason is there to believe this? I know of no good reason. You do not need me to remind you of the enormous and wide success of Shakespeare, Dickens, and Verdi.

Finally let me take up one criticism of television that is made very often, but whose point continues to escape me. Television is alleged to damage everything from wholesome family life to the social polity, and specifically it is accused of destroying the community of appreciation. Because watching television is often a solitary occupation, and because it does not bring together large audiences to share an appreciation of something, it is charged with subverting artistic appreciation. What a strange indictment. Except for theatrical performances, movies seen in theaters, musical performances, perhaps architecture of certain kinds, and a few other things, art typically is experienced by people who are either alone or in very small groups (groups of about the size, say, of a family watching television together). But the indictment is not only strange; it is completely wrongheaded. Television frequently creates an audience of a kind and on a scale absolutely unprecedented. For a number of years, every Monday night at 9 p.m., and every Thursday night at 9 p.m., respectively (both Central time), millions of people watched *Cagney and Lacey* and *Hill Street Blues*. They did not watch together in the same space, but they did watch together at the same time, *and they knew that one another were watching*. On the following Tuesdays and Fridays, thousands of viewers engaged one another in conversation about what they saw the preceding nights. What more could be wanted of an audience? An appealing idea of Dewey's is that the occasions for what he calls 'aesthetic experience' should not be confined to special places—concert halls and museums—but should be more prominent and pervasive in daily life. I put it to you that television has done just that, although in a way undreamt of by Dewey, or by Benjamin in his early speculations about what art would be like as it became "mechanically reproducible."

RETURN TO THE TOPIC

Once we have freed ourselves of preconceptions about the possibilities of television, let us try for a fresh look. An early question ought to be, What shall we look at? For an illustration of the subtlety of this question, permit me one last dip into the rejuvenating well of baseball.

Baseball is not the same as baseball on television: baseball-on-television is not merely baseball that happens to be televised. From the standpoint of the spectator the rhythm of the experience is different. This is never more obvious than when the spectator must make a choice that substantially determines his experience. An example presents itself when there is a batted ball with a runner on base. Suppose that the Chicago White Sox are playing the Oakland Athletics, with the A's at bat. José Canseco is on first base. The batter sends a line hit toward the gap in right-center field. Now what will you watch? Do you want to see what kind of jump Canseco gets off first base, and how well he makes the turn at second? Will you want to see the third-base coach giving signals? Do you want to see how Canseco tries to keep track of the ball and the coach as he decides whether to try for third? Or will you watch Harold Baines in right field, noting how good a jump he gets on the ball, how cleanly he fields it, and how well he throws to third (or maybe, if he decides that Canseco is not going to try for third, Harold will throw to second behind the runner)?

All those things are taking place so near to simultaneously that you cannot watch them all. You will likely wind up asking your companions whether Harold slipped, or Canseco stumbled, or the coach underestimated Harold's arm, even if you have the wit and the knack to check on all these things sequentially as the play develops.

There is no choice to be made by the television spectator. The program director will decide what you see. And then he will show you all the other things, the things he decided against showing you "live," and you will see in some temporal sequence the things that happened simultaneously. This is quite a different viewing experience from the one to be had in the ball park, and its principal visual constituent is a different object.

Some matters of choice are approximately the same for the ball park viewer and the television viewer. When you are watching a fielder or a runner or a batter you can concentrate your attention on his hands, his arms, his feet, his overall posture, his face, etc. That's up to you whether you are a home viewer or in the stands at the game. And sometimes even when you are concentrating you will not see everything that happens. During a Chicago Cubs game a few years ago, Ron Santo was a runner at first, with less than two out, when the batter grounded to the left side of the infield. Santo figured to be an easy force-out at second base, but the second baseman dropped the ball. Santo was still out, however, because he slid well past the base and was tagged by the second baseman. Cub fans booed, thinking that they had seen a sloppy slide cost them an out and a baserunner at second. It seemed to me, however, that Santo had quite reasonably taken himself to be a dead duck at second and he was bent on preventing a double play. To do so he needed to slide right past the bag into the legs of the fielder. Alas for Santo, if he had made the kind of unimaginative slide that would have guaranteed a double play and gotten him booed for failing to break up the play, he would have been safe. The booing fans did not *see,* and that failure to see is as much a possibility for a television viewer as for someone at the game.

The rhythm baseball exhibits is, in the first instance, a matter of movement through space, and the estimate of visual space is different on television. When the center field camera with its telephoto lens shows you the pitcher throwing to the batter, it looks as if the ball has such a short distance to go that it should reach the catcher immediately after the pitcher lets it go. With a little viewing experience, however, we have all learned to "understand" this episode. Early on, at least for me, the ball seemed to be going more slowly than I had expected. Then, gradually, I began to see the television ball traversing, not the sixty feet traveled by a real baseball, but the four or five inches separating television pitching rubber from television home plate, and the whole thing began to look and feel right. Nolan Ryan and Dwight Gooden look faster in the park than Orel Hershiser does, and they also look faster on television.

A different phenomenon arises when television renders baseball space discontinuously. When television shows all the space between a throw and a catch, viewers adapt readily, but it is different when the intervening space is not shown. Of late television has begun to treat base-stealing threats in this way: the television screen is split, right down the middle, I think, and on the left you see the pitcher holding the ball and peering over at the runner, and on the right you see the runner taking an ever-longer lead off first. When the pitcher throws to first, the ball simply disappears for an instant as it departs the left side of the screen, and one has no visual clues as to when to expect it to reappear on the right side of the screen. I have never been able to get the hang of this visual array, and I wish they would cut it out; but I may have an underdeveloped sensibility.

Baseball has been a brilliant subject for television, in some respects. It is not necessary, for instance, to interrupt baseball—or at least not the part of a baseball game when the ball is in play—in order to show commercials. The half-inning and full-inning breaks are enough, and they last long enough, especially when a few other interruptions occur naturally, as when a relief pitcher comes in. This is not to say that the experience of a baseball game in a baseball park is simply the experience to be had when the ball is in play. Absolutely not. A spectator has much to look at and think about, and many choices to make, during all those breaks. But television baseball is grafted onto real baseball, as, for instance, television football is not quite grafted onto real football. A football game must introduce additional pauses and delays into its own rhythm to accommodate commercial interruptions. Hence the "television time-out," which leaves the television audience with the choice of whether to go to the bathroom, go to the kitchen, or endure the commercial, all of which are consistent with the game-on-television, but drops the live audience out of the rhythm of the game.

That is enough of baseball, at least for this paper. What about television? What are television's objects of possible appreciation? I don't know the answer to this question, but I think I do know that what we should look at are not isolated thirty- or sixty-minute segments.[2] We should not look exclusively, that is, at particular episodes of *Lou Grant* or *Moonlighting* or *All in the Family* or *Slap Maxwell*. One of those episodes will be an audiovisual array of an hour's or a half hour's duration with two, three, four, or five interludes filled with commercials, announcements, etc. None of these is the principal thing in television. What is that thing? What do you think? Is it a series? A season? As

2. The only sustained, philosophical treatment of television's "formats" I know is Stanley Cavell's exceptionally useful "The Fact of Television," which first appeared in *Daedalus*, Fall 1982, and is reprinted in Cavell's *Themes Out of School: Effects and Causes* (San Francisco: North Point Press, 1984).

many seasons as a show lasts? Here are some significant thematic elements in *Cagney and Lacey*: Cagney's alcoholism and her relationship with her alcoholic father; Lacey's not-so-ambivalent relationship with her father; the coming of age of Lacey's military-minded older son; Cagney's aggressive but equivocal sexuality; the racial and ethnic tensions of the detective squad; Lacey's feminism; Cagney's loyalty to the force. You could not see half these things appear in any whole season, much less watch them develop. Just what does it come to, then, to say that *Cagney and Lacey* is one of the things on television?

Cagney and Lacey is not uniquely typical of what is on television, and although I will make no survey here, I will note that there are a number of different formats, and we ought to pay attention to what *works* on television. This does not seem to me principally a matter of judgment; it is just a question of looking. Most programs last either thirty minutes or an hour, although for a while hour-and-a-half programs were not uncommon (my memory may be faulty, but I think that *Columbo,* at least for a while, was part of a rotating series, each of whose programs was ninety minutes long). Consider only the programs that are fiction. Some of them present entirely self-contained episodes. Many situation comedies are like this, although some display a connectedness as the characters and their situations change. *All in the Family* was like this, and so is *The Cosby Show,* although less dramatically. Archie became less or differently bigoted, Edith became a proto-feminist, the Huxtable children grow up. It is not only situation comedies that are thus self-contained, episode by episode. *Harry O* and *The Rockford Files* were like that. Occasionally one of these self-contained programs will extend itself, but always for a specified time, usually just for two episodes, called 'Part One' and 'Part Two.' This kind of extension has appeared, to my knowledge, in a number of series, including, for instance, *Magnum, P.I.* and *Cagney and Lacey.*

Other programs are not self-contained, but spread out indefinitely. The most obvious examples are soaps, but *Hill Street Blues* was like this, and so is *L.A. Law.* What difference does it make? One difference is an alteration in what I think of as the rhythmic expectations of viewers. When you watch a self-contained episode, you expect a resolution by five minutes before either the half- or the full hour. Sometimes you are surprised, and perhaps exasperated, when the resolution does not come and in its place you read "to be continued." But your expectations are quite different when you watch a non-self-contained episode. *Hill Street Blues, St. Elsewhere,* and *L.A. Law,* for instance, almost always contain, in any episode, a number of sub-narratives. Some of these narratives are begun in the current episode and some are continued from earlier episodes; some of them will resolve in the episode at hand and others will not. You don't know which are which, and so you find yourself less able to anticipate developments as the episode nears its end. These programs have been able to secure an audience engagement sufficient to permit—if only very infrequently—a sub-narrative to begin in one episode and then to be entirely absent from the next episode but to be picked up again in a later episode. (A variation on this kind of construction, with an empty middle, is currently present in a commercial. I cannot remember just what headache remedy is being advertised. Someone appears complaining of a headache and then doses himself with the favored pills. Next you see other commercials, and only after that does the headache sufferer reappear, claiming that the pills have restored him.)

A certain kind of philosopher will insist, at this point if not long since, that if television is to pretend to be art, or like art, or significant as a medium, then it must be appropriate to say what is special about television, or at least one of its forms—to lay out an Aristotelian definition. Just as Aristotle tells us what is special about tragedy by way of a definition and its implications, so we should have a formulaic, definitive description of television. I think this is a mistaken project, not only inadequate to the task at hand, but also faithless to Aristotle's own project. Aristotle does not set out his definition *in advance*. Aristotle persistently is a methodological conservative. At the time Aristotle undertakes the philosophy of the *Poetics*, tragedy is securely in place in his culture, with a well-known history, considerable agreement about which of its examples are salient, and a significant understanding of how tragedies work. Aristotle reflects upon all this and then produces his analysis. Tragedy has already worked itself out when Aristotle attempts a philosophical understanding of it. Television has not worked itself out; it is doing so right now. We are not in a position to say what television is, and what is the best that television can do. Imagine trying to say these things about movies in the 1920's, or about music in the seventeenth century. What we can do is begin to ask questions.

It is not my task here to go into these things in detail. I would like to induce you to believe that there is some point, and some difficulty and perhaps a reward, in trying to describe what is on television. A focal point has to be what seems to work on television. Why are game shows enduringly popular? Why do Westerns sometimes work and sometimes police, doctor, or lawyer shows? Why do soap operas work, as well as other infinitely extended dramatic series? What is it about the medium that supports these things? How are we to understand the abiding interest in re-runs? When someone attached to *Harry O*, as I am, watches reruns, it may be in hopes of seeing an episode missed when it first showed, but not infrequently the viewer has seen every episode at least once before. I am like this. What am I doing when I watch these episodes again? Is it like re-reading a book, in hopes of understanding more? Or is it like visiting an old, comfortable friend (not that this is absolutely different)?

And how is it that television creates a character, and what kinds of characters can it create? This is one question I will go into briefly, although I will leave it, like the others, in considerable need of attention.

Let me begin with a three-part story. (1) The first part is autobiographical. Eight years ago my family made its first trip to Poland. While we were staying in Lublin, a provincial capital near the eastern border, we attended a party given for us by a number of marvelously generous and cordial academics. During the evening my children entertained themselves part of the time playing with the dog who belonged to our host. It was a basset hound, and my children remember him under the name they gave him, "Long and Low," because of their great difficulty in tumbling him off his feet. His Polish owners, however, had named him "Columbo."

(2) Recently the journal *American Film* published Michel Ciment's interview with Marcel Ophuls, dealing principally with Ophuls's recent movie, *The Hotel Terminus: The Life and Times of Klaus Barbie*. When Ophuls attempts to articulate the difference in conception between this movie and others, in particular his own *The Sorrow and the Pity* and Claude Lanzmann's *Shoah*, he says this:

> The series "Columbo" is very popular in France. I myself am a great "Columbo" fan, just as Truffaut was, and "Columbo" probably influenced me in the way that I constructed this film. The principle of "Columbo" is taking Hitchcock's idea that suspense is not the same as mystery—so much that in the first five minutes you know who the guilty person is. The rest is watching Peter Falk investigate the crime and seeing how people lie and how the crime was committed.[3]

(3) In Wim Wenders's recent movie *Wings of Desire* all the actors are European—mostly German, I think—with the exception of Peter Falk, who plays himself (whatever this means) as the-actor-Peter-Falk come to Berlin to be in a movie being made there. When he is not busy on the set he strolls around Berlin, frequently being recognized and always being called "Columbo."

3. *American Film*, September 1988, p. 41.

What are we to make of this? Well, first there is the wide appeal of the character Columbo. He is known to French film makers, a Polish philosopher of science and his friends and colleagues, and German construction workers. By itself that may be no more striking than the availability of Big Mac's in Paris, Belgrade, and Tokyo. But more is going on. Note the way in which Columbo is spoken of. During his description of the typical *Columbo* episode, Ophuls says that Peter Falk investigates the crime. But in *Columbo* it is Columbo who is the detective. This easy movement between the actor and the role is typical of discussions of movies, and it is at its most significant when the actor is one of those actors especially suited to the movies. (When I have written and lectured about *North by Northwest,* for instance, I have more often called the main character "Cary Grant" than "Roger Thornhill," and I am not at all unusual in this.) Television has made a character, Columbo, and it is misleading to think of Peter Falk as playing the role if that suggests a relationship like one in which Laurence Olivier plays Hamlet. In *Wings of Desire,* one of the angels decides to give up his angelic nature and become a human. After he does this, Peter Falk reveals to him that he himself once did the same thing, cashing in his armor in a pawnshop on Lenox Avenue. At this point the audience is invited to understand the personality of this man in terms of his angelic, pre-human background, and the choice he once made to be human. But what man is being understood in this way? Columbo? Peter Falk? This man has a deep, unhurried appreciation of details—the taste of coffee and cigarettes, the looks of streets and alleys and hats. And he has an abiding awareness that along with the concrete sensuality of life's objects there are things unseen, waiting to be revealed, perhaps by being induced to reveal themselves. The man with those characteristics is Columbo.

Much of what is in *Wings of Desire* eludes me, but I will venture the guess that Wenders wants this character to epitomize America and something that America stands for. When he chooses a character to do this, he chooses Columbo. It is a good choice. And this character exists because television created him.

How significant a creation is this? How profound and memorable is Columbo?[4] No doubt this remains to be seen, but there is no doubt

4. If you are embarrassed to be caught doing critical analyses of television characters, let me reassure you by noting that a friend of mine, Richard Strier, a distinguished professor of English literature and an expert on George Herbert, has suggested that the model for Columbo is Porfiry, the police inspector who persists to the end in *Crime and Punishment,* and that the structure of the program's episodes itself is taken from the dramatic psychological structure of the book. As fascinating as this suggestion is, I

that Columbo is specifically a television creation. He is something like a character created in fiction, like someone wrought in a long novel. One might think of Mr. Micawber from *David Copperfield,* and certainly one thinks of Sherlock Holmes as he is developed in the fifty-six short stories and four novels. But Columbo has a specific appearance, a visible concrete physicality, and in this respect he is like a character presented in a movie. But a movie does not have the expansive and discontinuous dimensions that permit the development of a character by accretion. As long as we see television in terms of single continuous units we will think of it as more confined and restricted than movies, but once we see television in terms of extended series we see it as more ample than movies.

It is not so clear what it means for a character to develop or be developed, in a novel, or a play, or a poem, or a movie, or on television. Sometimes the character has a personality essentially intact when the character is first presented, and he remains unchanged throughout the text. Aspects of this personality may be revealed cumulatively throughout the text, thereby enriching the character and showing how a character with this personality acts and feels as new situations appear, but in such a case we have character development only in the sense of developing the character *for the audience.* Columbo is like this. During the entire sequence we learn considerably many facts about the man, many of which reveal aspects of his personality. Some of them are facts about his current life, for instance the car he drives, the dog he owns, how he cares for his car and for his dog, the relatives he has and how he is involved with them, particularly the relatives who have come to him through his wife. Some of the facts, although not nearly so many, concern his history. In one episode Columbo

---

have been willing to credit the suggestion to Professor Strier and leave its defense to him. This is partly because I have been able to recall only one episode of this type, one in which Johnny Cash is the murderer, but a murderer whose religious nature is about to force him to confess when Columbo traps him. Recently, however, Professor Strier has fortified his case by noting a piece on the revival of *Columbo* in which the author of the piece says, "According to a press handout, the actor says he modeled the role on Porfiry Petrovich, the excessively polite, psychologically probing investigator, who works so insidiously on Raskolnikov in *Crime and Punishment* [*New York Times*, March 2, 1989]. According to Professor Strier, this not only makes his case but it also demonstrates that a literary thesis can be proved.

The most useful writing on *Columbo* I have seen is in David Thorburn's "Television Melodrama." I am not sure of the publication history of this piece. I think it first appeared in *Television as a Cultural Force,* edited by Douglass Cater and Richard Adler (New York: Praeger Publishers, 1976), but I have used it in *Television: The Critical View,* fourth edition, edited by Horace Newcomb (New York: Oxford University Press, 1987). It is especially good on the American character of Columbo, virtually anticipating the sense of the character that Wenders exploits.

needs access to a suspect's car, and so he contrives to disable the car, thereby inducing the suspect to leave it in a mechanic's garage over night. Columbo stymies the automobile engine by jamming a potato into its exhaust pipe. Near the end of the episode Columbo confides to the man whose wife was murdered by the suspect that he, Columbo, learned this trick with potatoes and exhaust systems when he was a boy hanging out with other boys who went in for such tricks.

Facts like these make good sense in the life of a man who is also the kind of man who would get a good price for armor when selling it in a pawnshop on Lenox Avenue.

When one of these facts is presented, the audience is delighted, perhaps, but not surprised, as one would be surprised to learn that a person had done something entirely unexpected and unpredictable, because these facts are congruent with the Columbo character who has been in place since the first episode in the series. It is as if an outline were continually being filled in. This kind of character development, which is character revelation, so to speak, is not a peculiarly television kind of device. It is to be seen in Mr. Micawber in *David Copperfield,* I think, and in Regan and Goneril in *King Lear.*

It is different with the character of Levin in *Anna Karenina* and the character of Michael Corleone in the *Godfather* movies. In both those cases it is arguable that the character himself is developing, perhaps changing and certainly growing. The story does not merely reveal more and more of the character; it is also the context in which the character alters as he reveals himself.

I see no reason why television should not be capable of both kinds of character development, and in fact I think it has succeeded with both kinds. Alexander Nehamas has not been sanguine about the achievement of character development in television. In his recent, stimulating piece "Plato and the Mass Media," he first says,

The characters' personalities are usually the same,[5]

and then he adds this reservation:

This statement needs to be qualified in light of shows like *Hill Street Blues, St. Elsewhere,* or *L.A. Law,* which allow for some character development. Such development, however, is both slow and conservative.[6]

In this assessment I think that Professor Nehamas goes too quickly and may have stumbled. It is not at all clear how to measure the speed with which a character develops in traditional mediums. Who develops

5. *Monist* 71 (April 1988): 229.
6. Ibid., 234, n. 54.

faster, the king in *Oedipus Rex* or the king in *King Lear*? In these cases I suppose we might actually time performances of the plays and note the time elapsed when Oedipus first seems to begin self-realization or when Lear first moves from being a parent to being a child, and we might time the development of the count in a performance of Mozart's *Marriage of Figaro,* too, but I doubt that this is what Professor Nehamas has in mind. In plays and operas we don't have to take an actual performance as the time frame, do we? And in novels, stories, and poems, we have no such possibility. Does it matter how long it takes us to read? How fast does Marlow develop in *Heart of Darkness?* As rapidly as he does in *Apocalypse Now?*

These are not the pressing questions about speed of character development, however, although they are intriguing. The pressing question is, what counts as speed of character development in television? What counts as speed of anything in television? Speed has to do with getting from one place to another. What are the places in television? The beginning and end of a thirty-minute episode? The ends of coherent segments within a whole series, which may or may not be congruent with the beginnings and ends of particular episodes? The point of this paper is that we do not know just what the *object* is when we discuss television, and so we certainly do not know how to measure speed and location in terms of that object. It is not a point of this paper, alas, to answer these questions. I hope it is an achievement to ask them.

If television has a special capacity for the development and delineation of characters (as I am suggesting in the case of Columbo), then does it not also have related capacities for the exploitation of temporal sequences, in particular interrupted ones, ones whose continuities span the gaps of two-minute commercial interruptions and the gaps of weeks between installments?

This year a television station in Chicago has been showing *Hill Street Blues,* rerunning the episodes in their proper order but showing one every night. I had previously watched reruns of *Hill Street Blues,* but always with the usual week interlude between episodes. The show is changed by being shown every night, and I think it is damaged. Weekly showings induce the audience to think and feel that time has gone by since the characters were last seen, and that the characters have existed during that time and been going about their business. There has been adequate time for LaRue's drinking problem to have gotten better or worse, for Belker's aging father to deteriorate, for Renko's feelings about Bobby Hill to change, for tension to build on the Hill. Nightly showings defeat this sense in the audience. *M*A*S*H* survives nightly showings much better because its rhythms seldom stretch beyond individual episodes. If *M*A*S*H* is like the items in a song recital, then *Hill Street Blues* is more like a song cycle or an opera. Or perhaps *M*A*S*H* is like a collection of short stories and *Hill Street Blues* is like a novel. But these analogies are dangerous. We need to describe television if we are going to be able to talk about it with any depth, and we must describe it without assimilating it to something else. However helpful, and maybe necessary, it is to begin by thinking of things television resembles, television is different and so are its capacities.

Once these capacities are worked out—by television itself—and then seen by us, it will still remain for us to realize whether they underwrite anything worthwhile. Until then, we are in the dark, and I put it to you that those who announce that there is no artistic merit in television almost certainly do not know what they are talking about.

4   **Narcissus and Pygmalion:
Lessons of Two Tales**

KARSTEN HARRIES

1

The following remarks are part of an attempt to raise once more the question of the origin of art. That question has an obvious first answer: should we not look for that origin to the artists who created it? Thus we may look for the origin of a particular work of art in the psycho-history of its creator, as Freud did, when he interpreted the mysteriously ambiguous smile of Leonardo da Vinci's *Mona Lisa* as a repressed memory of the artist's mother, from whom he was separated at an early age.[1] If Freud is right, this artwork, at any rate, figures a quite specific lost, but still dreamed of, happiness. Leonardo's art is given its origin in the artist's quite specific eros.

But such an interpretation does not explain why *we* should still be interested in the painting and treasure it as art. The artwork's continuing appreciative reception demonstrates that what finds expression in it cannot be something that belongs only to this particular individual, shaped by quite specific circumstances and events; rather it must belong to all who respond to, understand, and care for that expression. Only such reception lets us consider artworks "art." To locate the origin of the work of art in what belongs to the particularities of an artist's life or historical situation is to miss what makes the work of art a work of *art,* is to miss its origin as a work of art. But where then are we to look for that origin?

To ask for the origin of the work of art is not quite to raise the question with which I began.[2] To ask for the origin of art is not just to inquire into the nature of art. This question refuses to stop at the

1. Sigmund Freud, *Eine Kindheitserinnerung des Leonardo da Vinci, Studienausgabe,* 10 (Frankfurt: Fischer, 1982), 87–159.
2. See Martin Heidegger, "The Origin of the Work of Art," tr. Albert Hofstadter, *Philosophies of Art and Beauty,* ed. A. Hofstadter and R. Kuhns (Chicago: Univ. of Chicago Press, 1976), 650.

riddle that is art. It wants to root the nature of art in something deeper and wider, wants to know what it is that lets human beings create and take delight in works of art as they do. Aesthetics has answered this question by pointing to beauty and the pleasure it grants, a pleasure that needs no justification and is its own reward. But should we stop with this pleasure? Recall once more Freud's study of Leonardo. His art is said to have its origin in a return to the natural auto-eroticism of the child, in a narcissistic love that reoccupies the place once held by the original object of the artist's love, the mother from whom he was separated all too soon, with his own self. Answering to this twofold love, the androgynous beauty so characteristic of Leonardo's art provides a figure of a now-lost state of blissful perfection.

With his interpretation Freud belongs to a tradition that we can trace back to Plato, who in the *Symposium* understands beauty as the object of love and love as the desire for a perfection denied to us by our present state, marked as it is by lack and desire. To be sure, Plato's paradigm is not a work of art, but a person, who by his beauty fills another with love, a love that wants to embrace and give birth. What does such beauty have to do with the beauty of art? Haven't Kant and Schopenhauer taught us to understand beauty as the object of an entirely disinterested satisfaction? Beauty and love, it would seem, must be divorced, for is not love by its very nature interested? Or is this divorce, as Freud hints, only apparent? Does art have its origin in love?

To approach this question, I would like to take a look at two tales that speak to this origin: the tale of Narcissus and the tale of Pygmalion.

2

Near the beginning of Part Two of Alberti's *On Painting,* the first treatise to give voice to the aesthetic sensibility that was to shape the evolution of Renaissance and Post-Renaissance art, we find the following remark:

Moreover, painting was given the highest honour by our ancestors. For, although almost all other artists were called craftsmen, the painter alone was not considered in that category. For this reason, I say among my friends that Narcissus who was changed into a flower, according to the poets, was the inventor of painting. Since painting is already the flower of every art, the story of Narcissus is most to the point. What else can you call painting but a similar embracing with art of what is presented on the surface of the water in the fountain?[3]

3. Leon Battista Alberti, *On Painting,* trans. and intro. John R. Spencer (New Haven and London: Yale Univ. Press, 1966), 64.

A strange remark! Why should Alberti want to claim Narcissus as his precursor? To call him the inventor of painting would seem to cast the art of painting in a very questionable light. Ovid, one of "the poets" of whom Alberti must have been thinking, describes Narcissus as a young man of extraordinary beauty, possessed by a pride that refused love, until one of those he scorned prayed to heaven that he, too, might feel the pain of unrequited love; punished by Nemesis, Narcissus fell in love with his own reflected image; slowly consumed by this love, he was transformed into the flower we call "narcissus."

Alberti's use of the Narcissus story invites us to seek the origin of painting not just in love, but in an inversion of love brought about by pride. But can this be how Alberti would have his readers understand his remark?

Given Ovid's tale, it's not surprising that medieval writers should have discovered a moral lesson in it. Alan of Lille's *Plaint of Nature*, for example, names Narcissus, along with Helen of Troy, Pasiphae, Myrrha, and Medea, as an example of pride overturning the order of nature. Alberti's remark hints that art has its origin in such pride.

Inseparable from pride is a refusal of our temporal condition:

What is the basis of this haughtiness, this pride in man? His birth is attended by pain, the penalty of toil lays waste to his life, the greater penalty of inevitable death rounds off his punishment. His existence is the matter of a moment, his life is a shipwreck, his world is a place of exile. His life is gone or giving assurance of its going, for death is exerting its pressure or threatening.[4]

Our finite, embodied self is vulnerable and mortal, but it is just this subjection to matter and time that pride refuses to acknowledge. And from pride, Alan of Lille tells us, issues envy, which measures what we are and possess by what is denied to us, first of all by the perfection that belongs to God. Among those subject to envy, Alan mentions Narcissus.[5]

While Alan of Lille may very well have been one of the poets Alberti had in mind, to locate the origin of art in pride hardly seems to serve his stated purpose: to prove that "painting is not unworthy of consuming all our time and study."[6] How does Alberti understand that worth? If we take him at his word, the worth of painting would seem linked to its self-sufficiency: to say that it is not unworthy of taking up all of our time is to suggest that the pursuit of art need not serve other activities, for if so, could it ever be worthy of taking up *all* of

---

4. Alan of Lille, *The Plaint of Nature*, trans. and commentary by James J. Sheridan (Toronto: Pontifical Institute of Mediaeval Studies, 1980), 187.
5. Ibid., 188–89.
6. Alberti, *On Painting*, 63.

our time? For the sake of art, Alberti seems to suggest, we may suspend all other concerns. To be sure, I may be placing too much weight on what would seem to be no more than a casual remark made in passing; just like the anecdotal reference to Narcissus, it seems no more than a rhetorical aside, hyperbolic, as such asides tend to be, certainly not weighty enough to warrant the kind of literal approach I am imposing on it. But just such rhetorical asides, where an author relaxes a bit, often reveal his deepest concerns better than his central argument.

As stated, Alberti's statement of purpose gestures in a direction that would have to have troubled a Christian thinker like Alan of Lille. Just as Narcissus has denaturalized eros, the person whose time is entirely dedicated to art would seem to have strayed from the natural end of a human. One could speak here with Kierkegaard of a teleological suspension of the ethical, although what is suspended is not just the ethical but the religious. Such suspension is indeed inseparable from the pursuit of art for art's sake. As Kierkegaard knew, there is something demonic about such suspension; and there is something demonic about dedicating one's whole life to art.

I would like to call special attention to Alberti's claim that art is not unworthy of consuming all our time. Art apparently is capable of consuming, i.e., of abolishing, time. Do we get here a hint of the worth of painting as Alberti understands it? Is its dignity linked to its ability to defeat, or perhaps only to let us forget, if only for a time, the tyrannical rule of time? First of all and most of the time, care and desire, fear and hope let us reckon with time; first of all and most of the time, we find ourselves in the world as interested actors; but as long as we thus look ahead to the future, we are not truly at one with ourselves. We get here a hint as to why human beings should be so very interested in the pursuit of the disinterested satisfaction granted by the beautiful. In time aesthetic experience promises to lift the burden of time.

But let me return to the traditional understanding of the tale of Narcissus as a tale of pride subverting the natural order. That Alberti is aware of this reading, a reading that has to invite criticism, is suggested when he tells the reader that he tells his playful determination of the origin of painting only to his friends (where the reader, being let in on the secret, is thereby included in Alberti's circle of friends).

What readers was Alberti addressing? First of all, his fellow painters. The science of perspective taught by Alberti was to render them the masters of appearance. Recall that Alberti's *On Painting* appeared in 1435/36, at a time when a new approach to art was beginning to challenge the older medieval approach, which had blurred the boundary between art and craft and placed art in the service of religious truth. The book's prologue communicates something of the excitement that then pervaded the artistic world. Alberti tells us that he, too, used to believe that "Nature, the mistress of things, had grown old and tired. She no longer produced either geniuses or giants which in her more youthful and more glorious days she had produced so marvellously and abundantly."[7] But the Florence of Brunelleschi, Donatello, and Masaccio taught him better. Here were once again true giants. And the credit for this flowering Alberti no longer gives to nature, but to the person. A new prideful self-assertion lets him claim that "the power of acquiring wide fame in any art or science lies in our industry and diligence more than in the times or gifts of nature."[8] It is this pride that places the reader on the threshold not just of a new art—it is hardly an exaggeration to say that, down to the present, painting has acted out the scenario set by Alberti and his friends—but of a new world. Alberti's revaluation of Narcissus presupposes a changed self-understanding, especially a new understanding of the relationship of humanity and nature. This new self-assertion will not hear nature's lament.

Giving voice to the artistic revolution that overthrew medieval art, Alberti's *On Painting* helps mark the beginning of the aesthetic approach to beauty and art that has shaped the development of art ever since. Alberti's mention of Narcissus forces us to question this approach's ruling ethos: should we locate the origin of Renaissance and Post-Renaissance art in love, more precisely in that inversion of love brought about by the pride of which Ovid's tale tells?

3

Consider once more Alberti's remark:

... I say among my friends that Narcissus who was changed into a flower, according to the poets, was the inventor of painting. Since painting is already the flower of every art, the story of Narcissus is most to the point.

Narcissus was changed into a flower. As we read in Ovid:

The pyre, the tossing torches, and the bier, were now being prepared, but his body was nowhere to be found. Instead of his corpse, they discovered a flower with a circle of white petals round a yellow center.[9]

7. Ibid., 39.
8. Ibid.
9. Ovid, *Metamorphoses*, trans. and intro. Mary M. Innes (Harmondsworth: Penguin, 1955), 87.

It is significant that Narcissus was changed not just into a flower, but into the flower that now bears his name. As a matter of fact, the myth of Narcissus may well represent a response to the flower, an attempt, if you wish, to read in the book of nature. This, at any rate, is argued by Friedrich Wieseler: the core of the myth, he suggests, is nothing other than the history of the narcissus. That beautiful flower loves the water and turns its head downward. The flower also helps to explain the parentage of the mythical Narcissus, whose father is Cephisus, god of the main river of Boeotia, while his mother is called Liriope, because the narcissus was considered a kind of lily (*leirion*). The myth would then be an extended figure of the flower known in antiquity not only for its beauty, which returns every spring, but for its benumbing odor. As Wieseler points out, "The name, doubtless, has to do with *nárke, narkan,* words which in Greek are mainly used to refer to the effects of frost, terror, fainting, death."[10] Persephone is raped by Hades when absorbed in the beauty of the narcissus. The ancients thus associated the flower with both beauty and death. And these associations return in the mythical figure of the beautiful Narcissus, who in antiquity was considered a symbol of death.[11] The images of Narcissus on grave monuments suggest that Narcissus was understood not only as an incarnation of pride, but more positively, as a symbol of a metamorphosis that offers consolation for the pain inflicted by the terror of time. Narcissus's metamorphosis into a flower rescues him from total annihilation and grants him a semblance of immortality.

The flower is the metamorphosed Narcissus, we can say, his metaphor. In this metaphor Narcissus continues to live. Thus his final wish is granted after all. I quote Ovid's Narcissus:

"I am cut off in the flower of my youth. I have no quarrel with death, for in death I shall forget my pain: but I could wish that the object of my love might outlive me; as it is, both of us will perish together, when this one life is destroyed."[12]

The wish is paradoxical: while ready to die, Narcissus yet wishes that the object of his love might outlive him; but that object is of course he himself. Narcissus accepts death and yet wishes for continued life. And this paradoxical wish for life in death is granted. As the flower he has become, Narcissus is reborn every spring and thus rescued from total destruction.

10. Friedrich Wieseler, *Narkissos* (Göttingen: Verlag der Dieterichschen Buchhandlung, 1856), 79.
11. Ibid., 9.
12. Ovid, op. cit., 86.

Note that this reading invites an interpretation of the flower as a figure of painting. By embracing with art what is presented on the surface of the fountain,—these are Alberti's words—the artist gives what he embraces permanence, allows the mirror image to remain when its original has long ceased to be. Is this then part of Alberti's reason for invoking Narcissus? Is art the ambiguous figure of both death and the victory over death, a victory the artist does not owe to nature, or to God, but to skill?

4

Reconsider the line: "What else can you call painting but a similar embracing with art of what is presented on the surface of the water in the fountain?" The artist does not just re-present what is in the mirror but embraces it, where we should recall that just this was denied to Narcissus. The artist may thus be said to succeed where Narcissus failed. The offspring of that embrace is the work of art. Art allows narcissistic eros to become procreative after all.

The painter's embrace of what appears in the mirror subjects this appearance to a distinctly human order. The science of perspective provides the artist with a mathematical form into which must be fitted whatever is to be represented, if such representation is to present convincing illusions. This science determines a priori how things in objective space must appear to the eye. In this sense the science of perspective may be said to exhibit the logic of visual appearance. It is phenomenology, as Lambert understood it.[13] To understand that logic is also to understand that whatever we see is no more than appearance, dependent on the perceiving subject's specific point of view. The objects themselves disclose themselves only to the mind, which is capable of transcending the limitations of perspective. Inseparable from Alberti's insight into the power of perspective and from the artistic tradition that this insight helped found is thus a dissociation of the visible and the real. Its very medium cuts painting off from a pursuit of reality as it is. With this recognition beauty is severed from truth. The realm of art is appearance. Sight is incapable of granting us objective understanding. This dissociation of the visible and the real is equally a presupposition of the mathematization of nature that was to become a defining characteristic of the new science. Insight into the logic of appearance leads inevitably to demands for a more adequate under-

13. See Johannes Hoffmeister's introduction to Georg Wilhelm Friedrich Hegel, *Phänomenologie des Geistes* (Hamburg: Meiner, 1952).

standing of reality. In this sense Alberti's *On Painting* belongs to the prehistory of modern science.[14]

Like his contemporary, Cardinal Nicolaus Cusanus (given the biographies of these two seminal thinkers of the early Renaissance, I find it inconceivable that the two did not meet, although I know of no documented encounter), Alberti, too, knows that neither objective space nor its subjective appearance allows us to speak of the absolute size of things. This would presuppose some absolute measure, but such a measure is nowhere to be found. All things, Alberti insists, just as Cusanus was to do about five years later in *On Learned Ignorance*, are known by comparison.[15] This leads Alberti (once again the slightly older Cusanus was to follow him) to claim the sophist Protagoras as a forbear—another surprising choice, given the ill repute in which the sophist had long been held, beginning with Plato and Aristotle.[16] Perhaps, Alberti suggests, Protagoras had gotten hold of a profound insight we would do well to heed: "By saying that man is the mode and measure of all things [he] meant that all the accidents of things are known through comparison to the accidents of man."[17] This invites the reader to renounce the claim to know things as they are. Such knowledge is the privilege of God. His insistence on the finitude of human knowledge, which denies us access to *the* truth, might have led Alberti to the kind of epistemological resignation characteristic of late nominalist thought. But there is no trace of resignation in Alberti's text. Instead we meet with a proud self-assertion. The renunciation of the claim to absolute knowledge leads to the conviction that by our own resources we can make ourselves the masters of appearance.

Alberti fails to mention what Narcissus saw in the fountain. (We should note that Ovid speaks not of a fountain, but of a pool, which may suggest that Alberti was thinking not so much of Ovid's version of the story as of medieval retellings of it, such as the accounts found in *The Romance of the Rose*.[18]) What Narcissus saw was of course his

14. See especially Leonardo Olschki, *Die Literatur der Technik und der angewandten Wissenschaften vom Mittelalter bis zur Renaissance* (Leipzig: Winter, 1919), 30 ff.

15. Alberti, *On Painting*, 55. Nicholas of Cusa, *On Learned Ignorance*, tr. and an appraisal by Jasper Hopkins (Minneapolis: Banning, 1981), chap. 1, 50.

16. *On Painting*, 55. Protagoras is also mentioned in book two of Alberti's *I libri della famiglia*. Nicolaus Cusanus mentions Protagoras in chapters 36 and 37 of *De Beryllo*. See Charles Trinkaus, "Protagoras in the Renaissance: An Exploration," *Philosophy and Humanism: Essays in Honor of Paul Oscar Kristeller*, ed. Edward Mahoney (New York: Columbia Univ. Press, 1976), 190–213.

17. Alberti, *On Painting*, 55.

18. Guillaume de Lorris and Jean de Meun, *The Romance of the Rose*, tr. Harry W. Robbins (New York: Dutton, 1962), chap. 6 by Guillaume, and chap. 94 by Jean, who contrasts Lorris's Garden of Mirth, which holds "The bitter, poisonous Fountain Per-

own beautiful face, which so filled him with desire that, unable to embrace himself, he slowly wasted away, consumed by the hidden fire of love. But there is a sense in which what man sees in the mirror of appearance is, according to Alberti, always also himself. His body provides him with a natural measure by which to judge the size of things; and whatever appears to us, appears as it does because of the accident of our location in space and time and the accident of the makeup of our senses and our mind. The accidents of things are indeed known through the accidents of man. Alberti's references to Protagoras and Narcissus thus belong together. Both give voice to the anthropocentrism that is a presupposition of the turn to perspective in art. Looking into the mirror of appearance we always see ourselves.

5

Alberti's description of art as an embrace of what is reflected in the water's mirror recalls Plato's discussion of Book X of the *Republic*—this, too, a text that challenges Alberti's celebration of painting.

And there is another artist,—I should like to know what you would say of him.
Who is he?
One who is the maker of all the works of all other workmen.
What an extraordinary man!
Wait a little, and there will be more reason for your saying so. For this is he who is able to create not only vessels of every kind, but plants and animals, himself, and all other things—the earth and heaven, and the things which are in heaven or under the earth; he makes the gods also.
He must be a wizard and no mistake.
Oh! you are incredulous, are you? Do you mean that there is no such maker or creator; or that in one sense there might be a maker of all these things but in another not? Do you see that there is a sense in which you could make them all yourself?
What way?
An easy way enough; or rather, there are many ways in which the feat might be accomplished, none quicker than turning a mirror round and round—you would soon enough make the sun and the heavens, and the earth and yourself, and other animals and plants, and all the other things of which we were just now speaking, in the mirror.
Yes, he said; but they would be appearances only.[19]

Alberti's artist embraces these appearances with his art and thereby grants them permanence. This embrace allows him to escape the

---

ilous / That killed the fair Narcissus . . ." with the fountain of paradise. See especially pp. 433 and 434.
    19. Plato, *Republic* 10.596c–e, tr. Benjamin Jowett.

proud self-isolation of Narcissus. The products of the painter's pride meet with the community's grateful acceptance. "Any master painter," Alberti suggests, "who sees his work adored will feel himself considered another god."[20] "In painting animals" Zeuxis is said to have set "himself up almost as a god."[21] Like Plato, Alberti, too, understands the artist as a maker of the gods, citing the authority of Trismegistus, who is supposed to have said that *"mankind portrays the gods in his own image from his memories of nature and his own origins."*[22] "Nothing," Alberti adds, "has ever been so esteemed by mortals."[23]

Socrates would have insisted that the objects of esteem here are only imitations of appearances. Alberti, of course, would not have disputed that. But why then should painting be so valued by mortals? The word "mortals" hints at the answer: Alberti observes that "painting contains a divine force which not only makes absent men present, as friendship is said to do, but moreover makes the dead seem almost alive. Even after many centuries they are recognized with great pleasure and with great admiration for the painter."[24] And a bit later: "Thus the face of a man who is already dead certainly lives a long life through painting."[25] Alberti thus places painting in opposition to death. It has its origin in that ill will against time Nietzsche calls the spirit of revenge. That ill will bids human beings translate themselves out of time. Art, as Alberti understands it, effects such a translation.

6

Nietzsche thought the spirit of revenge the deepest source of human self-alienation. We find it difficult to forgive ourselves that we lack the power to realize what we so deeply desire: a state of plenitude that would mean the coincidence of freedom and facticity, of will and necessity. But such coincidence is denied to us by our finitude and temporality. Desire, care, memory, and anticipation, all testify to a lack of power that is constitutive of being human.

Born of this inability to accept the limits of our power, the spirit of revenge has to turn against ourselves, has to turn especially against what most obviously subjects us to time, against the body off which we can read our aging, against sexuality, which forces us to acknowl-

<hr>

20. Alberti, *On Painting*, 64.
21. Ibid.
22. Ibid., 65.
23. Ibid.
24. Ibid., 63.
25. Ibid.

edge that we are not disembodied spirits that happen to have assumed bodily shape, but that we are our bodies and as such not masters in our own house. Perhaps the most obvious manifestation of this ill will against time is a refusal of the authority of eros.

The tale of Narcissus has its origin in such a refusal. It is significant that the tale began with a perversion of eros, with a rape. The mother of Narcissus, Ovid tells us, "was the nymph whom Cephisus once embraced with his curving stream, imprisoned in his waves, and forcefully ravished."[26] The sexual act here is divorced from love. We understand why the unwanted offspring of such violence should refuse the nymph Echo's aggressive advances, why his "soft young body housed a pride so unyielding that none of those boys or girls dared to touch him."[27] Refusing all embraces, Narcissus would rather die than allow himself to be touched. In the end of course even proud Narcissus cannot escape love and love demands an object beyond the self. Narcissus finds that object in the mirrored reflection of his own beauty.

"I am on fire with love for my own self. It is I who kindle the flames which I must endure. What should I do? Woo or be wooed? But what then shall I seek by my wooing? What I desire, I have. My very plenty makes me poor. How I wish I could separate myself from my body! A new prayer this, for a lover, to wish the thing he loves away! Now grief is sapping my strength; little of life remains for me—I am cut off in the flower of my youth. I have no quarrel with death, for in death I shall forget my pain: but I could wish that the object of my love might outlive me: as it is, both of us will perish together when this one life is destroyed."[28]

Narcissus says of himself that he has what he desires. He thus would seem to embody that state of plenitude that haunts the spirit of revenge as an impossible ideal. In this respect Narcissus is rather like the circle-men of whom Aristophanes speaks in Plato's *Symposium*. Just as Ovid's tale links the plight of Narcissus to his pride, so it was the pride of these circle-men, a self-assertion that would scale Mount Olympus, that provoked the punishment of Zeus, who split these proto-humans into two, thus doubling them. As the search for our lost other half, for a lost plenitude, love has its origin in this divine punishment of pride. Presupposed is once more the desire for a self-completion denied to us by our present condition. For the human being such self-completion would mean death.

The myth of Aristophanes interprets for us the awakening of love

26. Ovid, *Metamorphoses*, 83.
27. Ibid.
28. Ibid., 86.

that puts an end to what Freud called "the primary narcissism of the child,"[29] to the child's only apparent self-sufficiency. Plenty now proves to be poverty. The self-embrace for which Narcissus longs would mean the impossible recovery of a plenitude denied by our fragmented self. Recognizing the impossibility, yet refusing to let go of his dream, Narcissus makes his peace with death. But Narcissus is not quite ready to renounce life altogether. He wants both: to be and not to be. This contradictory longing lets him wish that the object of his love, his own fleeting image in the pool, might outlast him. Narcissus knows that this is a vain wish. The mirror image will perish together with what it mirrors. But Alberti could have consoled Narcissus: art is able to give permanence to what has only fleeting existence in the mirror. It allows the beauty of Narcissus to survive, unsullied by a love that would embrace to give birth.

Is art then born of a narcissistic self-assertion? That it is not necessary to read the story of Narcissus as a warning tale about pride and its punishment is shown by Marcuse, who links the defamation of Narcissus to a defamation of the pleasure principle. In opposition to the prevalent reading, Marcuse finds in Narcissus, as in Orpheus, "the image of joy and fulfillment; the voice which does not command, but sings: the gesture which offers and receives; the deed which is peace and ends the labor of conquest; the liberation from time which unites man with god, man with nature."[30] The story of Narcissus is read as preserving "the truth of the Great Refusal, or, positively, insofar as it protects, against all reason, the aspirations for the integral fulfillment of man and nature which are repressed by reason."[31] So understood, Alberti's remark invites an understanding of art as a figure of that integral fulfillment denied us by reason and the ruling reality principle and which we yet dream of and refuse to let go. Traditionally the dream of integral fulfillment has been the dream of paradise. Art thus appears as a figure of paradise.

The association of art with paradise and of both with Narcissus is made explicit by André Gide's retelling of Ovid's tale. Marcuse would have us read this retelling as a poetic preservation of the image of Narcissus as the joy bringer. But Gide also articulates the antagonism that must separate this dreamed of joy from time and thus from reality.

29. See Sigmund Freud, *Zur Einführung des Narzissmus, Studienausgabe*, vol. 3, 39–73.

30. Herbert Marcuse, *Eros and Civilization* (Boston: Beacon, 1966), 162.

31. Ibid., 160.

In Gide's retelling, the pool from Ovid's story becomes the river of time:

On the banks of the river of time, Narcissus has come to a stop. Fateful and illusory river where the years pass and flow away. . . .

The place where Narcissus is looking is the present. Out of the most distant future, things which are still only potential hurry towards existence; Narcissus sees them, then they pass him by; they flow away into the past. Soon it strikes him that everything is always the same. He wonders; he reflects. They are always the same forms that pass; the movement of the current alone differentiates them.—Why are they so many? or why are they the same?—It must be because they are imperfect, since they are always re-commencing . . . and all of them, he thinks, are striving and rushing towards a lost primeval form, paradisal and crystalline. Narcissus dreams of paradise.[32]

Paradise here names a state where "everything was perfectly what it ought to be." That of course is how the artwork has often been described and, indeed, the paradise Narcissus dreams of is remarkably like a work of art:

Eden! where melodious breezes were wafted, undulating in pre-ordained curves: where the sky spread its azure over symmetrical lawns; where the birds were the colour of time and the butterflies on the flowers made providential harmonies; where the rose was rose-coloured because the green-fly settled on it for the very reason that it was green. Everything was as perfect as a number and scanned according to a rule; concord emanated from the relationship of lines between themselves; over the whole garden brooded a constant symphony.[33]

To the dream of paradise corresponds the dream of Adam, the grown-up child, who, knowing nothing of desire, knows nothing of time. Here is how André Gide describes him:

Single, still unsexed, he remained seated in the shade of the great tree. Man! Hypostasis of the Elohim! Mainstay of the Divinity! For his sake, by means of him, forms appear. Motionless and central in the midst of this fairyland, he watches it unrolling.[34]

Just as Gide thinks paradise in the image of the work of art, he thinks Adam in the image of the aesthetic observer. Or perhaps we should say rather the reverse: Gide thinks the work of art as a figure of paradise and the aesthetic observer as a figure of Adam, who in turn is thought, as John Scotus Eriugena already thought him, in the image of Aristophanes' circlemen. But with Gide it is not pride first of all

32. André Gide, "Narcissus," *The Return of the Prodigal*, tr. Dorothy Bussy (London: Secker and Warburg, 1953), 4–5.

33. Ibid., 7.

34. Ibid., 8.

that puts an end to this state of perfection, but boredom. Adam grows tired of forever watching, he wants to see and thereby seize himself. Yet, are not pride and boredom linked? Gide's Adam wants to assert himself. Such self-assertion lets him refuse the plenitude of his original aesthetic state.

And man, terror-stricken, self-duplicated hermaphrodite, wept with anguish and horror, feeling surges up within him, at the same time as a new sex, the anxious, uneasy desire for that other half, so like himself—that woman who, in a blind effort to re-create out of herself the perfect being and then stop breeding, will nevertheless carry in her womb the unknown creature of a new race and soon push into existence another being, still incomplete and incapable of sufficing to himself.[35]

Gide's Narcissus, who dreams this version of the Aristophanic myth, refuses the other-directedness of procreative eros. Seeking to recover the plenitude of Adam, he seeks to embrace himself:

Narcissus, solitary and puerile, falls in love with the fragile image; with longing for a caress, he bends down to the river to quench his thirst for love. He bends down and suddenly, lo and behold! the phantasmagoria disappears; he can see nothing on the river now but two lips stretched towards his own, two eyes, his own, looking at him. He understands that it is himself, that he is alone and that he is in love with his own face. Around him is empty azure, which is broken through by his pale arms, stretching out with desire through the shattered apparition and plunging into an unknown element.[36]

His attempt to repossess lost plenitude fails. But what then is Narcissus to do? Gide would have him renounce eros altogether and contemplate. Following Schopenhauer, Gide understands contemplation here aesthetically. The inverted eros of Narcissus is quieted by beauty. To find satisfaction Narcissus must renounce the vain attempt to embrace himself and allow himself to become absorbed in contemplation of the plenitude of the work of art.

For the work of art is a crystal—a portion of Paradise in which the Idea reblossoms in its superior purity; where, as in the vanished Eden, a normal and necessary order has arranged all forms in a reciprocal and symmetrical interdependence. . . .
Such works can crystallise only in silence; but there are silences sometimes even in the midst of crowds, when the artist, taking refuge, like Moses on Sinai, isolates himself, escapes from things and from Time and wraps himself in an atmosphere of light above the busy multitude. In him, slowly, the Idea rests; then lucid and fullblown, spreads forth, outside of Time. And as it is outside of Time, Time has no power over it. Nay, more; one wonders whether

35. Ibid., 8.
36. Ibid., 14–15.

Paradise itself outside of Time was perhaps never anywhere else—never anywhere but ideally.[37]

Marcuse would have us understand Narcissus as symbol of a non-repressive erotic attitude toward reality. This presupposes that we can escape from time without losing reality. Just this Gide, whom Marcuse cites in support of his utopian reading of the Narcissus myth, would have us question: as long as human beings experience themselves as subject to time, and such subjection manifests itself most inescapably in the awareness that we grow older and eventually must die, they are denied the plenitude of paradise. But art, breaking, if only for a time, the rule of time, serves the ideal of pleasure as Marcuse understands it, by granting illusions of presentness.

This, however, raises the question: Must pleasure be placed in opposition to time? Such a placement will indeed suggest itself as soon as the ideal of pleasure is linked, as it is by Marcuse, to "integral satisfaction," for "integral" suggests wholeness: are we not truly satisfied only when truly at one with ourselves, complete, entire? Just this ideal of satisfaction is incompatible with our temporal existence. That is to say, the ideal of integral satisfaction must alienate us from ourselves. The same goes for art that serves this ideal. Gide would, I think, have granted this. But if so, he would have welcomed such self-alienation as a necessary condition of recovering at least a semblance of paradise. Has not Schopenhauer taught us to understand the *principium individuationis* as the stain of which we must cleanse ourselves to be granted that pure perception which is the gift of art? To thus cleanse oneself would mean to lose reality.

7

Nietzsche has subjected such an understanding of aesthetic experience to scathing critique. Zarathustra's sermon "On Immaculate Perception" unmasks these would-be pure perceivers as self-deceiving lechers:

"This would be the highest to my mind"—thus says your lying spirit to itself—"to look at life without desire and not, like a dog, with my tongue hanging out. To be happy in looking, with a will that has died and without the grasping and greed of selfishness, the whole body cold and ashen, but with drunken moon eyes."[38]

37. Ibid., 14.
38. Friedrich Nietzsche, *Thus Spoke Zarathustra*, *The Portable Nietzsche*, tr. Walter Kaufmann (Harmondsworth: Penguin, 1976), 234.

Recall Narcissus, lying down, bent over the pond's mirror, "spellbound by his own self, . . . motionless, with fixed gaze, like a statue carved from Parian marble." Narcissus, of course, refuses to remain in this state of motionless absorption. This refusal makes him lose the paradise of contemplation that was his before love awoke. This is why Gide would have Narcissus divorce beauty from love and thus recover paradise in art. Just this divorce, so often taken for granted by traditional aesthetics, Nietzsche mocks:

"This I should like best"—thus the seducer seduces himself—"to love the earth as the moon loves her, and to touch her beauty only with my eyes. And this is what the immaculate perception of all things shall mean to me: that I want nothing from them, except to be allowed to lie prostrate before them like a mirror with a thousand eyes."[39]

In the *Genealogy of Morals* Nietzsche bolsters his critique of the disinterested purity of aesthetic perception celebrated by Kant and Schopenhauer by appealing to another tale from Ovid, the tale of Pygmalion.

If our aestheticians never weary of asserting in Kant's favor that, under the spell of beauty, one can *even* view undraped female statues "without interest," one may well laugh a little at their expense: the experiences of *artists* on this ticklish point are more "interesting," and Pygmalion was in any event *not* necessarily an "unaesthetic man."[40]

The tale of Pygmalion does indeed tell us not only something about "what art was taken to be in antiquity, but what it can be according to its very nature,"[41] and it is hardly surprising that speculation on art should have returned to it again and again.

An especially thoughtful reading of the tale was provided by Ernst Gombrich in *Art and Illusion*. According to Gombrich the story challenges the emphasis on mimesis by speaking of "an earlier and more awe-inspiring function of art when the artist did not aim at making a 'likeness' but of rivaling creation itself."[42] The story of Pygmalion is said to be only the most famous of many tales "that crystallize belief in the power of art to create rather than to portray."

---

39. Ibid.

40. Friedrich Nietzsche, *Genealogy of Morals*, 3:6, *Basic Writings of Nietzsche*, tr. and ed. Walter Kaufmann (New York: Modern Library, 1968), 540.

41. Udo Kultermann, "Pygmalion und das Symbol des Künstlers," *Kleine Geschichte der Kunsttheorie* (Darmstadt: Wissenschaftliche Buchgesellschaft, 1987), 1.

42. E. H. Gombrich, "Pygmalion's Power," *Art and Illusion* (Princeton: Princeton Univ. Press, 1961), 93.

Without the underlying promise of this myth, the secret hopes and fears that accompany the act of creation, there might be no art as we now know it. One of the most original young painters of England, Lucien Freud, wrote very recently: "A moment of complete happiness never occurs in the creation of a work of art. The promise of it is felt in the act of creation, but disappears towards the completion of the work. For it is then that the painter realizes that it is only a picture he is painting. Until then he had almost dared to hope that the picture might spring to life."[43]

The artist's dream of creation is also a dream of godlike self-sufficiency. This dream can dispense with love for another, because the dreamer seems able to provide himself with the object of his love. Gombrich appeals to the authority of Leonardo da Vinci:

In that hymn of praise to painting, the "Paragone," he calls the painter "the Lord of all manner of people and of all things." "If the painter wishes to see beauties to fall in love with, it is in his power to bring them forth, . . ."[44]

This recalls Alberti's invocation of Narcissus, also in praise of painting. So understood the two tales attribute the same origin to art.

It is worth noting that the tale of Pygmalion, too, begins with a perversion of eros. This time we hear not of rape, but of prostitution. Ovid tells of the loathsome Propoetides, who

dared to deny the divinity of Venus. The story goes that as a result of this, they were visited by the wrath of the goddess, and were the first women to lose their good names by prostituting themselves in public. Then, as all sense of shame left them, the blood hardened in their cheeks, and it required only a slight alteration to transform them into stony flints.[45]

Turned by the sight of these wicked women against the female sex, Pygmalion "long lived a bachelor existence, without any wife to share his home. But meanwhile, with marvellous artistry, he skillfully carved a snowy ivory statue. He made it lovelier than any woman born, and fell in love with his own creation."[46]

The parallels between our two stories are evident: both tell of a displacement of love brought about by a revulsion with sex. In the case of Narcissus this leads to a replacement of the beloved other with the self's reflected image, where Alberti would have us replace that image in turn with the work of art. In the story of Pygmalion the ivory statue becomes the object of love, where the adjective "stony" is

43. Ibid., 94.
44. Ibid., 95.
45. Ovid, *Metamorphoses*, 231.
46. Ibid.

suggestive: the turn to art there suggests something like a freezing of love. Also born of a refusal to honor the divinity of Venus, Pygmalion's translation of living flesh into ivory resembles the Propoetides' metamorphosis into stony flints.

Both Narcissus and Pygmalion lay claim to self-sufficiency. Both fail, as they must. But while the love of Narcissus remains self-centered, Pygmalion, by imploring Venus to give him "a wife like the ivory maid," acknowledges the inability of art to satisfy what he most deeply wants: even the most successful work of art is only its figure. As that figure it holds a promise of a happiness that, while it does not imply a restoration of the plenitude of Aristophanes' circle-men, is available to us humans.

For the metamorphosis of artwork into a living person Pygmalion cannot take credit. That metamorphosis is the gift of Venus. As one might expect, modern appropriations of the story (from Diderot's celebration of the sculptor Etienne-Maurice Falconet as a second Pygmalion, who with his *Pygmalion and Galatea* repeated the miracle of the first, restoring this paradigmatic sculptor to life, down to *My Fair Lady*) have credited human creativity with the godlike power of metamorphosis.[47] Or, in keeping with Kant's understanding of the aesthetic, Pygmalion's very desire to embrace the artwork he has created has been understood as a betrayal of the purity of art. Goethe thus criticizes Rousseau's *Pygmalion* for blurring the boundary that separates nature and art in the mistaken hope of transforming the latter into the former:

We see an artist, who has achieved perfection, and yet finds no satisfaction in externalizing his idea according to the rules of art, granting it a higher life. No! It is also to be dragged down to his level into this mundane life. He wants to destroy the highest that spirit and deed have wrought by the lowest act of sensuousness.[48]

Ovid's Pygmalion is guilty of this aesthetic crime. Venus accepts his offering. The story ends with a marriage and the birth of a child. The tale of Pygmalion thus does not celebrate the godlike power of the artist to create. Quite the opposite. It invites us to understand the artwork's beauty as figuring not a utopian but a genuinely possible happiness, a happiness that does not mean self-integration, but rather is given only to those who know about the lack that is constitutive of being human, that lets one person seek out another, and fills one with

47. See Udo Kultermann, "Pygmalion und das Symbol des Künstlers," 9–12.
48. Johann Wolfgang von Goethe, *Dichtung und Wahrheit*, 3:11, *Sämtliche Werke, Jubiläumsausgabe* (Stuttgart und Berlin: Cotta, 1902), 24:51.

the desire to embrace and give birth (Plato's *Symposium* hints at the many senses in which "embrace" and "birth" should be understood). The tale thus tells of the transformation of narcissistic into procreative eros. To that transformation corresponds the movement from a beauty that invites us to lose ourselves in its self-sufficient presence— this is how André Gide, very much indebted to Schopenhauer, understands the beauty of the artwork—to another that would have us understand the artwork's beauty as pointing beyond itself to a happiness granted only to those who have learned that we find happiness by turning not to ourselves but to the other, not by retreating from reality, but by engaging it, by committing ourselves to a future that extends beyond the life of the individual.

Once more let me return to that passage in the *Genealogy of Morals*, where Nietzsche cites Pygmalion to poke fun at Kant's and Schopenhauer's understanding of beauty as object of an entirely disinterested satisfaction. Nietzsche wants to know what interest it is that lets some humans pursue with such passionate intensity what is supposedly an entirely disinterested satisfaction. The vehemence of Schopenhauer's diction gives Nietzsche a clue as to where to look, where we should locate the origin, not of art, but of a particular conception of art that has had a strong hold on both critics and artists. Consider this quite characteristic celebration of the aesthetic state found in the third book of *The World as Will and Representation*:

This is the painless condition that Epicurus praised as the highest good and the condition of the gods; for a moment we are delivered from the vile urgency of the will; we celebrate the Sabbath of the penal servitude of volition; the wheel of Ixion stands still.[49]

Nietzsche's gloss points to the origin of the interest that supports this understanding of the beautiful:

What images of torment and long despair! What an almost pathological antithesis between "a moment" and the usual "wheel of Ixion," "penal servitude of volition," and "vile urgency of the will!"[50]

Here we do indeed get an answer to the question: what interest supports the celebration of the disinterested character of aesthetic experience? Sought is a release from torture. But torture here should not be thought of as inseparable from the human condition. That condition appears as torture only given a particular utopian ideal of hap-

---

49. Nietzsche, *Genealogy of Morals*, 3:6, 6, p. 541, citing Schopenhauer, *The World as Will and Representation*, 1, book 3, 38.

50. Nietzsche, *Genealogy of Morals*, 3:7, 541.

piness. Everyday life, and more especially sexual desire, are vilified because of the presupposed ideal of integral satisfaction. That ideal has to turn us against time and thus against reality and love. But that ideal is itself born of a disappointment with life. Rather like Freud, Nietzsche thus invites us to look for the origin of Schopenhauer's aesthetic and ascetic ideal in what is most personal in his life, to that disgust that let him treat "sexuality as a personal enemy (including its tool, woman, that *instrumentum diaboli.*')"[51]

But such attention to what is all too personal should not obscure what is typical. The reception of Schopenhauer's ideas, especially of his ideas on beauty and art, in the second half of the nineteenth century, when his influence came to surpass that of his old archenemy Hegel, requires us to look beyond his life to the psycho-history of the society and the age to which he belonged: This brings us back to the spirit of revenge, which issues from a self-assertion that cannot forgive itself its final impotence. It offers the key to the narcissistic inversion of eros in which the aesthetic approach has its origin.

8

To conclude let me return to the question with which I began: the question of the origin of art. Developing hints provided by the Platonic understanding of beauty I suggested that art has its origin in love. This suggestion is challenged by Kant's and Schopenhauer's understanding of beauty as object of an entirely disinterested satisfaction. The tale of Narcissus leads us beyond the dissociation of beauty and love implied by this determination, hinting that such dissociation has its origin in a love turned by pride against the other, back to the self. The impossibility of this love leads to its transformation into the aesthetic impulse: at least a semblance of the satisfaction denied to us by our time-bound being is sought in the ideal plenitude of the work of art. So understood, art is Narcissus's dream of paradise. The tale of Pygmalion reminds us of the insufficiency of that understanding.

51. Ibid., 542.

The Nature of Art's Nature

JOSEPH MARGOLIS

To speak of the nature of art's nature rather than directly of art's nature is to flag a warning and a complication. It is, effectively, to recommend subordinating the usual question to an analysis of the constraints under which it may be perspicuously answered. It would not be unreasonable, therefore, to anticipate that alternative answers may be entirely welcome so long as certain compelling constraints are first satisfied. We shall indeed venture part of an answer about art's nature—in the process of speaking of the other; but there is a great advantage to be gained by isolating the constraints intended. The reason is simply that they are implicated in every strong discussion of the nature of art and yet unaccountably never met in those very discussions. This will be doubted, of course, which contributes to the charm of the charge. Let us, for the sake of economy, therefore, collect a bit of the force of the argument in advance of itself.

Two sorts of constraint will be favored: one, regarding the functional minima of discourse; the other, the match, both in discourse and in reality, between what we take the generic nature of artworks to be and what we may say of them in any way conceptually congruent with assigning them such a nature. Now, our thesis is that the best-known accounts of art's nature at the present time utterly fail to meet the second sort of constraint, and that the most fashionable dispute about the tolerances of the art of our own day badly confuses the sense of how the two constraints are linked to each other. To speak candidly: the argument is intended to show that such theorists as Arthur Danto, Nelson Goodman, and Richard Wollheim never meet the conditions of the second constraint in their analyses of artworks, though they themselves unmistakably draw attention to the need to do so—and, in failing, fail to give a good account of their own claims; also, that the well-known controversy between modernists and post-modernists is best understood in terms of a confusion of both sides regarding the difference between the two constraints.

Since the discussion will be principally occupied with the theorists mentioned, we may safely postpone more detailed remarks about them here. The lesson about the second issue may be safely risked, however, because of the sheer sprawl of the accumulating literature. In any case, our claim is that modernism, meaning to satisfy the first constraint, wrongly supposes the need for an extremely conservative fixity regarding the second; and postmodernism, grasping a viable new openness regarding the second, incoherently supposes that it can eschew the first. If our argument holds, then, among other things, neither modernism nor postmodernism is tenable and we need to search further. And if the defect shared by our specimen theorists is reasonably imputed, then analytic philosophies of art tend to be peculiarly impoverished. Let this much serve as a double provocation.

1

One can no longer theorize about the nature of art or artworks in the innocent workman-like spirit of simply improving particular definitions of art or of discovering once and for all art's essence. The history of the effort is against it. Morris Weitz once tried, notoriously, to show, some thirty-five years ago, that a definition of art was out of the question because of the "openended" nature of the world of art.[1] Weitz was quite wrong about this, as he dimly came to realize: for, *if* we fix the boundaries of the field for which we seek an apt definition fitting the interests of a certain kind of inquiry, then it becomes an empirical question whether a definition can be had (for Greek tragedy, for instance). He wrongly supposed that definitions that sought closure in terms of necessary and sufficient conditions, or in terms of genus and difference, had to presume to be essentialist or realist or "platonic"; and he also assumed that all realist definitions (wrongly) presupposed the validity of platonic closure, the need for and the availability of real necessary and sufficient conditions. In spite of these oddities, Weitz did grasp the historically evolving nature of the world of art, the sense in which definitions or the explication of concepts (two notions that can never be sharply sorted, except along essentialist lines) must conform to the changing interests and salient experience of those who follow the arts, and that there is no vantage or cognitive privilege from which one could convincingly claim definitional progress. Weitz wrongly insisted on the *logical* peculiarities of definition,

1. See Morris Weitz, *The Opening Mind: A Philosophical Study of Humanistic Concepts* (Chicago: University of Chicago Press, 1977); and "The Role of Theory in Aesthetics," *Journal of Aesthetics and Art Criticism* 15 (1956).

whereas the truth is that there is no essential canon of definition. Different kinds of definition may, in informal ways, be said to fit the *real* nature of a given domain. Weitz subscribed to a theory about the *ontology* of art, which he failed to support explicitly. He never united in one account an analysis of art's ontology, its openendedness, and our changing conceptual interests in the arts in the face of its changing history. He sensed the connection among these themes but he never brought them together to center stage.

In a memorable passage, Arthur Danto indicated a much more promising, logically more relaxed and historically more resilient view of the concept of art when, some ten years later, he remarked that "to see something as art requires something the eye cannot descry—an atmosphere of artistic theory, a knowledge of the world of art: an artworld."[2] A full appreciation of Danto's proposal would reveal that art, the perception of art, the history of art, and the theory of art are all artifacts of an evolving historical experience. There is no essentialism, no fixity about definitions, no transhistorical privilege in Danto's view. Nevertheless, Danto does appear to hold that art has a distinct ontological standing—or, at any rate, a conceptual or rhetorical relation to what has ontological standing—and that, so seen, art's history has now reached a point at which, in a Hegelian sense, art (a fortiori, art's history) has "come to an end." First of all, Danto claims that "a work such as Duchamp's *In Advance of the Broken Arm* [a work which could not in an earlier age have even been 'seen' or 'perceived' as an artwork—the required artworld not having yet been born], even when accepted as a work of art, [still] retained its identity as a quite ordinary snow shovel."[3] The flexibility of Danto's conceptual recommendation is considerably dampened by his failure to explain the sense in which the "something" that is "seen" or "perceived" as a work of art remains numerically identical with a mere snow shovel (the *In Advance of the Broken Arm*), when the mere snow shovel is *not* an artwork and the *In Advance is.*

The apparent inconsistency is provisionally resolved by denying that the "'is' of artistic identification" is the same as the "'is' of numerical identity."[4] Notoriously, however, Danto never explains that difference, or shows that it can be consistently maintained. It looks as if (on Danto's view) artworks are *not* objects or entities of any sort; it looks as if

<hr>

2. Arthur C. Danto, "The Artworld," *Journal of Philosophy* 61 (1964).

3. Arthur C. Danto, "The End of Art," *The Philosophical Disenfranchisement of Art* (New York: Columbia University Press, 1986), 82.

4. Danto, "The Appreciation and Interpretation of Works of Art," *The Disenfranchisement of Art,* 44–45.

we can only talk about talking about things *as* artworks—which *nothing* ever *is*. But that also would be a very strenuous claim about art, for which Danto offers not a word of support.

Secondly, on the basis (one supposes) of *this* conception, Danto implies that the essentializing definitions of art are all mistaken in failing to grasp the nature of "art's philosophical history," that is, art's "being absorbed ultimately into its own philosophy" (in a Hegelian sense), its "self-theoretization." The upshot, for Danto, is that "if we look at the art of our recent past [that is, 'late productions'], what we see is something which depends more and more upon theory for its existence as art, so that theory is not something external to a world it seeks to understand, so that in understanding its object it has to understand itself [so that the objects of our latest production] approach zero as their theory approaches infinity, so that virtually all there is at the end *is* theory, art having finally become vaporized in a dazzle of pure thought about itself, and remaining, as it were, solely as the object of its own theoretical consciousness."[5] What we see, therefore, is the need to separate Danto's conceptual recommendation from his own peculiar use of it. Artworks depend on a sensorily indiscernible artworld all right, on a sense of historical and conceptual context; but we cannot go the distance with Danto unless he first explains what, favoring his own claims, *are* the pertinent ontological limitations of the actual world, what *are* the merely "rhetorical" uses of language applied to actual things, what *is* the sense in which the "subject" of history *is* real and understands its own history. Hegel never convincingly explained the historical thesis, and no one has to this day. Nevertheless, on the fate of that undeveloped claim appears to hang the very death of art.[6]

The important point to appreciate is that Danto does not escape the complications of ontological involvement in treating art as he does; and yet, the intended advantage of his evident ingenuity appears to be to save at one and the same time the robust reality of the physical *world* and the ineluctable encumbrance of our culturally entrenched art-historical and art-critical discourse that implicates that world. Readers will find provision, in Danto's picture of human discourse, for everything we might wish to feature in our world; and so, somewhat inattentively, they may suppose that Danto also wishes to save and identify those same "things" *as actual entities in our world.* But the truth is he does not—and therein lies an ontological quarrel worth pressing. For, if the form of discourse suited to the physical world

5. "The End of Art," 110–11.
6. See Berel Lang, ed., *The Death of Art* (New York: Haven, 1984).

were inadequate for our discourse about art, then we should need to know why that fact does not seriously matter, whenever we speak of art as we do.

A similar but decidedly minor complaint arose, some ten years after the appearance of Danto's essay, in Nelson Goodman's frankly essentialist conception of art—what Goodman entrenches with the pronouncement: "art without representation or expression or exemplification—yes; art without all three—*no.*"[7] Goodman's point is to forestall, by the formula he advances, all the "desperate attempts" (that "litter" aesthetics) "to answer the question What is Art?" That question, he says is "the wrong question—[the trouble lies] in failing to recognize that a thing may function as a work of art at some times and not at others. In crucial cases, the real question is not 'What objects are (permanently) works of art?' but 'When is an object a work of art?'— or more briefly . . . 'When is art?'"[8] Goodman's idiom, like Danto's— though more sparely or more thinly—provides for all the usual discourse of art; but it collects such discourse in the conceptual bag addressed only to "When is art?" never to "What is Art?" Apparently, there *are* things about which we may ask, "What *are* they?" but art or artworks are never among them: "*When* is *an object* a work of art?" is the form of the question Goodman pointedly recommends.

The parallel with Danto is perfectly transparent and fails for essentially the same reason. In fact, it fails even more completely, since Danto resists, though Goodman does not, venturing an essentialized account of the finitely many alternative functions a "thing" must perform, failing which, any such "thing" "is not" an artwork. We lack, in Goodman's story, an account of what it is to function as an artwork, just as we lack, in Danto's, an account of what it is to identify something as an artwork. Goodman's apparent worry about "permanent" substance does not take us very far: similarly, his enumeration of "five symptoms of the aesthetic" does not explicitly address the question of the sense in which anything really does exhibit those symptoms or has the properties said to be thus exhibited.[9] Even if we supposed that semiotics could replace ontology—which is doubtful, since we sometimes wish to know whether there *are* symbols, whether anything actually functions symbolically, and what it is to do so—we still have need for the explanatory or legitimating argument. Goodman never supplies it. We never know, with Goodman, what it is to be a thing

7. Nelson Goodman, "When Is Art?" *Ways of Worldmaking* (Indianapolis: Hackett Publishing Co., 1978), 66.
  8. Ibid., 66–67.
  9. Ibid., 67–68.

that, in addition to being that, may also function (and we never know how it functions, when it functions) as an artwork.

Consider, finally, Michel Foucault's well-known discussion of *Las Meninas*—which was published at about the same as Danto's "Artworld" paper. Foucault is remarkably explicit and assertive in his description and interpretation of that painting's representational function, in his account of what the painting represents. He begins *Les Mots et les choses (The Order of Things)* quite abruptly in the middle of an analysis of the painting, as if we had already laid a groundwork for it: "The painter," he says, "is standing a little back from his canvas."[10] He moves with confidence to the finding: "Perhaps there exists, in this painting by Velázquez, the representation, as it were, of Classical representation, and the definition of the space it opens up to us."[11] The account seems absolutely straightforward until we recall the nagging fact that, on Foucault's view, "before the end of the eighteenth century, *man* did not exist—any more than the potency of life, the fecundity of labor, or the historical density of language. He is a quite recent creature . . . there was [in the seventeenth and eighteenth centuries] no epistemological consciousness of man as such. The Classical *episteme* is articulated along lines that do not isolate, in any way, a specific domain proper to man."[12]

We are suddenly at sea regarding what it is to describe and interpret a painting; what the sense is in which we can say, correctly and knowledgeably, what a seventeenth-century painter is representing in painting *Las Meninas*, if we—post-eighteenth-century creatures—think in an utterly different way from Velásquez; we are at sea about how Foucault (or anyone) could correctly specify the difference between Velásquez's mode of thought and our own; and about what we mean by identifying eighteenth-century paintings, representations, inventions, and interpretations, or about what we mean in supposing that what we say in these regards is capable of being true or false or confirmably such. Foucault never answers these questions, but it is clear that he has baffled every relevant issue by radicalizing the historical processes Weitz and Danto more conventionally acknowledge.

Weitz and Danto are modernists, after all, according to the current idiom. Goodman is a modernist in some respects at least (for instance, in *Languages of Art*, certainly in *Fact, Fiction, and Forecast*), but he also "drifts" toward postmodernism (in *Ways of Worldmaking* and in *Of*

<hr>

10. Michel Foucault, "Las Meninas," *The Order of Things; An Archaeology of the Human Sciences*, trans. (New York: Vintage Books, 1973), 3.

11. Ibid., 16.

12. Foucault, "Man and His Doubles," *The Order of Things*, 308–9.

Minds and Other Matters). Foucault is distinctly poststructuralist or, even more drastically, he is the early vivifier of the Nietzschean source of what was later to become poststructuralism. In that respect, Foucault severely worries the question with which we first began, the question of how to theorize about the nature of art. In Foucault's case, but not in Weitz's, Danto's, or Goodman's, we are now no longer sure what it means to theorize about the nature of art (or about knowledge or history or reality—or about the analysis of artworks). Still, the effort to theorize *now* must take account of Foucault's puzzle even as we attempt to compensate for the lacunae of the other accounts mentioned.

Foucault's own lacuna is the monumental one that results from our (and his) not being able to understand just what he has given us in supplying an apparent analysis of *Las Meninas*. For, by the time Goodman's *Ways of Worldmaking* appeared, Foucault had come around quite openly to acknowledging—but hardly resolving—the essential *aporia* of his entire professional endeavor: "What is history [he asks himself], given there is continually being produced within it a separation of true and false? . . . what historical knowledge is possible of a history that itself produces the true/false distinction on which such knowledge depends?"[13] That aporia is insoluble in Foucault's terms, though it is and must be resolved if discourse may be said to be coherent at all. It also clearly infects the standing of the efforts of our other three theorists.

In any event, if we take these four accounts of the last thirty-five years to fix fairly accurately the fortunes of our continuing efforts to analyze art's nature, then it is plain enough that we have hardly budged from square one.

2

The conceptual therapy required may be painful but it is hardly futile. It begins with the homely instruction that debate about art's nature—as about anything else—requires a reasonably disciplined adherence to the minima of discourse. Whatever else we may say of natural language, it must preserve what is needed for that family of functions variously named *statement, assertion, affirmation, declaration, judgment, claim, constatation, énonciation,* that is, the purely formal min-

13. "Questions of Method: An Interview with Michel Foucault," trans. Alan Bass, *Ideology and Consciousness,* 8 (1981); reprinted in Kenneth Baynes, James Bohman, and Thomas McCarthy, eds., *After Philosophy: End or Transformation?* (Cambridge: MIT Press, 1987), 111.

ima of reference and predication: we must be able to fix effectively what we are talking about and what we declare to be true of it. Foucault's puzzle confirms the formal incoherence of what he actually says. It is quite impossible that Foucault's description and analysis of *Las Meninas,* for instance, should be historically accurate about Velásquez's representational achievement in the seventeenth century if the very idea of its accuracy is merely a local item of some sort generated within Foucault's own contingent history, a history radically discontinuous with Velásquez's, and subject to similar contingencies in terms of further such histories. Foucault never explains the intelligibility of the very histories he produces—which, it cannot be denied, he treats as having captured the actual, now-superseded features of the various quite alien ages he works so strenuously to recover. In fact, his essential theme is the writing of "the history of History"—what, now, takes the form of being normalized or "trapped" within an *episteme,* "the laws of a perspective which, while allowing a certain apprehension—of the type of perception or understanding—prevents it from ever being universal and definitive intellection."[14]

Part of Foucault's theme is captured by the now-familiar notions of preformation, horizon, loss of privilege, prejudice, *habitus,* and the like. Foucault himself alludes to the relevance of phenomenological, hermeneutic, structuralist, Marxist, historicist, and perspectivist ingredients in the recovery of history.[15] But he also means to radicalize these admissions by internalizing them all within the space of discontinuous *epistemes* whose own processes elude the continuities of discourse that would trace the "history of History"—until, that is, some emerging *episteme* is, serially, sufficiently normalized once again to make at least local sense of the newly perceived past. In effect, the apparent incoherence of Foucault's thesis results from his having intruded something distributively—a Nietzschean-like flux or chaos into a particular history—that cannot be regimented there in terms of the minima of discourse it itself requires. It is, therefore, a *mythic,* a nonconstative element, though it is hardly uninstructive for that reason; it cannot play the critical role it appears to be assigned in the *aporia* Foucault constructs for himself. The recovery of the classical conception of history, or of the nineteenth-century "dehistoricizing" of man, or of Foucault's late account of shifting *epistemes* throughout that very process[16] presupposes a synchronic order of truth and falsity that cannot, at the moment of entry at which the sequence is identified, be

14. Foucault, "The Human Sciences," *The Order of Things,* 370, 372–73.
15. Ibid., 372–73.
16. Ibid., 366–70.

open to distributed, critical assignments of truth and falsity from above. There is no objectivity or neutrality to be recovered. The holistic worry of the historicizing of truth and falsity can never be more than a mythic theme, a global speculation about the context of all contexts within which the other functions, that alerts us to the need to revise our critical orientation unpredictably, even discontinuously, over time. The limits of our world remain the unutterable limits of our world, wherever and in whatever way they obtain. We live horizonally, but we cannot formulate the boundaries of our own horizon. *That is the best of what may now be called postmodernism.* And, as we may laboriously claim, the theory of art's nature must now accommodate that particular theme.

The weaknesses already discerned in Weitz, in Danto, and in Goodman are largely local. They also share, however, the weakness of what we may now call *modernism*—in the sense that, although they do oppose privilege and acknowledge the historicity of the human or cultural world, they do not directly address the postmodern challenge, and they remain altogether too sanguine—sanguine without defense— about the essential nature of art (Weitz) or the true meaning of the history of art (Danto) or the extensionalized docility of any of art's properties (Goodman). An adequate theory of the nature of art will have to thread its way between the illicit recovery of privilege among the modernists and the excessive risk of incoherence among the postmodernists.

To some extent, this is already prefigured by acknowledging the fixities of reference and predication. First of all, there are no natural languages that lack the constative function. Secondly, there can be no such function, effectively, without meeting the conditions of reference and predication. Thirdly, those constraints are entirely formal and by themselves yield no questionable claim of cognitive privilege. Fourthly, they require the staple individuation and reidentifiability of linguistically apt subjects and numerically distinct referents (whatever their natures may be supposed to be), and they require stable predicables that may be rightly ascribed to just such unitary subjects and objects. Fifthly, such subjects and objects must be sufficiently unified in their own natures (but not more) to support such reference and predication. These and similar invariances are instructive because they appear to be ineliminable; because they are entirely general, compatible with indefinitely varied cognitive strategies and indefinitely varied theories of the population of the actual world; because they are only formal and entail no determinate cognitive claims about particular entities; and, most important, because they signify that there may well be a minimal metaphysical constraint entailed by the very nature of discourse itself.

So seen, they accommodate such claims as those of Weitz and Danto and Goodman without prejudice, and they resolve the unnecessary *aporia* of Foucault's puzzle, again without prejudice to the deeper historicity Foucault himself invokes. To put the point this way is to challenge all those who claim to see in metaphysical discourse of any sort an inescapable concession to cognitive privilege. On the argument, there must be a metaphysics of constatation entirely distinct from a metaphysics of privilege—one relatively neutral to the quarrels of naturalism, hermeneutics, phenomenology, deconstruction, and genealogy.[17] Here one finds a decisive clue to a third option, lying between or beyond modernism and postmodernism, well suited, of course, to our original question of the nature of art but not in any way restricted to it.

These maneuvers draw attention to the complexity of discussing art's nature, but they say nothing of a distinctive sort about it. What they confirm are the following two strategic findings at least: first, that the unicity and unity of whatever we posit as artworks (that is, the conditions of numerical identity and the ascription of an internal nature to whatever is capable of numerical identity) may be attenuated in a formal way as far as we care, so long as they permit the referential and predicative needs of constatation to continue to obtain; second, that whatever we do posit as the ontic nature of artworks within such constraints must count as no more than salient or horizonal invariances, effective or notable only in terms of their dialectical or competitive standing within and across historical horizons. The first of these findings is surprisingly important, for it affords a very nice maneuver by which to escape all the usual prejudices of physicalism and associated doctrines—to which both Danto and Goodman are distinctly prone.[18] The second is the direct benefit of resolving Foucault's *aporia*.

17. See, for instance, the influential thesis advanced in Martin Heidegger, *Being and Time*, trans. from 7th ed. John Macquarrie and Edward Robinson (New York: Harper and Row, 1962), Introduction.

18. Perhaps the most supple form of physicalism so far formulated may be found in John F. Post, *The Faces of Existence; An Essay in Nonreductive Metaphysics* (Ithaca: Cornell University Press, 1987). See, also, Joseph Margolis, *Texts without Referents; Reconciling Science and Narrative* (Oxford: Basil Blackwell, 1988), chap. 6. The best evidence of this, in Danto's work, appears in Arthur C. Danto, *Analytical Philosophy of Action* (Cambridge: Cambridge University Press, 1978). In Goodman's case, it is more by default than by explicit claim that the charge is made: Goodman's nominalism, extensionalism, and his functional account of intentionality within those constraints tend to favor the prejudices

We may now risk a very large conceptual gain. Every ontology, let us say, formulates a theory of the nature of a family of things—consistent with the constative function—that, on an argument, perspicuously integrates whatever we take it we may say distributively and truly of such things. The essential ontological concern—an entirely formal distinction in itself—centers on what we may call adequation, *ontic adequation,* the conceptual congruity between whatever we predicate of any particular thing of some domain, and the intrinsic nature we assign it as the individuated thing it is in that domain. Clearly, this is a general constraint that hardly singles out artworks among things of other kinds, but it does apply to artworks as well as to other things. The intended economy invites us to concede that what are most salient about artworks are the varieties of intentionally complex properties that the entire history of man's interest in the arts has always featured, and that *that* is what the ontic adequation of art must suitably collect: representational, expressive, symbolic, exemplaristic, stylistic properties, properties usually collected as semiotic or rhetorical or linguistic or historical or simply intentional.

The point is that the most important puzzle that confronts us in the artworld is precisely what we may reasonably claim *is* art's nature—adequationally—if we regularly ascribe properties to works of art drawn from such a list as the one just given. Most theories of art—as of culture in general—founder on that condition. Having said that, we may concede at once that any essentializing of art is entirely contingent on the saliencies of prevailing discourse and on our recollection and anticipation of its own historical contingency. Its invariances, in this sense, are merely "indicative," empirical, reflexive, provisional; though the point of risking an ontology is to propose at a level of second-order legitimation an account of art's nature suited to the inclusive requirements of ontic adequation. In an obvious sense, the exercise here sketched constitutes a third option between the excessive confidence of modernisms like Weitz's, Danto's, and Goodman's to "recover" art's nature once and for all and the excessive anarchy of postmodernism and poststructuralism that repudiates too quickly (or renders impossible, as in Foucault's *aporia*) any such second-order reflection.[19] Plural options are a distinct advantage here, hardly a mark

---

of physicalism, in spite of the fact that he clearly does not commit himself to any such ontology. The best clue may well lie in the fact that Goodman insists that art's possession of expressive properties *must* be "metaphorical." See Nelson Goodman, *Languages of Art; An Approach to a Theory of Symbols* (Indianapolis: Bobbs-Merrill, 1968), 85–95. We shall come to these matters shortly.

19. On this postmodernist issue, see, for example, Jean-François Lyotard, *The Postmodern Condition: A Report on Knowledge,* trans. Geoff Bennington and Brian Massumi (Minneapolis: University of Minnesota Press, 1984).

of failure or conceptual "misprision." There is also no reason to suppose that, if one ontology can satisfy the conditions of adequation, there might not be indefinitely many such, even incompatible, ontologies to choose among. The point of pursuing adequation is quite simply to arrive at an adequate model of the entire referential and predicative commitments of our first-order discourse. Even a provisional model would improve our sense of the rigor, coherence, mutual intelligibility, and order of whatever we have to say—without in the least foreclosing on improvisations among the arts themselves or among our philosophical theories. Please notice that Danto had actually featured a related theme in his account of the philosophical history of the arts; and the entire movement of so-called postmodern architecture and painting is clearly informed by conceptual possibilities the so-called modernists had resisted, partly at least, on the strength of philosophical considerations.[20] In any case, it is only an illusion of rigor, or an impossible objection to the sort of rigor we seem capable of, to disallow second-order conjectures about ontic adequation on the grounds, first, that they cannot fail to be horizonal and contingent, and, second, that they cannot fail to be hospitable to pluralistic and relativistic options. Neither constraint precludes the search for ontic invariances or disallows their distinct conceptual benefit. The refusal to admit this is just the arbitrariness of philosophical postmodernism.

Having said all this—which is still only preparatory to a direct discussion of art's ontology—we may as well suggest a further benefit of the argument: to theorize about art in the way we have is also to address, metonymically, the whole of human culture. Artworks are certainly among the most complex of human artifacts: any analysis of art is bound to yield essential clues about the nature of human persons, language, history, tradition, culture itself. Furthermore, the existence of human persons is the existence of creatures apt for producing art, language, texts, actions, practices, histories: the nature of the one will have to be adequated to the nature of the others.

3

Dialectically, the single most important—and most strenuous—contest centered on the issue of the adequation of the arts concerns the

20. See Robert Venturi, *Complexity and Contradiction in Architecture*, 2nd ed. (New York: Museum of Modern Art, 1977); Hal Foster, ed., *The Anti-Aesthetic; Essays on Postmodern Culture* (Port Townsend, Wash.: Bay Press, 1983); Rosalind E. Krauss, *The Originality of the Avant-Garde and Other Modernist Myths* (Cambridge: MIT Press, 1985).

vindication or defeat of every form of physicalism. In addressing it, we must bear in mind that we have recovered the validity and viability of ontology by a variety of reasonably uncontroversial maneuvers: by abandoning every presumption of cognitive privilege or transparency; by drawing out the relevant second-order adequational issue as a distinctly empirical question, or as a question idealized from empirical considerations, addressed to the salient referential and predicative practices of our own society; and by making a conceptual virtue of the horizonally shifting and relativized models of adequational invariance any domain is likely to support. If it could support more than that, our maneuver would actually vindicate philosophical modernism; and if it could not support even that much, it would vindicate philosophical postmodernism. A fair way of putting the point is to construe our proposal as a way of recovering the general coherence of all philosophical argument that concedes intransparency, preformation, historicized existence, horizonal incommensurabilities and the like—of which perhaps Thomas Kuhn's specific notion of paradigm shifts is the single best-known but still quite fuzzy and distinctly modernist-inclined instance.[21]

Consider, now, four representative texts that should help us understand the strategic importance of the issue of adequation, the inadequacy of all physicalisms, and what would be required of any apt model of the arts or cultural phenomena in general, given the failure of physicalism.

To make a start, in *Art and Its Objects,* Richard Wollheim identifies himself as one attracted to the "physical-object hypothesis"—"the hypothesis that works of art are [simply] physical objects"—which he nevertheless finds unsuited to literature and music (unsuited to *Ulysses* and *Der Rosenkavalier,* for example) but which he is persuaded *is* apt for paintings and sculptures.[22] Wollheim implicitly acknowledges the adequational worry, when, considering arguments that may be brought against his hypothesis, he observes:

This identification [of artworks and physical objects, the *Donna Velata* and Donatello's *St. George,* for example] can be disputed in (roughly) one or other of two ways. It can be argued that the work of art has properties which are incompatible with certain properties that the physical object has; alternatively it can be argued that the work of art has properties which no physical object could have: in neither case could the work of art be the physical object.[23]

21. See Thomas S. Kuhn, *The Structure of Scientific Revolutions,* 2nd ed. enl. (Chicago: University of Chicago Press, 1970).

22. Richard Wollheim, *Art and Its Objects,* 2nd ed. (Cambridge: Cambridge University Press, 1980), §§4, 9.

23. Ibid., §10.

Wollheim means to consider whether the representational or expressive properties of paintings can be squared with the physical-object hypothesis. Thus: "We say of the *St. George* [he observes] that it moves with life (Vasari). Yet the block of marble is inanimate. Therefore the *St. George* cannot be that block of marble. . . . We say of the *Donna Velata* that it is exalted and dignified (Wölfflin). Yet a piece of canvas in the Pitti cannot conceivably have these qualities. Therefore the *Donna Velata* cannot be that piece of canvas."[24] A moment's thought should persuade us that his question is a version of the general question of which Danto's worry about the "is" of artistic identification and Goodman's about "when" is art are alternative versions.

Nevertheless, Wollheim's argument is quite different from theirs— and, we may claim, utterly indecisive. Wollheim, it is true, does examine objections to the view (which the others do not) that representational properties may be accounted for entirely in terms of the phenomenon of what he calls "representational seeing," "seeing-as," seeing something as a representation in the sense of its then being "a visual sign, or reminder, of [whatever it is taken to be a representation of] . . . [probably] a culturally determined matter."[25] At the very least, Wollheim's finding here cannot but be incomplete, since, first, it depends on whether the capacity for seeing-as, for representational seeing, *can* be suitably ascribed to human beings whenever they are construed as mere physical objects. If that maneuver cannot be defended—which is also an adequational matter—then the force of Wollheim's proposal must be reviewed again. It is certainly possible to try to give a reductive (or physicalist) account of painting, an account impoverished in this sense from what might otherwise be proposed if the richer ascriptions required (granting the actuality of representation) could in principle be accommodated by a suitably enriched notion of human beings. Unfortunately, Wollheim nowhere attempts the labor, so we cannot really say what his own ingenuities might produce. But it is clear enough from *Art and Its Objects,* as well as from other sources,[26] that Wollheim does not favor (or at least does not favor in any clearly legible way) the notion that human beings are no more than physical objects. (We shall pursue this point in a moment. We may also recall that Wollheim specifically denies the adequacy of the physical object hypothesis for music and literature, which is already a

24. Ibid.
25. Ibid., §§12–18.
26. See Richard Wollheim, *The Thread of Life* (Cambridge: Harvard University Press, 1984), chaps. 1–2; "The Mind and the Mind's Image of Itself," *On Art and the Mind* (Cambridge: Harvard University Press, 1974).

very large [probably a disastrously large] admission affecting his thesis.)

A second consideration is this: in accounting for representation in terms of the seeing-as phenomenon, Wollheim must treat representation *relationally*, that is, as a relationship between a physical object and a human being. Now, such a view cannot fail to be dubious as well as desperate if, as seems reasonable, the spontaneous interest human beings show in paintings (collecting, buying and selling, exhibiting, interpreting, appraising, debating) could never (if construed in accord with the relational theory) supply a sufficient array of intrinsic and pertinent *non*-relational properties true of mere physical objects in virtue of which such further *relational* properties (variable, even idiosyncratic and arbitrary) could be intelligibly and pertinently imputed. There is nothing at all in Wollheim's account that provides the least clue regarding the obvious stability of the artworld and our interest in it, that suggests *how* to reconcile that fact and physicalism. The plain alternative would be to attribute representational properties directly to artworks, but then the physical-object hypothesis would fail; alternatively put, if human nature were not reduced physicalistically just when it was adequated to the entire range of the culture experience we must account for, then there would be little reason to hurry to impoverish the ontology of art as well.

In fact, the reasonableness of resisting Wollheim's thesis is unintentionally betrayed by Wollheim himself. For Wollheim divides his own argument regarding representation and expression:

Though there is nothing [he says] other than a physical object that has representational properties, there is something other than a physical, or at any rate a purely physical, object that has expressive properties: namely, a human body and its parts, in particular the face and certain limbs. So now we wonder, How can anything other than this be expressive? More specifically, How can anything purely physical be expressive?[27]

It is most important to notice that Wollheim insists that the expressive qualities of the Brancacci frescoes, the Granduca Madonna, the Isenheim Altarpiece "cannot be . . . mere attributes of the experiences or activities of Masaccio, of Raphael, of Grünewald [or of ourselves, we may add]—they inhere rather in [those works]."[28] So Wollheim actually divides his account of representational and expressive properties or qualities—which concedes the force of objections against at least *some* relational renderings of artistic attributes; and he attempts to

27. *Art and Its Objects*, §14.
28. Ibid., §15.

account for expressive qualities in terms of an adequational theory that, at least incipiently, rejects any purely physicalist account of humans—which suggests the force of a corresponding concession regarding the artworld. (Wollheim, however, nowhere addresses the adequation of human nature, the relation of nature and culture, the difference between *homo sapiens* and persons.)

Put most briefly, Wollheim's account of expressive qualities depends, first, on something akin to Wittgenstein's notion of "natural expression" and, second, on what he specifically calls "correspondence" (which need not involve natural expression); that is, in the second instance—presumably suited to painting—his thesis requires a perceived fit between some putative expression and "what we [may, under other circumstances] experience inwardly."[29] But that won't do at all: first, because to admit the matching expression is already to invoke attributes that, on the hypothesis, are not merely physical in the required sense; and second, because the putatively intrinsic, expressive properties of artworks are then only inferentially (or in some other relational sense) imputed to the works in question. It is difficult to resist the conclusion that Wollheim's argument is a complete disaster.

Goodman's prejudice along related lines is remarkably transparent. Goodman conveys it in a single line: "What is expressed [he says] is metaphorically exemplified."[30] The curious thing is that nowhere in all of Goodman's work is there the slightest effort to explain *why* expression must be a metaphorical ascription or why, in particular, it must be an ascription of metaphorical exemplification. Goodman's "reason" for resisting a literal ascription is simply that he wishes to avoid the plain thesis that "expression is . . . mere possession," that is, that artworks are expressive in the sense that they literally possess expressive qualities.[31] The only plausible reason (we may conjecture) for so insisting is to avoid the logical complications of a too-generous picture of cultural or intentional complexities.

Here is what Goodman says by way of defining exemplification: "An object that is literally or metaphorically denoted by a predicate, and refers to that predicate or the corresponding property, may be said to exemplify that predicate or property."[32] It is reasonably clear, then, that Goodman has our adequational question in mind, since he very strongly affirms that expressive properties are to be analyzed as metaphorical exemplifications (he thinks of a tailor's sample cloth swatches as exhibiting the exemplification-relation in a literal sense). Neverthe-

29. Ibid., §18.
31. Ibid., 52.

30. *Languages of Art*, 85.
32. Ibid.

less, his claim is utterly arbitrary on its own terms, since he nowhere gives an account of objects, or of objects "when" they function as artworks, in virtue of which, expression must be construed in terms of exemplification or of metaphorical possession or of metaphorical exemplification. It is most extraordinary—though nevertheless true— that Goodman neglects to address the essential issue he himself raises. But he is right to raise it, even if coyly.

We may, perhaps, here usefully sample certain telltale analogues of the mismanagement of the adequational issue. The most blatant recent example appears in John Searle's solution of the mind-body problem:

[O]n my view [says Searle], the mind and the body interact, but they are not two different things, since mental phenomena just are features of the brain. One way to characterize this position is to see it as an assertion of both physicalism and mentalism. Suppose we define "naive physicalism" to be the view that all that exists in the world are physical particles with their properties and relations. The power of the physical model of reality is so great that it is hard to see how we can seriously challenge naive physicalism. And let us define "naive mentalism" to be the view that mental phenomena really exist. There really are mental states; some of them are conscious; many have intentionality; they all have subjectivity; and many of them function causally in determining physical events in the world. The thesis of this first chapter can now be stated quite simply. Naive mentalism and naive physicalism are perfectly consistent with each other. Indeed, as far as we know anything about how the world works, they are not only consistent, they are both true.[33]

What is extraordinary about this passage is just that Searle obviously takes it that he is addressing the adequational question and yet he resolves it by merely announcing that there is no other option worth considering except the one he offers. The trouble is, he nowhere shows what the sense is in which "mental phenomena" *can* be adequationally ascribed to the brain. It's clear, in context, that Searle opposes reducing mental attributes to non-mental attributes: he opposes all versions of the identity thesis; but he nowhere rises to the challenge he himself appears to be responding to in announcing that unreduced mental attributes can be directly ascribed to the brain. On any adequational thesis, one must be able to show that the attributes ascribed to the brain—attributes that the brain can actually have—are conceptually congruent with the intrinsic nature of brains. The parallel with the artworld is clear enough.

The subtlest, most skillful defense of the general position of which

33. John R. Searle, *Minds, Brains, and Science* (Cambridge: Harvard University Press, 1984), 27.

Searle's is a poor cousin appears in John Post's account of non-reductive physicalism. Informally put, Post's strategy runs as follows: "We can tighten our inventory of what there is so as to include just the physical, without presuming reducibility of everything, or even of very much, to physics, and therefore without presuming that everything is nothing but a physical thing. A monism of entities is entirely compatible with a pluralism of properties and with everything the pluralism implies for the autonomy of domains beyond physics and beyond all the sciences, as we lately noted in connection with works of art."[34] For one thing, Post is a materialist, in the restricted sense—a sense hospitable to *non*-physicalists—that "what there is" is, however constituted, constituted of nothing but matter or of whatever physical things are constituted. He is also, however, a physicalist—a nonreductive physicalist—in the sense that, although materially constituted objects possess whatever conceptually complex properties cultural and human phenomena do possess, those properties are not themselves identical with or reducible to mere physical properties. The difference between Searle and Post is simply that Post (but not Searle) actually tries to defend the nonreductive physicalist's position. Post fails in this, as we shall see—which yields a very nice economy for our own arguments. He fails because he actually tries (where Searle does not) to obviate the need for an adequational account of unreduced mental and cultural properties, by demonstrating (nonreductively) the adequacy of what would otherwise have been a reductive physicalism applied to whatever anyone who was a nonreductive materialist (also a non-physicalist) would claim. This is an ingenious maneuver—well beyond anything Searle has attempted; also, (doubtless) one that Searle would never have been willing to accept.

Post's maneuver is to claim that there is—that we may count on—an extensional equivalence (not an identity) between what would otherwise have been a reductive physicalist account (now employed only operationally; hence, nonreductively) and a *non*-physicalist account of the unreduced psychological and cultural properties of artworks, persons, and similar phenomena. His intended solution is given in the following formula: first, informally put, "Given the way things are physically, there is one and only one way they can be nonphysically";[35] then, put in a more formal way,

TT. Given any two *P*-worlds [that is, physically possible worlds], if the same *P*-sentences are true in both, then the same *N*-sentences [that is, sentences employing nonphysical predicates] are true in both,

34. Post, *The Faces of Existence*, 203.
35. Ibid., 185.

or, more explicitly,

TT*. Any two *P*-worlds indiscernible as regards the physical properties and relations of the things in them are also indiscernible as regards their things' nonphysical properties and relations.[36]

Notice that Post does not actually address the adequation problem: he bypasses it by showing us how to construe physicalism nonreductively without it being the case that an (otherwise) reductive physicalism would fail to determine all relevant truth values. Notice also that, in advancing the thesis, precisely because he does not address the adequational problem (or, in fact, the logical peculiarities of nonphysical properties), he cannot but fail to be entirely arbitrary (though ingenious) in resolving the question of the nature of psychological and cultural properties.

The truth is that Post's defense is drawn from the alleged superiority and adequacy of physical explanation through all of the natural or actual world: "Any explanatory power the nonphysical truths have [he says] will be, in some derivative sense, part of the explanatory power of physics, or at least a manifestation of its comprehensiveness. If no aspect of life is left out of account, the reason is that the nonphysical truths which describe or explain some such aspect are themselves determined by truths at the level of physics, even when there is no explanation proper at that level."[37]

Post is absolutely right in drawing our attention to the fact that to resist nonreductive physicalism is to reject the unity-of-science program in all its guises, the entire thesis of the explanatory adequacy of physics.[38] In this sense, our little discussion about the ontological fortunes of art is but a metonym for a large quarrel about the whole of man's world. Make no mistake about that. Furthermore, *if* Post were right, then there would be no real need to explain the ontology of art: the required account would, effectively, explain (and explain away, at least ontologically) Danto's "is" of artistic identification—which, as we have already seen, *is* committed (whether it means to be or not) to construing discourse about art as (mere) discourse about essentially physical objects. Either, then, there *is* a reductive program in Post and Danto or else their respective programs are deficient on the critical issue.

As it happens, there is one decisive consideration that neither Post

36. Ibid.
37. Ibid., 181.
38. See Joseph Margolis, *Science without Unity; Reconciling the Human and Natural Sciences* (Oxford: Basil Blackwell, 1987).

nor Danto nor Goodman nor Wollheim nor Searle ever directly examines; it either defeats their variations on the physicalist thesis, or shows that the adequational issue cannot be sidestepped, or both. Consider, first, that none of our theorists is willing to commit himself to any form of the identity thesis, that is, to the identity of physical and nonphysical properties. (Think of nonphysical properties as psychological or cultural or artistic properties.) Of course, if any of them had favored identity, then he would have committed himself thereby to an extensional equivalence of the strongest sort. The trouble is that there is no known conceptual strategy by which to show in a distributed and empirical way either that there is such an identity (mind-body or culture-nature) or that there is any alternative extensional equivalence for the domains in question. Consider, second, that if identity fails (which, in effect, is an adequational thesis) and if extensional equivalence fails (which [Post's option] bypasses the adequational question), then, on the argument already supplied, we must, in all philosophical candor, attend to the question afresh. Now, the consideration that decisively goes against both reductive and nonreductive physicalism is simply what Herbert Feigl—who at times supported both reductive and nonreductive physicalisms[39]—used to call, thirty or more years ago, "the many-many problem."[40]

The "many-many" thesis holds that there are always indefinitely many nonphysical properties appropriately "associated" or "linked" with any given physical property, and that there are always indefinitely many physical properties appropriately "associated" or "linked" with any given nonphysical property. For example, one can make the same chess move in indefinitely many physical ways (by postcard, by moving a piece with one's toes, by ordering someone to move the right piece, and so on); and one can do indefinitely many different things in making a particular physical movement (signalling, imitating someone signalling, making believe one is signalling, accidentally making a movement that would in context have been rightly construed as signalling but lacks the pertinent intention, and so on). There is no known way to defeat the "many-many" thesis—which is to say: (i) that Post's version of nonreductive physicalism is entirely arbitrary and unsupported; (ii) that the empirical evidence (such as it is) strongly favors a nonequivalence between physical and nonphysical ascriptions; and (iii) that, therefore, the adequational problem cannot be avoided and can-

<hr>

39. See Herbert Feigl, *The "Mental" and the "Physical"; The Essay and a Postscript* (Minneapolis: University of Minnesota Press, 1967).

40. I have heard Feigl use the expression—and explain it—several times; but I have been unable to locate its use in his actual papers.

not be settled in any way favorable to physicalism, if the reality of human culture, artworks, and persons be conceded.

Of course, the important point in the context of our own discussion is to reinstate the issue of art's nature or art's ontology. We have, in effect, clarified the nature of art's nature but not art's actual nature; and we have done so in a perfectly straightforward way that shows the empirical relevance of ontology without appeal to any speculative fandango that the crisper philosophical skeptics of our day would have cheerfully knocked down.[41] By parity of reasoning, if we think of Michelangelo's *Pietà*, there is no known set of purely physical traits of the marble in which the sculpture is cut that can be independently shown to be coextensive with the expressive pathos of the sculpture, and there is no argument to show (again on independent grounds) that the sculpture's expressive quality could only have been "linked" with the particular physical properties of the cut marble. In fact, there is no sense in which the expressive quality of the sculpture can even be segregated from the physical properties of the marble—which is not equivalent to holding that the same expressive quality could not have been manifested in different physical properties or that the same physical properties could not, in another art-historical context, have yielded other expressive qualities. This is a profound puzzle to which we shall return briefly. (Notice, also, that we have deliberately left the conceptual relation between the two sorts of property and the two sorts of entity entirely vague.)

4

Having come this far, we must pause to appreciate two very reassuring findings that may be drawn from the foregoing argument. For one thing, it appears that it cannot be altogether necessary to state once and for all what the nature of art is; all that we really need is the evidence that it would be both reasonable and coherent to construe artworks (in fact, all culturally and psychologically endowed phenomena) in a way that went entirely contrary to the physicalist alternative. For a second, once given the intransparentist theme of our own age (the rejection of cognitive privilege of every sort), there is no reason to resist the possibility that if there were at least one ontological proposal fitting the artworld perspicuously, there might well be indefinitely many alternative such proposals that would fit as well, given

41. See Richard Rorty, *Philosophy and the Mirror of Nature* (Princeton: Princeton University Press, 1979).

art's historicity and openendedness along the lines Weitz and Foucault and Danto (in rather different ways) have made so much of. In any case, the attraction of the ontology of art (and of culture) cannot fail to be affected by the repudiation of privilege.

With those two caveats in hand, it turns out to be exceedingly easy to identify the *sole* counterstrategy that our sort of inquiry must pursue. Once admit the reality of artworks and their actual possession of nonphysical properties, once admit that a dualism of substances or "stuffs" from which everything actual is composed or constituted is unconvincing—an admittedly difficult but arguable issue in its own right—then the adequational issue can be resolved only by admitting the emergence of pertinently indissoluble complex entities: in particular, persons, artworks, and, by extension, actions, institutions, histories, and the like.

Before we go further, we must resolve a troublesome equivocation that Post has reinforced, that most discussants are never entirely clear about. "Nonphysical" properties, in our present context, are rightly construed as properties that do not yield to physicalist analysis, not (or not necessarily) as properties that have no physical aspects or features at all. For example, as already remarked, the expressive quality of Michelangelo's *Pietà* need not be—as it might be thought to be in Goodman's semiotized account—a merely abstract, functional, informational, or metaphorically ascribed property; it might, instead, be an indissolubly complex property that included among its discernible features the physical qualities of the marble as well as the emergently expressive quality of the sculpture. That is, the expressive quality obtains only in the space of human culture—just as human language and human history do—but, obtaining there, it is, *qua* manifested, inseparable from (that is, it emergently incorporates), the pertinent physical properties of the marble. There are no instances of high Renaissance pathos of Michelangelo's sort in mere physical nature (unless, of course, either reductive or nonreductive physicalism successfully gains the day). The puzzle about the cultural emergence of language and art may be acknowledged (and may be explained). But for our present purpose, it is enough to understand that the adequational question requires that there *be* (emergently, indissolubly) complex entities (persons and artworks preeminently) at the level of cultural life, and that they *possess* correspondingly (emergent) complex properties. Conveniently, such entities may be said to be *embodied* in physical things and their properties, *incarnate* in physical properties.[42]

---

42. A fuller account of these distinctions appears in Joseph Margolis, *Art and Phi-*

We gain a double benefit thereby. For one thing, our constatational constraints on reference and predication are easily honored; for another, the adequational puzzle is solved in general. There may well be different ways of putting the answer needed, but there is reason to believe that the viable alternatives cannot be very diverse on essentials. Furthermore, the solution appears to be entirely hospitable to whatever the history of art may yield: it does not restrict in any obvious way what we may say in the analysis or appreciation of particular artworks. On the contrary, it is very much less confining than any physicalism could possibly be. In fact, it would be fair to say that no physicalism could possibly escape the pretensions of an extreme modernism (at best).

Let us collect the argument a little more trimly. We raised the question of art's nature by conceding an array of familiar properties (representational and expressive properties, for instance) that we usually say artworks actually possess. Discourse of this sort is constative in the sense in which, to be viable and efficiently spontaneous, it must conform to certain referential and predicative conditions. To be construed in a realist sense as well, what we speak and what we say of it (in particular, what falls within the entire world of human culture) must meet the further adequational condition that the properties things are said actually to possess (artworks, for instance, and their representational and expressive properties) must be conceptually congruent with the natures imputed to them. Nevertheless, in accord with a policy of refusing cognitive privilege, the resolution of that question yields regularities or invariances only relativized to the saliencies of our own horizon and cannot ensure any unique answer. Ontology, then, is the general (second-order) empirical effort to formulate an account of the nature of things such that our constative discourse may be inclusively adequated to the natures thereby ascribed to things. Our interest in these matters is obvious, and the strategy recommended escapes the threatening pretensions of modernism and the threatened incoherences of postmodernism.

In particular, we have claimed that physicalist solutions are surprisingly widespread but demonstrably inadequate for the artworld (and more). Given the usual intentionally complex properties ascribed to artworks and the failure of physicalism of every sort, the adequational constraint obliges us to admit that, in the space of the human world, there are to be found entities that are culturally emergent;

---

losophy (Atlantic Highlands, N.J.: Humanities Press, 1980), *Culture and Cultural Entities* (Dordrecht: D. Reidel, 1984).

indissolubly complex; complexly embodied in the physical phenomena in which they emerge or are manifested; possessing natures that include indissolubly complex properties complexly incarnate in the physical properties in which they emerge or are manifested; and possessing further properties that they can be shown to be capable of possessing because those properties can be adequated to their imputed nature. A sculpture, for example, is not a physical object (as Wollheim affirms); it is a real, culturally complex object produced in a humanly apt world and embodied in a physical object of some sort. In being thus complexly embodied, "it" cannot be segregated from its embodying materials—which is not to say that, as with Dürer's *Melancholia I*, "it" cannot be plurally embodied in a variety of different materials (indissolubly so, among its distributed instances). But it will possess properties (expressive properties, for instance) of a kind that mere physical objects cannot possess, unless some form of physicalism is true.

Beyond that, what is important to see is that ontologies of this sort are more liberating than confining—they set a hospitable context for, rather than restrict, the entire range and rigor of our critical discourse about artworks. In fact, it is a great irony of the history of the philosophy of art that, in one of the best-known models of the discipline of literary criticism, the model championed by Monroe Beardsley at least thirty years ago, in the spirit of the so-called New Criticism and constructed to accord with the requirements of a physicalist model—though not explicitly with physicalism itself—a concession is honorably allowed that betrays at a stroke the implausibility of modernist constraints on criticism (guided by physicalism) and the openness of the alternative model we have just sketched. Thus, in *The Possibility of Criticism*, published in 1970, when, in the United States, there was barely a glimmer of an alternative strategy, Beardsley openly admits:

the boundaries of textual meaning . . . are not all that sharp. Some things are definitely said in the poem and cannot be overlooked; others are suggested, as we find on careful reading; others are gently hinted, and whatever methods of literary interpretation we use, we can never establish them decisively as "in" or "out." Therefore whatever comes from without, but yet can be taken as an interesting extension of what is surely in, may be admissible. It merely makes a larger whole.[43]

Beardsley believed, of course, that the accommodation was due to the ambiguities of reading a text, to evidentiary and cognitive difficulties

---

43. Monroe C. Beardsley, *The Possibility of Criticism* (Detroit: Wayne State University Press, 1970), 36.

on the part of readers; whereas what we now see is that it is an ineluctable feature of the very nature, the ontology, of cultural phenomena. The quarrel is in a way the analogue of the quarrel between early relativity and quantum physicists, between the limits of what we know of nature and what we may take nature to be really like. The model here barely sketched obliges us to consider that *if* the physical world *is* determinate in the way the physicalist assumes (already a fatally flawed thesis), we may be reasonably sure that the world of human culture is not like that at all—hence, that the appreciation of art helps us to understand possibilities of discursive rigor that a slimmer philosophy (physicalism, in particular) would never admit.

6   Some Issues in a Neothomist Philosophy of Art

FRANCIS J. KOVACH

It is a curious fact, if not a paradox, that modern and contemporary schoolmen, the intellectual descendants of the medieval authors of superbly systematic summas, have systematically treated of the philosophy of art no better and no more frequently than modern and contemporary non-scholastic aestheticians. One finds only a few scholastic and non-scholastic authors in, say, the last one hundred years who more or less systematically deal with philosophical problems of fine art or work of fine art. In the early part of this period Joseph Jungmann is one such;[1] in recent decades, Jacques Maritain and Etienne Gilson qualify in this respect.[2]

To my mind, the most fundamental issues in any scholastic and, especially, Neothomist philosophy of art include the essence, the basic division[3] and the first causes[4] of the work of fine art; the relational character, the basic relations, the properties, the modes of being,[5] analogy, and the hierarchy of the basic classes of the work of fine art;[6] the questions of the nature of art and the mystery of artistic creation.

1. Jungmann, *Aesthetik* (Freiburg i. Breisgau: Herder, 1884), 321–950.

2. Even these few authors (1) prefer the treatment of a series of loosely connected topics to a rigorously systematic discussion of some or all major issues of the philosophy of art and (2) favor philosophically discussing some branches of fine art, like painting and music, rather than the work of fine art in general and each of its basic genera or classes in particular.

3. Paul Weiss eloquently argues for the importance of the definition and division of the work of fine art in the philosophy of art: *The World of Art* (Carbondale: Southern Illinois University Press, 1961), 103.

4. A magnificent treatment of the material and formal cause of painting is to be found in E. Gilson, *Painting and Reality* (New York: Pantheon Books, 1957), 70–170.

5. According to Gilson, the philosopher should ask about how painting is related to its mode of existence. (Op. cit., 27).

6. Among the few aestheticians who deal with the hierarchy of fine arts is Béla von Brandenstein, who is the author of an excellent analysis of this issue in his *Philosophy of Art (Művészetfilozófia* [Budapest: The Hungarian Academy of Sciences, 1920], 308–17).

99

In this essay, I wish to discuss four problems: the definition and division, the relational character, the generic properties, and the modes of being of the main genera of the work of fine art.

A. DEFINITION AND DIVISION OF THE WORK OF FINE ART

1.

Relying on empirical knowledge of artworks and on certain relevant and indisputable principles of Aristotelian-Thomistic metaphysics, work of art in general[7] may be defined as an entitatively accidental being composed of matter and form (definition by essence), intentionally made by man according to an idea or form that is determined by a human purpose[8] (definition by efficient, exemplary, and final causes).[9]

The basic division of the work of fine art rests on the following considerations. It is true that, being extrinsic to the artwork, the purpose or final cause of the work of art is not an essential part of the artwork.[10] Yet, as St. Thomas points out, it is precisely the purpose that determines the quasi essence of the artwork.[11] For the final cause determines the form or formal cause of the artifact, whereas the form, one essential part of the nature of the artwork, determines the quasi essence of the individual artwork. All this can be seen from the fact that the material cause or artistic medium, say, clay, will receive radically different forms (arrangements) according to whether the purpose of making an artifact out of that clay is to furnish man with a pot for cooking or a little statue, like a Hummel figure, to have something delightful to look at.

This fundamental role of the artwork's final cause in turn justifies

---

7. Only a few authors take the term "work of art" in the broadest possible sense in given contexts. One of them is Maritain, *Art and Scholasticism*, chap. 3, trans. J. W. Evans (New York: C. Scribner's Sons, 1962), 8.

8. Cf. Aristotle, *Phys.* II, 2, 194a34–35 and Thomas Aquinas: Nos enim sumus quodammodo finis omnium artificialium (*In II. Phys.* Lect. 4, Marietti edition, n. 173) and *In I. Eth.* 8, 101.

9. For an explanation and greater details see F. J. Kovach, "Neothomist Reflections on the Nature and Kinds of the Work of Fine Art," *Proceedings of the American Catholic Philosophical Association* (henceforth: *Proceedings*), 57 (1983), 116–34.

10. Cf. Maritain, op. cit., note 40, p. 158.

11. Thomas: Ostensum est . . . in artificialibus, quod formae ordinantur ad usum sicut ad finem. (*In II. Phys.* 5, 186.) (Artifex) considerat ipsum (*sc.* artificiatum) in fine suo prout scilicet videt quod posset ad talem finem per tale artificiatum devenire. (*De veritate*, 2, 8c.) In artificialibus enim ratio ordinatur ad finem particularem quod est aliquid per rationem excogitatum. (*Summa theologiae*, I–II 21, 2, ad 2.) Sed usus est cuius causa fit artificiatum. (*In II. Phys.* 4, 173.)

the most basic and most important division into useful, beautiful, useful and beautiful, and novel work of art. The first kind is technological; the second, fine;[12] the third, mixed (being per se both useful and beautiful); and the fourth, the product of twentieth century artists, experimental (being per se neither useful nor beautiful but only interestingly novel).[13]

Concentrating henceforth solely on the work of fine art—the proper object of the philosophy of art—one may define it as (a) a beautiful, entitatively accidental being, (b) the artistic medium of which is arranged by the maker according to a model or preconceived idea for the sake of cognitive delight. Part (a) constitutes the quasi-essential definition identifying the material and the formal causes of the work of fine art, whereas part (b) is the definition of the fine artwork by efficient cause, exemplary cause, and final cause.[14]

2.

The Aristotelian-Thomistic division of being into real and mental is a division according to the essential mode of being. Correspondingly, the same division of the work of fine art into physical and mental is undoubtedly the conceivably most basic of all divisions. Similarly, the exemplary cause significantly, although not completely, determines the form of the artwork and, through it, not only the generic and specific but also the individual character of the work of art. Accordingly, the division of the work of fine art into creative and reproductive artworks is also fundamental and second only to the division into physical and mental works of fine art. By creative work of fine art I mean one that is not made according to a work of another *kind* of fine art as an exemplary cause. In contrast, a reproductive work of fine art is meant to be one made according to a work of another kind of fine art used as an exemplary cause.

12. Various authors name these first two genera more or less differently. E.g., Johann A. Eberhart calls them mechanical and free artworks (*Theorie der schönen Wissenschaften* [Prague, 1786], 2); Carl Lemcke, technical and higher artworks (*Populäre Aesthetik* [Leipzig: E. A. Seemann, 1879], 279); Jungmann, mechanical and fine artworks (op. cit., 325); DeWitt H. Parker, industrial and fine artworks (*Theory of Aesthetics* [New York: Appleton-Century-Crafts, 1946], 271); R. G. Collingwood, useful and fine artworks (*The Principles of Art* [New York: Oxford University Press, 1958], 36); and E. Gilson, industrial and fine arts (*The Arts of the Beautiful* [New York: C. Scribner's Sons, 1965], 20–22).

13. Cf., for instance, Marcel Duchamp's urinal called "Fountain" and Walter del Maria's "High Energy Bar"—a piece of stainless steel *certified* as a work of art, in George Dickie, *Aesthetics* (Indianapolis: The Bobbs-Merrill Co., 1971), 103–6.

14. For a detailed explanation and defense of this "total" definition, see F. J. Kovach, "Neothomist Reflections," 125–26.

Combining the two dichotomic divisions, the principal division becomes fourfold in the following manner:

Work of Fine Art

Physical		Mental	
Creative *(Visual Fine Artwork)*[15]	Reproductive *(Artistic Performance)*	Reproductive *(Interpretive Work of Fine Art)*	Creative *(Liberal Work of Fine Art)*

Using history and empirical knowledge of works of fine art, one can inductively add the following *lists* of artistic subclasses to the above four artistic genera:

Visual works of fine art include aesthetically two-dimensional artworks (painting, drawing, etching, etc.) and aesthetically three-dimensional artworks (statue, collage).

Liberal works of fine art comprise poetic works (those of both poetry and literature), musical compositions (e.g., sonata, song, symphony, choral composition, etc.) and choreographed dances (both solo and team dances).

Interpretive works of fine art include poetic works mentally made by stage directors and film directors; musical compositions mentally made by conductors; and choreographed dances mentally made by dance directors or dance masters.

And finally, artistic performances and motion pictures made of artistic performances consist of recitals of poems or epics; acting (theater performances); singing and playing music (concerts by solo singers, choruses, and solo musicians or orchestras, respectively); and cinematic works (a combination mainly of acting and photography).

Art philosophers in modern times mostly *list* various genera of works of fine art, and various numbers of such genera, whereas some others offer various *divisions* of fine artworks. For these reasons, it is necessary at this juncture to do two things. One is to argue for the necessity and completeness of the above fourfold division. The other is to point out that the four artistic genera are necessarily what they are and cannot be increased in number, although the number of the respective subgenera or subclasses may constantly increase, as time goes on.

15. I must concede that this name is not satisfactory, because most artistic performances are also *visual*. However, the name *"plastic"* work of fine art, used by numerous German aestheticians, as well as Gilson (*The Arts of the Beautiful,* 122), is equally inadequate. Therefore, I consider the name *"visual* artwork" only tentative.

3.

The argument for the necessity of the fourfold division in question is the following. As seen, the fourfold division is the combination of two twofold classifications of artworks: physical and mental, and creative and reproductive. Now, it is clear that a beautiful work of art must be either in the artist's creative imagination (mental work made in imagined matter) or outside the artist's mind—a physical work made in physical matter. There is no conceivable third genus of artwork. Similarly, it is obvious that an artist either does or does not use a generically different kind of work of fine art as an exemplary cause for his own artwork. If he does, he mentally enriches, as will be shown, that other kind of artwork with his own interpretation, as Toscanini or Furtwängler does Beethoven's Fifth (prior to holding rehearsals with an orchestra). If he does not use such another artwork as an exemplary cause, the artist produces his work completely and solely by the use of his creative imagination. Again, there is no third kind of artistic genus besides the creative and the reproductive. Adding up the two conclusions, one inevitably realizes that every work of fine art must belong to one of the above-derived four artistic genera: the creative-physical; the reproductive-physical; the creative-mental; and the reproductive-mental. Consequently, there are necessarily four artistic genera and necessarily these four—the visual artwork, artistic performance, liberal artwork, and its direct interpretation in the mind.

The argument for the other thesis (that there cannot be more than the four listed artistic genera) may be stated as follows.

There are only two kinds of genetic relations conceivable between any two genera of fine artwork: a passive, that is, the relation of being inspired in its becoming by a work of another of the four genera; and an active, namely, the relation of inspiring the becoming of an artwork of another genus.

In these two respects, the visual work of fine art is neither inspired nor inspiring, except per accidens.[16] For paintings and statues can be made and, in most cases, are made without their makers' use of any other genus of artwork as a particular exemplary cause. On the other hand, the finished work of painting or sculpture, however great it may be artistically, by its nature does not give rise to an artwork of another genus, except per accidens, as, for example, Moussorgsky's piano composition, "Pictures at an Exhibition," shows by having been orches-

---

16. The per accidens use consists in the artist's free decision to use the work of another genus of fine or mixed artworks as a model or exemplary cause, as is the case with Monet's *The Rouen Cathedral*.

trated by four different composers. In partial contrast, works of liberal fine arts are per se uninspired by works of *other* genera of fine arts[17]; yet, they per se can and often do inspire, and give rise to, interpretive artworks and/or artistic performances.

Artistic interpretations of poetic, musical, and choreographic works by stage directors, conductors, dance masters, and film directors, respectively, are both inspired and inspiring in the strict technical senses of the terms. For unless there are, say, plays, screen plays, symphonies, and choreographed dances, the stage director, the film director, the conductor, and the dance master have nothing to interpret in their minds and nothing to communicate to a cast of actors, musicians, or dancers. On the other hand, interpretive artworks are created in the minds of various artists *only* if there are performing artists to be guided in their performances by the respective interpretive artworks. Evidently, then, interpretive artworks are necessarily modelled by liberal artworks, and always serve as models for performing artists.

Finally, artistic performances are always inspired by interpretive and/or liberal artworks (as just stated), but they themselves do not give rise to generically different or any other artworks. In this sense, they do not inspire any other kind of artwork, although they do cause cognitively delightful images in the mind of the beholder.

These findings may be summarized as follows:

1) Visual Artwork: Uninspired by, and uninspiring, other artists;
2) Liberal Artwork: Uninspired by, but inspiring, other artists;
3) Interpretive Artwork: Inspired by, and inspiring, other artists; and,
4) Artistic Performance: Inspired by, but uninspiring, other artists.

Evidently, these are the only four alternatives in the genetic order of fine artworks. For the first genus is doubly negative; the third, doubly positive; the second, negative and positive; and the fourth, positive and negative. No additional artistic genus is possible or conceivable. Consequently, the listed basic classes in our division of the work of fine art are the only four possible artistic genera.

---

17. Operatic music is not an exemption from this truth. For while opera needs a libretto, i.e., another class of artwork, libretto is not of a genus other than that of music (since both are works of liberal artists). Nor is Gustav Mahler's Second employing a chorus in imitation of Beethoven's last symphony a proof to the contrary. For both the inspiring and the inspired works are of the same artistic genus (and species). Moreover, even if they were not both of the class of musical composition, it was Mahler's own decision, not a musical or compositional necessity, to imitate Beethoven in the use of a chorus in his symphony; and this fact renders the Ninth a per accidens model of Mahler's Second.

In sharp contrast, as the recent history of art shows, there are constantly newer and newer subdivisions being produced in each of the four artistic genera. Cinema is the best known and most important such art form as an addition to the subclasses of artistic performances. But there are such also in the other three artistic genera, as collage and the combination of statue and painting are under the visual artworks. Analogously, it is not inconceivable that, in the future, new genera will be added to useful, beautiful, mixed, and novel artworks.

4.

One more question needs to be answered before we turn to the second main topic in this essay. Following Benedetto Croce, someone may assert that the division into physical and mental artworks is arbitrary, since it is arguable that all works of fine art are made in the artist's mind, so that there is no such thing as a physical work of fine art.

In reply one may list three reasons for maintaining, as the division does, that some artworks are, in fact, mental, whereas others are actually made in physical matter. One such reason is that, contrary to the makers of liberal and interpretive artworks, a painter or sculptor never completes his work in his mind[18] and, accordingly, never claims to have made a painting or a statue before he completed his work in physical matter. Similarly, no performing artist performs a liberal artwork in exactly the same manner, even if he performs it twice on the same day, say, at a matinee and an evening concert.[19] This fact clearly shows that what the performing artist has in mind is not the complete, but the almost complete, work of fine art. Instead, only the live performance involving the artist's body in various ways and the completed and edited motion picture are completed, final, and unique artworks. Moreover, however much the performing artist may know every word or bar or step of the liberal artwork, as long as he is merely *going to* perform it either at rehearsals or on stage, he does not consider himself an actual performer of the liberal artwork in question. This fact is a tangible proof that, to the artistic performer's own mind, his completed work is one made in physical matter—in his own body or in the tones of the musical instrument he plays—rather than in his mind.

18. Cf. Gilson: "The execution of their (sc. the painters') work is not preceded by its perfect precognition in their mind." *Painting and Reality,* chap. 5, n. 2, p. 151.

19. Cf. Gilson: "No man signs his own name twice in identically the same way" (op. cit., chap. 2, n. 3, p. 81).

A third reason is, perhaps, the strongest and decisive: Once all written texts or notes of, say, a poetic, musical, or choreographic work are destroyed, that work is still "around," provided that somebody remembers the composition *in toto*.[20] In sharp contrast, if, say, a painting or statue is physically completely destroyed, even if its maker or a beholder remembers it well or if photographs showing it from every possible angle are extant, that visual work of fine art does not exist anymore, and is not considered to exist any longer. The reason for this difference cannot be anything except this: By its nature, the visual work of fine art is a physical work and, as such, it must exist in its original artistic medium in order to be a finished and unique artwork; so that mere remembering of it would not qualify it as existent. However, the liberal and the interpretive artworks are per se made and completed in the mind, whether or not they are ever externally expressed by their makers; and for this reason as long as somebody remembers such an artwork, that artwork is in its own proper way, that is, in imagined matter.

Therefore, artworks by painters and sculptors, as well as performing artists, are, in fact, physical works of fine art; the liberal and the interpretive artworks are not.

B. THE RELATIONAL NATURE OF THE WORK OF FINE ART

Reflecting, first, upon the twofold division of the work of fine art and, secondly, on the relational character in the genetic order of the four basic genera of fine artworks, one can realize the implications of these two facts in terms of the relational nature of each of the four artistic genera of artworks.

1.

In terms of Aristotelian-Thomistic metaphysics and logic, every being, as well as every concept, is either a singular or a universal—the former being predicable of only one thing, *this one* unique and, as such, indefinable being; the latter, of *many* beings pertaining to the same group of individuals. And, if a being or concept is a universal, it is either a genus or a species.

Analogously applying these terms to works of fine art, one can immediately realize that every member of both the visual works of fine

20. For an excellent treatment of the issue, although limited to the work of poetry, see René Wellek and Austin Warren, *Theory of Literature,* 12 (New York: Harcourt, Brace, and World, 1956), especially 129–31.

art and of artistic performances is a singular, like "David" as *this* one work by Michelangelo or *this* one performance tonight at Carnegie Hall of Beethoven's *Emperor* Concerto by Arthur Rubinstein.

In contrast, all works of all liberal and interpretive artists, being conceived and completed in the mind, are universals for the following reasons. Every poetic work, like every musical composition and every choreographed dance, once externalized, is capable of being enriched by receiving additional specifications in the creative imagination of an interpretive artist—a stage or film director, conductor, or dance master. This creative process of enriching the liberal work of fine art consists in mentally adding qualities or differences to a poetic, musical, or choreographic work very much like adding qualities or differences to a genus—like "rational" or "white" or "wise" to the genus "animal." This is to say that, analogously, the liberal artwork has the character of genus; the interpretive work of art, the character of a species. Moreover, it is commonly known that the interpretive artist changes the artistic genus, the work of the liberal artist, into an artistic species— his own work—only to communicate it to performing artists through words, gestures, etc.; and the performing artists, in turn, further enrich the specified generic work with their own voices, enunciations, gestures, physical appearances, and with the particular kind of musical instruments they play (Bösendorfer *vs.* Steinway; Stradivarius *vs.* Amati *vs.* a violin made in Mittenwald, etc.). The process of transforming the originally generic and the interpretively specified artwork leads to the performing artist's own unique work, viz., an artistic singular or individual, like this one unique performance.[21]

Summing up, visual works of fine art and, analogously, artistic performances are all per se artistic singulars; the works of liberal artists have the character of genus; and the works of interpretive artists, the character of species.

2.

Notice that I said not that the work of the liberal artist *is* a genus (or the work of the interpretive artist a species), but that the former has the character of genus, and the latter the character of species.

21. I may add here that there is a significant difference between the ways in which artists giving solo performances (e.g., a pianist playing Schubert's *Wanderer Phantasie*), and those performing together with other artists in a team produce their respective artistic singulars. For the solo performer must, all by himself, both specify and individualize the artwork of a playwright, composer or choreographer—thus doing his own specific *and* individualizing interpretation. In contrast, the team performer needs only to individualize the original poetic, musical, or choreographic work, since the specification of such a work is done for him by the interpretive artist.

This is to say that liberal artworks are similar to a genus, and interpretive artworks to a species. The reason for asserting that the two genera of fine artworks "have the character of " genus and species, respectively, is the following.

On the one hand, works of liberal and interpretive artists bear genuine resemblance to genera and species in nature, insofar as the work by every artistic interpreter of, say, Mozart's *Jupiter* Symphony has one and the same artwork at its core, and participates in the same, although each interpreter enriches that participated core differently— just as both man and brute participate in the same generic nature, even though each participates in it differently—one in a rational way, the other in an irrational manner. Therefore Ormandy's and Stokowski's Jupiter are truly like species with respect to their common core, Mozart's *Jupiter*; and Mozart's *Jupiter* is truly like a genus in which the other two participate. Nevertheless, the two interpreted versions of Mozart's last symphony are not exactly the same way the two species of the work of Mozart's genius, as, say, man and brute are the species of "animal." For "animal" is a nature predicable of many and, as such, is a *concept* abstracted from individual men and brutes by the rational mind and inhering in the rational mind. Not so is the case with either one of the two versions of the *Jupiter* in the minds of the named two conductors. Instead, each version, just like the original Mozartian model, is a unity of a large number of *images,* the product of one of man's sensory powers; and being a sensory picture composed of nothing but sensory images,[22] the interpreted work cannot possibly be a species in the univocal sense, nor the liberal artwork a genus in the univocal sense.[23]

Consequently, while not being a genus or species in the strict sense, an order of images making up a mental work of fine art *has the character* of either one of the two kinds of universal; as such, it can lead to an indefinite number of concrete artistic performances—artworks having the character of singular.

22. Only in the work of poetry are there universals—the meanings of the words constituting the material cause of the poetic work.

23. Another and more metaphysical argument for this truth is this: Every work of fine art is an accidental being, i.e., one that, strictly speaking, has no essence, except for the essence(s) of its material cause(s) (Thomas, *In II Phys.* 1, 142). Instead, it has a quasi essence, namely, the unity of its parts made not by an intrinsic principle (substantial form) but by an extrinsic principle—the artist as its maker (efficient cause). Now, that which has no essence has no intrinsic formal cause, which alone is, by nature, a universal. Therefore, the work of fine art, having the ontological status of an accidental being, is not a universal in the strict traditional sense; and consequently, the liberal work of the poet, composer, and choreographer is not a genus in the strict sense, nor the interpreted version of it a species.

C. GENERIC PROPERTIES OF THE WORKS OF FINE ART

Once it is established that visual works of fine arts, as well as artistic performances, are concrete individuals made in physical matter, whereas creative and interpretive works of fine arts are *like* universals in the imagination and intellect of their makers, the generic properties of the physical and those of the mental works of fine art can be readily recognized.

Both the properties of the physical works of fine art and those of the mental artworks can be divided into objective (absolute) and subjective (relative) properties. The former group of properties characterize works of fine art independently of beholders or considered in themselves; the latter, artworks considered in regard to the beholder, the subject of aesthetic delight, which delight works of fine art elicit in him.

1.

To begin with the *objective* or absolute properties of *physical* works of fine art, the very first such property follows from the concrete individual character of such artworks. For an individual artwork includes not only its quasi-genus and quasi-specific difference, as a given performance of *Hamlet* does the generic work of Shakespeare and the specifications of a stage director, but also innumerable additional features, which no liberal or interpretive artwork can have on its own, however great artists may have made them.[24]

This fact, in turn, means that being analogous to concrete individual beings, visual works of fine art and artistic performances are both entitatively and aesthetically entirely determined or, shall we say, complete, whereas the mental works of fine art are per se, by reason of their artistic quasi universality, entitatively indeterminate and, in re-

---

24. Such are Titian's *Assumption of the Virgin* and Rodin's *Thinker*, as well as, say, the performance of Alban Berg's *Lulu* by Anneliese Rothenberger and the Hamburg State Opera under the baton of Leopold Ludwig in the Metropolitan Opera House at the Lincoln Center Festival 1967 on Saturday, July 1, 1967, beginning at 8 p.m. For, with regard to that memorable performance of *Lulu*, the size and shape of the stage, its acoustics and decorations, the voices of Rothenberger and the rest of the cast, their physical appearances, their facial expressions, their gestures, their enunciation of words, their singing and acting, their dresses, the way the orchestra played following Leopold Ludwig's instructions, and many, many other factors are the features rendering the Ludwig-interpreted work of Alban Berg more beautiful and more rich than either Berg's work alone (in its printed score) or its interpretation by Ludwig were. For a good discussion of the difference between written and performed work of fine art, see, e.g., Warren E. Steinkraus, *Philosophy of Art* (Beverly Hills: Benziger, 1974), 36–37.

lation to their artistic interpretations or performances, aesthetically incomplete.

This incompleteness does not mean aesthetic imperfection in the sense that no poet, composer, choreographer, or artistic interpreter, however great he may be as an artist, can ever produce an aesthetically truly great work of art. Instead, what this incompleteness does mean is that even the greatest liberal or interpretive artwork naturally lacks certain aesthetic qualities, which only its artistic performance can actually possess. Or, to put it differently, artistic performances naturally entail aesthetic qualities with which they enrich, that is, aesthetically enhance the interpreted and/or original work of a poet, composer, or choreographer.

To those who may think that declaring works of even the greatest liberal and interpretive artists to be aesthetically per se incomplete is an arrogant and insulting position, the following may be pointed out. If interpreted original artworks were not aesthetically richer than the originals themselves, or if performed originals were not aesthetically richer, more beautiful, and more delightful than either the original artworks or their interpreted versions, then neither the interpreting nor the performing artist would have any contribution to make to the original works of liberal fine arts or to the interpretations of those works of liberal arts—a truly absurd consequence, indeed. For which music lover does not find the voice of Feodor Chaliapin or Lili Pons, the tone of a Stradivarius or the organ of the Cologne Cathedral, the way Isaac Stern plays the violin, Wilhelm Kempff the piano, and Leonard Bernstein conducts the *Rosenkavalier,* exquisitely beautiful even *apart* from the artwork they sing, play, conduct, etc.? Evidently, all this beauty is added to the work of a composer, and is put into the service of showing the beauty of the original composition in all its glory. Moreover, ordinary experience shows that merely reading the score or a written screen play, however delightful in itself, causes less, or less intensive, cognitive delight than listening to its actual performance in a concert hall or on record, or watching the finished motion picture of that screenplay, as the fruit of a team work of the playwright, the film director, actors, film photographers, *et alii.*

The entitative and aesthetic inferiority of the mental artwork rooted in its quasi-generic or quasi-specific universality is, in the language of metaphysics, the per se indefiniteness, indetermination, or privative infinity of potential or mental beings. Such beings lack the principle or principles of determination and, as such, are indeed imperfect or incomplete by not having everything they can have and that is due to them.[25]

25. Cf. Aristotle, *Phys.* III, 6, 206b32–207a2; *Met.* V, 16; and Thomas: Secundum

The second and third objective properties of physical and mental artworks directly follow from their entitative and aesthetic completeness and incompleteness, respectively. For that which is complete is not completable anymore and, as such, needs no other kind of artist or technician to complete it.[26] Correspondingly, that which is incomplete can be completed or is completable by other kinds of artists, and perhaps also by technicians. And, as such, it does need other kinds of artists or technicians. The performance of certain musical compositions, like Beethoven's *Missa Sollemnis* or Mahler's Second requires a conductor and a large number of musicians and singers, not to mention technicians; and some operas need conductors, singers, musicians, dancers, and even painters, as well as creative experts of staging, lighting, and so on.

Finally, since that which is complete and needs nobody else to enrich or perfect it cannot be multiplied in any way, such as by various interpretations, the visual artwork and the artistic performance are interpretively immultiplicable. On the other hand, since that which is incomplete and needs other kinds of artists to enrich it entitatively and perfect it aesthetically, the mental work of fine art is per se multiplicable by interpretation and, one may add, indefinitely multiplicable.[27] With this realization in mind, the analogy of the mental fine artwork to Plato's concept of Idea is too obvious not to notice it. For the work of the creative artist and, secondarily, of the interpretive artist, is the "eternal," unchanging exemplar according to which artistic performances are done.[28]

Contrary to works of mental fine arts, a finished painting and an actual stage performance cannot be artistically multiplied, only technically copied by, say, students of painting or relatively untalented performing artists.

2.

Turning next to the *relative* or subjective properties of physical and mental works of fine art, again one must start out with the entitative nature of each of the two highest genera of fine artworks.

---

hoc enim dicitur aliquid esse perfectum, secundum quod est actu, nam perfectum dicitur, cui nihil deest secundum modum suae perfectionis (*Summa theologiae*, I, q. 4.a 1, c). Also, Sed quia in his quae fiunt, tunc dicitur esse aliquid perfectum, cum de potentia educitur in actum, transumitur hoc nomen perfectum ad significandum omne illud cui non deest esse in actu (Ibid., ad 2).

26. For a confirmation of this unique value of physical artwork with regard to painting, see the remarkable story about the British painter Constable and one of his customers in Gilson, *Painting and Reality*, chap. 3, n. 3, pp. 103–4.

27. Cf. Gilson, op. cit., chap. 1, n. 4, p. 59.

28. Cf. e.g., Plato, *Phaedo* 100b–e; *Tim.* 28–30.

Physical works of fine art, precisely because they are made of physical matter, are directly knowable—mainly through vision and hearing.[29] This is the reason for the second subjective or relative property of the physical artwork: the lack of need for symbols to make it knowable to beholders.

As can be expected, the two subjective or relative properties of mental works of fine art are the contrary opposites of the two above-named properties. For being per se in the mind, all liberal and interpretive works of fine art are directly unknowable, and only indirectly knowable—through physical symbols.

This gives rise in turn to the second subjective property of the mental artwork: the need for symbols through which the artist enables the beholder (and, in cases of interpretive artworks, the performing artist) to recognize the work of fine art which the liberal or interpretive artist has in mind.

The symbols in question, as history shows, in case of poetry are written words using various alphabets as conventional (i.e., purely arbitrary) signs of articulate sounds; in case of music, musical notes (like those used in Gregorian chant and those employed at least since the early baroque times), which are predominantly arbitrary and, to some extent, natural signs.[30] The externalization of choreographed dances is relatively recent, with labanotation being the presently preferred system of dance notation.[31] In the absence of any such system, the choreographer must verbally explain the single steps and the whole of the dance—or else he himself must dance at least the most important or most difficult sequences of steps.[32]

The interpretive artist externalizes his mental work mostly by describing in words and gestures how to act any line, scene, etc., or how to sing or play each part of the liberal artwork.

---

29. For the reasons why the beautiful material object, whether a natural thing or an artifact, is perceived precisely through the eye and/or ear, see F. J. Kovach, "The Role of the Senses in Aesthetic Experience," *Scholastic Challenges*, Essay 17 (Stillwater, OK: Western Publications, 1988), 281–94.

30. The poet and the composer have, of course, also another way of communicating their mental works to others—by directly reciting them, singing them, or playing them on a musical instrument.

31. The first to describe such a method of dance notation seems to have been Guglielmo Ebreo of Pesaro; and the first notator of dancing, the French choreographer Raoul Feuillet in his *Choreographie* of 1701, who was followed by a few in the nineteenth century. The method at the present widely in use, especially in this country, was developed by the Hungarian Rudolf von Laban in his *Kinetographie* (1928), and is named after him "labanotation." For these and additional data see G. B. L. Wilson, *A Dictionary of Ballet* (Penguin Books, 1957), 88–91 and *passim*.

32. This latter and traditional expression of choreographed dance is clearly analogous to the poet or the composer personally performing his own artwork.

D. THE MODES OF BEING OF WORKS OF FINE ART

There is one more important issue that may be discussed here on the basis of the twofold division of the work of fine art into physical and mental, and of its fourfold division into visual, liberal, and interpretive artworks and artistic performance. It is the issue of the various ways in which the four genera of fine artworks exist.[33]

This problem arises from the following consideration. It is a rather obvious fact that some works of fine art exist in physical matter as their material cause, whereas others are completely in the mind. This being so, the following question can be asked: Can one and the same kind or individual work of fine art have both modes of being, namely, being in the mind and being in physical matter? The answer will be given separately with respect to each of the four genera of fine artworks.

1.

The visual work of fine art exists in reality by having been made of some physical medium. This is a matter of sensory evidence. However, every painter and sculptor makes his artwork according to an idea in his mind (which idea may be relatively original, not based on any individual material being, or else the partial creative modification of a chosen object, like a certain seascape, landscape, or person to be portrayed.[34]

Now, if the creative idea in the artist's mind has a concrete, particular model in the physical world, as Rembrandt had for his self-portraits, or Peter Paul Rubens had for *Helena Fourment with her son Francis,* or Anthony van Dyck for *Cornelius van der Geest,* or Goya for *Donna Isabel de Porcel,* or Jean A. D. Ingres for *Madame Moitessier,* then that model is the extrinsic exemplary cause perceived by the artist; and the unique way in which the artist partly alters, partly enriches that model in his own creative imagination is the intrinsic and direct exemplary cause of the would-be painting, according to which the

33. To Croce this problem does not exist, since he holds that no work of fine art exists as a physical object, and the entire artistic creation is a mental process or activity (op. cit., chaps. 1–2, pp. 11, 12–13).

34. I am fully aware of certain avant-garde painters who, imitating Salvador Dali, use paint guns in chance-producing paintings on canvases without any preconceived idea or image. However, even though some of such pictorial products may happen to be more or less beautiful—mainly through pleasing color combinations—such pictorial works are *not* works of fine art in the strict, proper sense.

artist directly makes his work in some physical medium.[35] All this holds true, naturally, not only for portraits, but for all kinds of painting and sculptural work.[36] If, however, the maker of a visual artwork does not use any concrete physical model for his work, and instead has only a "minimal" creative idea for it, as when he decides to paint a still-life or a mountain or to sculpt a nude in marble, then that broad idea is the remote but intrinsic exemplary cause of his work, and that idea gradually particularized with details of his would-be work is the proximate intrinsic exemplary cause.[37] (All this holds true even for artistic improvisations in music.)[38]

Summing up these details, one may say the following: In any case, the visual artwork is, first, in the maker's mind as a generic exemplary cause. Second, it is, as a direct exemplary cause of the would-be visual artwork, *almost* completed in the artist's imagination.[39] Third, it exists

35. Cf. Oskar Kokoschka's following lines from a letter (1917/18) to Hans Tietze: "And so I now use as models the faces of people . . . whom I know inside out, so that they torment me almost like nightmares, to build up compositions showing the struggle of man against man, . . . and in each picture I search for the dramatic accent that will weld the individuals into a higher unity..." (from *Painters on Painting*, Eric Potter, ed. [New York: Grosset and Dunlap, 1963], 214). Juan Gris is also to the point: "Nor is a painting which is merely the faithful copy of an object a picture, for . . . it . . . has no esthetic, that is to say, no selection of the elements of the reality it expresses" ("On the Possibility of Painting" [1927] in *Painters on Painting*, 217).

36. For instance, Eugene Fromentin (*Les maîtres d'autrefois*, 1775) remarks on the great landscape artist Jacob von Ruisdael, "Such is the sole cause of Ruisdael's superiority, and this cause suffices; there is in the painter a man who thinks, and in each one of his works a conception." (Trans. Mary C. Robbins [Boston: Houghton, 1882], 186). Antoine Watteau concurs on this point when writing his patroness, Madame Julienne, "I mean to begin work on it again after midday on Monday, because, during the morning I shall be busy putting down ideas *in sanguine*" (*Painters on Painting*, 86).

37. Cf. the painter Sir Thomas Lawrence's words: "I can only use a model when the picture is already made; then I can look at the model to get some detail which the vision failed me with. . . . The picture must all come out of the artist's inside, awareness of forms and figures..." (Quoted from *The Creative Process*, Brewster Ghiselin, ed. [The New American Library, 1964], 212).

38. For instance, in a letter giving his father account of a recent concert he had given, Wolfgang A. Mozart wrote, "I then played . . . a fugue in C minor and then all of a sudden a magnificent sonata in C major, out of my head, and a Rondo to finish up with." *The Letters of Mozart and His Family*, II, Letter No. 228b of 1777, trans. E. Anderson (London: Macmillan, 1938), 498.

39. A contemporary French painter, Georges Braque, disagrees with the view that there is a "first" and a "second" mode of being to a painting: "The picture makes itself under the brush. . . . There must be no preconceived idea. . . . When I tackle the white canvas I never know how it will come out. . . . I never visualize a picture in my mind before starting to paint" (*Je Jour et la nuit*, 1952, quoted from *Painters on Painting*, 210). However, these lines must not be taken as asserting more than that the painter completes his work on canvas, rather than in his mind. Braque himself indicates this truth in a sentence added to the above quotation: "I believe that a picture is finished only after one has completely effaced the idea that was there at the start"; and, elsewhere, he openly speaks of "impregnations" (subconscious inspirations?), which came to him in early youth and "which have since pursued me until this final realization" (ibid., 209).

in physical reality directly knowable to the beholder. To these three modes of being there comes a fourth one just touched upon: When the artwork finished in physical matter is intuited and beheld by somebody as a beautiful artwork, that artwork is also in the mind of the beholder in a partly objective (truthful) and partly subjective manner, dependent upon certain features of the observer's personality.

Altogether, then, the visual artwork has four modes of being: (1) Being in the mind of the painter or sculptor as a generic and indirect exemplary cause; (2) being in his mind as an almost finished artwork to be used as a direct exemplary cause of the artist's physical artwork; (3) being in physical matter as a complete, individual work of painting or sculpture; and (4) being in the mind of the contemplator as a partly objective picture of the beheld visual artwork.

Out of these four modes of being only one is proper to the nature of the visual artwork, and only one is proper or suitable to the nature of the beholder. Since the visual artwork is by its very nature a physical work of fine art, the third of the above four modes of being (being in physical matter) is its entitatively or metaphysically proper mode of being. And since the nature of the human beholder is such that he knows nothing unless it first becomes known to him through the sense perception of material things or objects, the cognitively or epistemologically proper mode of being to the visual artwork is also being in physical matter.

2.

Turning next to liberal fine artworks, one can say that their modes of being are analogous to those of visual artworks. First, at least analytically, the creative idea comes into the mind of the poet, composer, or choreographer.[40] Next, the liberal artist works out the details and completely finishes his artwork in his own mind. Then, inasmuch as he wishes that his work become known to others, and known not by his acting as the performer of his own work, the liberal artist externalizes his mentally completed work in sets of symbols[41] (alphabet used

---

40. For example, Beethoven tells von Haslinger in a letter about a canon that "came into my head" while he was asleep on his way to Vienna (see *The Creative Process*, 51).

41. No less authority than W. A. Mozart attests to the first three modes of being with regard to musical composition: "When I am as it were, completely myself, entirely alone and of good cheer . . . it is on such occasions that my ideas flow best and most abundantly. *Whence* and *how* they come, I know not. . . . Those ideas that please me I retain in memory . . . to hum them to myself. If I continue in this way, it soon occurs to me how I may turn this or that morsel . . . to make a good dish of it. . . . All this fires my soul and, provided I am not disturbed, my object enlarges itself, becomes

in handwritten or printed forms, musical notes, and dance notations), which enable any would-be beholder to come to know and enjoy the liberal artwork and any interpretive and/or performing artist to specify and/or individualize them. And finally, the work of the liberal artist exists in the minds of beholders and reproductive artists as a more or less objective mental picture of the poetic, musical or choreographic work.

The second of these four modes of being is entitatively proper to the nature of the liberal work of fine art. For such a work is completed, and is, in the mind, even if the artist forgets to externalize it or is prevented from doing so.[42] The third mode of being cannot be entitatively proper, for absurdities would follow from it. One such absurdity would be that, say, Shakespeare has millions and millions of *Hamlets*, and Beethoven thousands and thousands of *Eroicas*. From this it is clear that the printed work is not the work of the liberal artist, but is only the indefinitely multiplicable external manifestation of it in symbols. In contrast, the third mode is the *cognitively* proper mode of the liberal work of fine art, since the beholder, as well as the interpretive and performing artists, can directly recognize and enjoy the poetic, musical, or choreographic work only in its written or printed form.

3.

For similar reasons, the work of the artistic interpreter also has four modes of being. The analytically and chronologically first is the work of the liberal artist as it is recognized through physical symbols, and as it serves in the role of direct intrinsic exemplary cause for the work of the artistic interpreter. The second mode is being in the mind of the interpretive artist as his own mentally completed work. The third mode is the external manifestation to a group of performing artists, of, say, the stage director's or conductor's mental work through words, gestures, and so on. Finally, the fourth mode is being in the mind of a certain kind of beholder—the performing artists, to whose minds the communicated interpretive artwork is partly an enjoyable mental

---

methodised and defined in my mind. . . . For this reason the committing to paper is done quickly enough, for everything is, as I said before, already finished; and it rarely differs on paper from what it was in my imagination" (*The Creative Process,* 44–45). Cf. also Roger Session's account of "inspiration," "conception" (i.e. the vision of the whole composition) and "execution" (i.e. the process "of listening inwardly to the music as it shapes itself; of allowing the music to grow" (*The Creative Process,* 47–48).

42. Beethoven says of the canon mentioned in n. 40 above, "But scarcely did I awake when away flew the canon" (*The Creative Process,* 51).

knowledge and, more importantly, the direct exemplary cause of the would-be performance by actors, singers, musicians, and dancers.

As in the case of liberal artworks, the entitatively proper mode of being to the artistic interpretation is unquestionably the being in the interpreter's mind as his own completed work of fine art. On the other hand, the cognitively proper mode of being is the external communication of the interpreted work through physical signs to performing artists.

4.

As can be expected, the artistic performance also has four modes of being. One is the interpreted work which is in the mind of the performer as a direct intrinsic exemplary cause, according to which he must form in his mind the particular way in which he will make his artistic contribution by performing every part (word, tone, step, etc.) of his performance, being guided by the interpreted artwork. The second mode is the nearly completed artwork in the mind of the performer, which artwork will guide him in executing his part of the originally liberal artwork. The third mode, evidently, is the actual artistic performance as a work of fine art made in physical matter (such as the body of the performer or parts of his body, the tones of musical instruments played upon, the photographic camera, and the finished and edited cinematic work). And the fourth mode is the artistic performance's being in the mind of the beholder as the direct cause of his aesthetic delight. The third of these four modes is both entitatively and cognitively the proper mode of being to the artistic performance and cinema, and to the beholder, respectively. For, by its very nature, performances are produced and truly completed only in the body of the artist or in musical instruments used by his body. On the other hand, only the actual performance is directly knowable and enjoyable to the spectator.

* * *

I wish to bring this brief study to conclusion by doing a few things I consider important at this juncture.

First, I would like to point out that probably the most basic truth I have attempted here to throw light on is that while aestheticians generally treat of arts or fine arts, this short Neothomist paper has the *work* of art and the *work* of fine art as its principal object. Exploring the latter rather than the former is basic to the proper understanding of artworks and works of fine art, because it is the artwork (or its externalization in physical symbols), rather than art or fine art, that is directly knowable to man. One would not even know of the existence of art or fine art (unless he himself is a maker of *mental* artworks) if artworks were not, in some way, sufficiently knowable to him. The other basic truth that underlies all the issues treated above is that artwork of any kind, including the work of fine art, is basically an accidental being—a truth that facilitates the proper categorization of the work of fine art within the realm of reality and the proper understanding of what artworks are, how they exist, and how they are made. I may also mention here that in my analysis of the various modes in which works of fine arts exist I have endeavored, among other things, to do something long overdue—to do justice to the work of the interpretive fine artist, who is known, appreciated, and perhaps also praised by most art lovers only for his role of actual conducting, and not also for his being the maker of a mental artwork, without which he would not know how to conduct any musical composition in an aesthetically valuable fashion.

Finally, I wish to make a parting remark to my peers, many of whom may be reluctant to deal with the philosophical discipline of aesthetics out of fear of its object, beauty and art, being "too worldly" for the *inner sanctum* of metaphysical thought. For reply I will turn to my great and favorite authority, Thomas Aquinas, who early in his life realized and taught that all created beauty participates in God's infinite beauty;[43] and He, as the divine Artist, is the eternal primary analogue of all human artists and artworks.[44]

---

43. Filius habet claritatem, quae irradiat super omnia et in quo omnia resplendent. (Thomas, *In I. Sent.* 31, 2, 1, sol.) Cf. Thomas's *Commentarium de Div. Nom.*, c. 4 lect. 5, nn. 334, 337, 347.

44. Thomas, *In II. Sent.* 16, 1, 2, ad 2; *Summa contra gentiles*, II, 21, nn. 972, 977; *De pot.* 1, 2.

7

Who's Afraid of Marcel Duchamp?
JOHN BROUGH

In 1915 Marcel Duchamp purchased a snow shovel at a hardware store in New York, signed it, and inscribed it with the phrase, "IN ADVANCE OF THE BROKEN ARM." The snow shovel was an early example of what Duchamp called a "readymade," a manufactured article selected by the artist and introduced into the artworld. This particular shovel lay about Duchamp's studio for some time, finally disappearing. But despite its inauspicious career, the snow shovel and its brothers and sisters in the readymade family eventually came to have an enormous influence. "For," as George Heard Hamilton wrote in 1955, "of what other object, man-made and mass-produced (*pace* the plane and the bomb), can it be said that, because of one man's decision, the course of Western culture was altered?"[1] Even if one does not want to go as far as Hamilton, one must at least admit that almost all of the major art movements of the sixties, seventies, and even eighties show the unmistakable mark of Duchamp, and specifically of his readymades. But the impact of the readymades has not been restricted to the artworld. It has also been felt by the philosophers, particularly by those who pay close attention to what transpires in contemporary art. As Steven Goldsmith observes, the readymades "have become the central hurdle over which any attempt to define art must leap."[2] Why is this the case?

First, there is the cardinal fact that most of the key players in the contemporary artworld accept the readymades as works of art. And then there is what Duchamp said about them: that they were not selected for their aesthetic qualities—indeed, that their choice "is always based on visual indifference and, at the same time, on the total

1. George Heard Hamilton, "In Advance of Whose Broken Arm?" in *Marcel Duchamp in Perspective,* ed. Joseph Mashek (Englewood Cliffs, New Jersey: Prentice-Hall, 1975), 73.
2. Steven Goldsmith, "The Readymades of Marcel Duchamp: The Ambiguities of an Aesthetic Revolution," *The Journal of Aesthetics and Art Criticism* XLI (1983), 197.

absence of good or bad taste."[3] The challenge the readymades lay down to aesthetic theory, then, is to explain how an everyday manufactured object, not made by the artist and possessing no aesthetic value, is nonetheless a work of art.

Two philosophers who take Duchamp's readymades to be works of art and who attempt to meet this challenge are George Dickie and Arthur Danto. Dickie's response is his "institutional theory" of art; Arthur Danto's response is more difficult to label, although one might call it, inadequately, an "interpretation theory." I want to discuss in this paper how the pressure of the readymades, taken as works of art, has shaped these two theories in fundamental ways. The theories, of course, are intended to explain all works of art, certainly all works of visual art, and not just the readymades. But it is the demands of the readymades, not the demands, say, of Rembrandt's *Philosopher*, that determine the central positions the two philosophers take. In the course of this paper, I hope to show that while the focus on the readymades has opened a number of fascinating and significant possibilities for the philosophy of art, it has also led to some profound difficulties, exemplified in Dickie's and Danto's theories. These difficulties are serious enough to suggest that one might want to undertake a thought experiment, one that is admittedly irreverent to Duchamp's hagiological status but that might also be seen as in keeping with his spirit: What would be the significance for the philosophy of art if we denied—giving reasons, of course—that the readymades are works of art? This is a possibility that we will consider at the end of the paper. But first I shall look at George Dickie's institutional theory and then at Arthur Danto's interpretation theory in the light of the pressure exerted on them by the readymades.

I should mention that Duchamp's readymades fall into two categories: the "readymade aided" and the readymade unaided.[4] The readymade unaided is one to which the artist does not do anything, except perhaps sign, inscribe in some other way, or place in an unusual position. Examples would be the snow shovel (*In Advance of the Broken Arm*), the urinal (*Fountain*), and the bottle rack. The artist does something more dramatic or overt to the other sort of readymade, however: he "aids" it or assists it, as in the case of the bicycle wheel mounted on a stool. Sometimes this assistance may become rather extensive, as when Duchamp filled a bird cage with, among other things, what

3. Pierre Cabanne, *Dialogues with Marcel Duchamp,* trans. Ron Padgett (New York: The Viking Press, 1971), 48. See also Duchamp, *The Essential Writings of Marcel Duchamp,* ed. Michel Sanouillet and Elmer Peterson (London: Thames and Hudson, 1975), 141.
4. Duchamp, *Essential Writings,* 142.

appeared to be sugar cubes but which were in fact cubes of carved white marble. While I will discuss both sorts of readymades, it is obviously the unaided sort that poses the greatest challenge, at least when it is taken to be a work of art.

I. THE INSTITUTIONAL THEORY AND THE READYMADE

George Dickie's institutional theory has undergone considerable evolution since it first appeared. An episode in the theory's development gives an indication of the power over philosophy that the readymades can exercise. In an earlier version of the theory, Dickie held that the work of art is, among other things, a "candidate of appreciation." Dickie once thought that this was true of Duchamp's readymades, even of *Fountain*. When Ted Cohen challenged the claim that *Fountain* was something that possessed qualities that could be appreciated, arguing instead that it was a kind of gesture, Dickie replied that, even if it was a protest of sorts, it nonetheless could be appreciated: "Why cannot the ordinary qualities of *Fountain*—its gleaming white surface, the depth revealed when it reflects images of surrounding objects, its pleasing oval shape—be appreciated," Dickie asked. "It has qualities similar to those of works by Brancusi and Moore which many do not balk at saying they appreciate."[5] Arthur Danto later attacked this reply on the grounds that the possession of aesthetic qualities is not essential to something's being a work of art, and it does seem true that Dickie's remarks could be construed as a defense of *Fountain*'s status as a work of art in terms of its possession of aesthetic qualities. The really telling point here, however, is that Duchamp himself obviously did not think that the possession of an aesthetic dimension was essential to *Fountain* or to any other of his readymades. Quite the contrary, he viewed them as aesthetically neutral and thought that their neutrality was intrinsic to their sense as readymades. "A point which I want very much to establish is that the choice of these 'readymades' was never dictated by esthetic delectation."[6] Duchamp intended precisely to put forth something that was aesthetically indifferent. Now apparently under the pressure of the readymade thus understood (which is to say, as Duchamp himself understood it), Dickie changed his mind about the criterion of appreciation. For in the latest version of the theory he explicitly abandons it. This amounts to dropping the aesthetic as a necessary dimension of the art work.

5. George Dickie, *Art and the Aesthetic* (Ithaca and London: Cornell University Press, 1974), 42.
6. Duchamp, *Essential Writings,* 141.

Duchamp's readymade seems to have called the theoretical tune in this instance, whatever other arguments may have played a role. The transformation of Dickie's theory might be taken as a kind of paradigm of the force the readymades have had on at least some philosophical theories of art.

The Work of Art as Artifact

One element in his original definition of the work of art that Dickie has not abandoned is the condition that a work of art must be an artifact. "*A work of art*," he writes in the latest version of his theory, "*is an artifact of a kind created to be presented to an artworld public.*"[7] That the work of art must be an artifact Dickie takes to have been the traditional philosophical view until our own day, and he assumes that it is certainly the view of ordinary people.

The Sense of Artifactuality in Art

What does it mean to say that the work of art must be an artifact? First, it must be something made by a human being: "'Artifactual art' is the product of a certain kind of human activity: an activity of making."[8]

The activity of making something is hardly restricted to the artworld, of course; and while it may be true that works of art must be artifacts, it is also true that there are many artifacts that are not works of art, indeed, far more than there are artifacts that are works of art. The artifacts in question in the philosophy of art are artifacts of a certain kind, then.[9] Specifically, they are "artifacts which are or were intended by their creators to be art."[10] Spelled out in institutional terms, an artist produces a work of art by intentionally "creating an object against the background of the artworld."[11] This "status of being art . . . is achieved by the creative use of a medium."[12]

Dickie's stressing of the last point represents yet another development in his theory. In the earlier version, he had argued that artifactuality could be conferred. He argued, in fact, that this is precisely what happens in the case of readymades such as *Fountain*. The readymades are already artifacts before Duchamp chooses them to be transported to the planet of art, but they are not yet "art" artifacts. They

<hr>

7. George Dickie, *The Art Circle* (New York: Haven Publications, 1984), 80.
8. Ibid., 36.　　　　　　　　　　9. Ibid., 13.
10. Ibid., 34.　　　　　　　　　11. Ibid., 12.
12. Ibid.

are just ordinary things made in a factory somewhere: a snow shovel, for example. Now since Duchamp seems to do little or nothing to the artifacts he selects for readymade status, and since Dickie wanted to maintain that making on the artist's part is essential to art, he claimed that, in the case of the readymades, Duchamp "conferred" the artifactuality appropriate to art on the objects. Dickie now holds, however, that artifactuality is not the sort of thing that can be conferred. It must rather be achieved by actual work in a medium: by working in paint, for example, or by carving stone.[13] The work the artist must do in this connection does not have to be extensive, but *some* work must be done by the artist over and beyond what any non-artworker may have done before the artist came on the scene. This condition Dickie calls "the minimal work requirement."[14]

The Minimal Work Requirement and the Limits of Making

The minimal work requirement is supposed to be helpful in delimiting the class of things that can count as works of art.[15] Duchamp's readymades were powerful forces in promoting the notion that anything can be a work of art, but that is not a notion that Dickie shares. He does think that the readymades are works of art, but he does not think that means that just anything can be art. Dickie's view is that the readymades are works of art because they meet the minimal work requirement, and that only what meets this requirement has a chance of becoming art. Now it is precisely this view, as applied to the readymades, that deserves close scrutiny.

If the minimal work requirement segregates what is art from what is not art, then one must ask, " 'What are the limits of *making*?' . . ."[16] The question becomes acute when one confronts—to use Dickie's language—"actions which produce artifacts but which are not straightforward cases of making."[17] Dickie pursues an interesting and complex analysis here, the point of which is to gather the unaided readymades under the protection of the minimal work requirement. His analysis is worth pursuing in some detail.

Dickie first focuses on several cases involving a piece of driftwood. The criterion of artifactuality that seems to govern the discussion is a dictionary definition of artifact: " 'An object made by man, especially with a view to subsequent use.' "[18]

In the first case, one comes upon a piece of driftwood and simply

13. Ibid., 11–12.   14. Ibid., 12.
15. Ibid.   16. Ibid., 37.
17. Ibid., 44.   18. Ibid., 45.

tosses it aside in order to get it out of the way. No artifact is involved here.

In the second case, one carves a handle on the piece of driftwood so that one can use it as a spear. Here something useful has been made out of the driftwood by altering it. The product of the making is obviously an artifact, although it is not a work of art.

In the third case, one does not alter the driftwood in any way, but one does pick it up and use it as a weapon or as a shovel. Now Dickie claims that the driftwood *is* an artifact in this case, despite the fact that it has undergone no physical alteration comparable to the carving that occurred in the second case. It is an artifact simply because it has been *used*. "The artifact is the driftwood manipulated and used in a certain way."[19] The object in this case is complex, not because it has been worked on physically but because it has "undergone a change at the hands of an agent" in the sense of being used by someone to dig with or to fight with.

The final case is designed to benefit from the lessons of the other three and to lead us from the beach into the art world. Suppose an artist brings the driftwood home and hangs it on the wall, unaltered, "with the intention to display its characteristics as the characteristics of a painting are displayed."[20] At that point the driftwood becomes part of a more complex object: "the driftwood-used-as-an-artistic medium," and this complex object "is an artifact of an artworld system."[21]

The piece of driftwood is not a readymade because it is not a previously manufactured object, but the transition from the driftwood hung on the wall by the artist to the case of a genuine readymade, say, *Fountain*, is easy to make, according to Dickie. In *Fountain*, he claims, the urinal, like the driftwood, is used as an artistic medium. It is therefore "an artifact of an artworld system." As artistic media, the urinal and the snow shovel and the driftwood "are used as pigments, marble, and the like are used when more conventional works of art are made."[22] True, *Fountain* is a double artifact—made once in the factory, made again by the artist—but there is nothing unusual about that; after all, "a painting is made of pigments which in turn are manufactured."[23] *Fountain*, then, is just like a painting, or close to it. Have we therefore captured *Fountain* for the realm of artifacts?

Let us go back over these cases and their application to the readymades more closely. *Fountain* is obviously not like the piece of driftwood tossed aside just to get it out of the way (although Duchamp's original readymades did have the habit of getting lost, as happened

19. Ibid.
20. Ibid.
21. Ibid.
22. Ibid., 46.
23. Ibid.

in the case of *Fountain,* or of being dumped into the trash, which was the fate of *Bottle Rack* at the hands of Duchamp's sister). Dickie rather thinks *Fountain* is generically like the piece of driftwood used as a weapon without being altered, and specifically like the driftwood used as an artistic medium without being altered. In both cases, Dickie thinks that use, and use alone, is sufficient to create an artifact. But this seems to confuse artifactuality and utensility.

Recall the general definition of artifact that Dickie had in mind throughout his analysis of the driftwood: "'An object made by man, especially with a view to subsequent use.'" Now Dickie seems to be saying, in effect, that the using *is* the making. The object will become an artifact simply by being used, even if nothing is done to it.[24] But the definition does not identify making and using, and nothing Dickie has said about artifactuality has prepared us for such an identification. Indeed, the definition distinguishes *between* making and using. The piece of driftwood carved and used as a spear would fit the definition. The simple object used would not, and any claim that the use would render it something "made by man" is counterintuitive. What is intuitive is precisely that it is something not "made by man" but put to use by man for some purpose. Utensility and artifactuality are not the same.

The difference is nicely illustrated in the film *2001* by the ape-like creature on whom it suddenly dawns to use a bone as a weapon. The scene may be taken as illustrating a breakthrough in the evolution of intelligent life, but the breakthrough is not initially the production of artifacts but the glimmering realization that natural things already there can be used for a purpose. This discovery of utensility, of course, does launch us on the path to the discovery of artifactuality, for, on the whole, artifacts will serve us better as means in our projects than natural things will. Thus in *2001,* after using the bone to kill one of his fellows, the creature throws it high over his head and the camera follows it as it rises, rotating in its bony whiteness against the azure sky, until it dissolves into a twenty-first century space station, gently twisting in the black vastness of space. The station is an artifact; the bone from which it evolved was not. *Use* was the bridge between the two.

Medium and Artifactuality

The making that characterizes art, Dickie claims, involves the creative use of a medium. In the case of the driftwood hung on the wall by the artist or in the case of *Fountain,* the driftwood and the urinal,

---

24. Ibid., 45.

respectively, are said by Dickie to be used as artistic media and thereby to become artifacts of an artworld system.[25] He compares them to pigments or to marble. But is it true that the driftwood or the urinal really do function as artistic media?

Consider the case of the piece of driftwood hung on the wall. It is not worked on or changed (apart from its location) by the person who hangs it up. It does not enter into a larger whole, say, an assemblage of some sort, made by the artist. It is rather in the position of a piece of stone before the artist has approached it with his chisel. It is the sort of thing—non-artifactual thing—from which art could be made. But it would become a medium for art only when the artist actually used it in making something, and this making would have to involve some kind of actual work. The driftwood is not used in the making of anything and so is not really a medium and does not become an artifact or an ingredient in an artifact.

Now is the urinal in *Fountain* a medium? One could think of cases in which it certainly would be a medium: if it were incorporated into a larger work, as the bicycle wheel was in Duchamp's aided readymade of the same name, or if it were worked on itself in some way—painted, perhaps, or shattered into pieces and glued to a canvas in the fashion of Julian Schnabel's plates. But *Fountain* is not an assemblage, even a minimal assemblage like the bicycle wheel attached to the stool. As for saying that it is like manufactured pigments used as media in the making of a painting, one might cite Duchamp himself: "Since the tubes of paint used by the artist are manufactured and ready made products we must conclude that all the paintings in the world are 'readymades aided' and also works of assemblage."[26] Duchamp made this remark tongue in cheek (he preceded it with the comment: "A final remark to this egomaniac's discourse"), but the point it expresses is important. A painting is not a simple readymade. It is a readymade aided, as Duchamp said, which means that the manufactured paint is used in its making in ways quite different from the way in which the urinal is used in *Fountain*. A painting is a complex object, genuinely something made rather than something simply used. A great deal is done to and with the original artifact—the manufactured pigment from the tube—in making the second artifact—the painting that hangs on the wall. It is even possible for tubes of paint to enter rather literally into an assemblage, as they do when Arman—an artist whom Duchamp admired—crushes them under clear plastic. But here again

25. Ibid.
26. Duchamp, *Essential Writings*, 142.

a new artifact has been made by actual work. Nothing remotely comparable, as we have seen, is done to or with the urinal or the snow shovel. *Fountain,* then, is not like a tube of paint used by an artist to make a painting or assemblage. It is rather like a tube of paint bought in a store, signed and perhaps briefly inscribed by an artist ("In Advance of Critical Acclaim"), and then put on display without being altered in any other way. The tube remains a tube of paint, a first-level artifact—perhaps at most a kind of souvenir, like a signed baseball or an autographed copy of a book. It is neither a medium nor an "art" artifact. I think the same can be said of Duchamp's unaided readymades such as *Fountain* or *In Advance of the Broken Arm.*

The point of this discussion of Dickie's notion of artifactuality is not to show that there is something wrong with the claim that being an artifact made by an artist is essential to being a work of art. I think Dickie is absolutely correct in making that claim. The point is rather to show how difficult it is to accommodate the claim to Duchamp's unaided readymades. And Dickie thinks that it is important to make that accommodation if we are to avoid the conclusion that just anything can be a work of art. But given what we have said so far, can Dickie avoid that conclusion?

Artifactuality and Specification: The Limits of Art

Salvador Dali, Dickie notes, is reported to have pointed at some rocks, called them works of art, and claimed that they thereby became works of art.[27] Man Ray said that anything he signed was a work of art, just "like a painting or a sculpture."[28] And, on the plane of philosophy, Dickie cites Timothy Binkley's assertion that ". . . in order to 'create' a work of art it is necessary only to *specify* what the artwork is."[29] Binkley illustrates his position with Robert Barry's making of "a work of art by saying (specifying) that it is 'all the things I know but of which I am not at the moment thinking—1:36 P.M.; 15 June 1969, New York."[30] Binkley thought that Duchamp was using the same kind of simple specification when he made *Fountain.* Now if simple specification is sufficient to create a work of art, then anything could be a work of art. Had Dickie been able to show convincingly that Du-

27. Dickie, *The Art Circle,* 30.
28. Statement by Man Ray in *Dada,* a film produced by Procine for the Ministry of National Education, Brussels. Released in the U.S. by International Film Bureau, 1969.
29. Timothy Binkley, *Culture and Art,* ed. Lars Aagard-Morgensen (Atlantic Highlands, N.J., 1976), 92; quoted in Dickie, *The Art Circle,* 57.
30. Dickie, *The Art Circle,* 59.

champ's unaided readymades are indeed art artifacts, he would be able to refute Binkley's claim. But as it is, his replies face difficulties.

With respect to Dali's rocks, for example, Dickie argues that "there does not seem to be any sense in which something is *made* by 'pointing and calling.'"[31] The thing pointed at and called art is not altered in any way and it is not used in any way. This is a sound point, but one wonders if it is sufficient to save the readymade for artifactuality. Consider first the question whether Duchamp's urinal or snow shovel is altered—beyond merely being used—in some way. In discussing the Dali case, Dickie suggests that alteration is not really important in determining whether something is an artifact. "In the cases such as the unaltered driftwood digging tool and *Fountain* we seem to have come to the limit of artifactuality; the driftwood and *Fountain* are just barely artifacts."[32] This amounts to an admission that the urinal in *Fountain* is not altered in any significant way, which is in keeping with Duchamp's own distinction between aided and unaided readymades. We are left with use, then, as the criterion for determining whether something is an artifact. But we have argued that mere use will not make something into an artifact; using is not making any more than pointing and calling is. It becomes difficult to see how Dali's rocks and Duchamp's readymades differ. We just have not found "the gap which marks the dividing line between artifact and nonartifact" that Dickie rightly seeks.[33]

Of course, one might argue that the readymades are at least signed, often in intriguing ways, and that this is a sufficient alteration to render them artifacts. So Dali's pointing and calling would be excluded from artmaking activity while Man Ray's profligate signing would be welcomed. But why would not speaking and writing—that is, signing or even inscribing—be logically equivalent here? Dali could have signed his rocks, even written on them, "These are art." I assume that Binkley thinks that Duchamp really did nothing more with the urinal and the snow shovel. Whether or not the specifying goes on in written or in verbal form would seem to be irrelevant. Dickie, of course, thinks that more than specifying is going on: making by using is also taking place. But again, we have argued that using is not making. So it seems we have no grounds for excluding either Dali's rocks or Man Ray's signed objects as works of art.

In handling Barry's "thought piece," however, Dickie gets closer to a genuine defense of the readymade in terms of artifactuality, that is,

31. Ibid., 46.   32. Ibid.
33. Ibid.

in terms of actual making. Letting use recede for a moment into the background, Dickie returns to his original thesis that "making art has had at its center working with a medium,"[34] which involves an actual process of crafting on the artist's part.[35] Barry, in referring to those of his thoughts of which he is not thinking at a particular time, is not working with a medium. He crafts nothing and therefore produces no artifact. Dickie writes that Duchamp, on the other hand, does craft something using a urinal as an artistic medium, "although the crafting involved in creating *Fountain* is at an absolute minimum."[36] Now Dickie thinks that conceptual artists such as Barry "seem to have decided that if Duchamp can create art by working with such a medium as a urinal, they can create art with no medium at all."[37] But this decision is false because Duchamp—Dickie claims—did work with a medium: "Duchamp at least caused the urinal to change place and to be displayed within the artworld framework."[38] One is inclined to say to this claim: Some work! Dickie's numerous concessions that the readymades are just barely artifacts, and his statement here that "Duchamp did not do much by way of applied skill, but he at least did something with something"[39] suggest an unease with the idea that the urinal really was a medium that Duchamp worked on. So little is done with the urinal or with the snow shovel that it is questionable at best whether work on or with a medium really applies in their cases at all.

Dickie makes a compelling point when he claims that the intention to create a work of art, even when combined with the would-be artist's saying that something is a work of art, is not, by itself, sufficient to bring a work of art into existence. The intention must be combined with the actual making of an artifact. But it is questionable whether Duchamp, in "producing" his unaided readymades, has actually made an artifact at all. Indeed, if Duchamp's *Fountain* and *In Advance of the Broken Arm* are works of art, it is more likely that Binkley's notion of specification better explains how they managed to achieve that status, given what they are, than Dickie's attempt to show that they really are artifacts. What Duchamp does is more like "saying something is a work of art" than like making a work of art.

Dickie struggles—it seems to me unsuccessfully—to show that Duchamp's unaided readymades are artifacts made by Duchamp himself. His strenuous efforts to demonstrate that *Fountain* really is an artifact, despite all appearances to the contrary, are reminiscent of his earlier and abandoned efforts to show that the readymades do indeed man-

34. Ibid., 61.   35. Ibid., 60.
36. Ibid.   37. Ibid., 61.
38. Ibid.   39. Ibid.

ifest appreciable aesthetic qualities. The pressure of the readymades themselves, and of what Duchamp said about them, forced him to abandon the position that appreciability is a condition of something's being a work of art. I suspect that a similar situation prevails with respect to the artifactuality of the readymades. Just as it is incongruous to argue that aesthetic appreciability is somehow essential to items selected precisely because of their aesthetic indifference, so there is something incongruous about trying to prove that things called "readymades" are really artifacts *made* by the artist himself. If that is the case, why did Duchamp call them "readymades" to begin with? The very word suggests that they were in fact intended by Duchamp to be understood precisely as things *not* made by the artist, that is, already made when the artist chose them to be offered to an artworld public. As Duchamp himself said of the term "readymade": "That is the name, as you know, that I gave to those works which in effect are already completely made."[40]

This would seem to leave Dickie in a bind. Either he is going to have to give up saying that works such as *Fountain* are artifacts made by an artist with the intention that they be art (in which case, assuming that he wants to maintain his artifactuality condition, he should conclude that the unaided readymades are not works of art—something he seems unwilling to do) or, if he wants to go on maintaining that the readymades are works of art, he should give up his artifactuality condition (thereby opening the door to the claim that anything can be a work of art—something he is equally unwilling to do). The pressure of the readymades is again making itself felt, this time on the claim that the work of art must be an artifact made by the artist.

One philosopher who may be read as making a definite decision in the face of this pressure is Arthur Danto. I think that Danto gives up the artifactuality condition—with interesting, if disturbing, consequences.

II. DANTO'S INTERPRETATION THEORY

George Dickie, it is worth noting, thinks that "Danto . . . is talking about artifacts,"[41] but Dickie's discussion of Danto is restricted to articles published before *The Transfiguration of the Commonplace*. In the preface to that book, Danto unfolds a sequence of points that makes it plain that he does not regard artifactuality as a necessary condition

40. Duchamp, *Essential Writings*, 134.
41. Dickie, *The Art Circle*, 29.

of art. He starts, of course, with the readymades, which he views as paradigmatic examples of the transfiguring of the commonplace. In faithfulness to Duchamp's declared intentions, he insists that aesthetic considerations have nothing to do with the readymades' status as art. He then turns to one of the readymades' progeny that clearly is an artifact: Andy Warhol's *Brillo Box* from 1964. Warhol's boxes displayed in a New York gallery are said by Danto to be visually indistinguishable from real Brillo boxes sold in grocery stores. They were, however, made by Warhol out of plywood. They are not readymades, therefore, and they do satisfy Dickie's criterion of artifactuality. But that artifactuality is not a criterion for Danto is made clear by his next move. The fact that Warhol made his boxes out of wood while the real Brillo boxes are machine-made out of cardboard is simply not germane to their being works of art. "*No* material differences," Danto writes, "need distinguish the artwork from the real thing."[42] Warhol illustrated this by taking actual cans of Campbell's soup from the grocery store shelf and signing them. "But even were he laboriously to have fashioned them by hand—hand-made cans so faultlessly fashioned as to be indistinguishable from the manufactured article—he would not have advanced them one degree *in the category of art they already occupied* [emphasis mine]."[43]

The soup cans, unlike the wooden Brillo boxes, are nice examples of readymades unaided; it is clear from Danto's remarks that he regards them as works of art but does not think that they are artifacts made by the artist. (The distinction he implies between hand-made and readymade reminds one of an exchange between Paul Cabanne and Duchamp. Cabanne asked about an awning Duchamp had made for his house in Spain: "Is this your last readymade?" Cabanne asked. Duchamp replied: "It's not readymade, it's hand-made.")[44]

For Danto as for Dickie, then, the readymades, whether Duchamp's or Warhol's, are works of art. But for Danto, apparently, the "subtle miracle of transforming"[45] something ordinary into art has nothing to do with making: something can be a work of art without having been made by the artist working in a medium, just as it can be a work of art regardless of whether it possesses aesthetic qualities. Why are such things art, then (if they are)?

Danto's answer to this question in *The Transfiguration of the Common-*

---

42. Arthur Danto, *The Transfiguration of the Commonplace* (Cambridge and London: Harvard University Press, 1981), vi–vii.

43. Ibid., vii.

44. Cabanne, 105.

45. Danto, *Transformation*, vi.

place and subsequent writings is subtle and many-faceted; it is also, to this reader at least, elusive. I will focus on what I take to be the core of his reply, acknowledging that Danto would surely object that I have simplified his account to the point of distorting it.

Danto claims that what distinguishes a work of art from an object that is not a work of art, even if the two things are perceptually indistinguishable, is interpretation. Danto uses many examples to illustrate his claim, but a significant number involve the readymades; and all, one suspects, were inspired by the spirit of the readymades or were molded under their pressure. Thus in a recent essay he asks us to imagine three snow shovels, one of which is a work of art while the other two are not.[46] He means, I assume, that all were produced in the same manufacturing plant and are identical in every material respect. We might even assume that all were available and perhaps purchased from the same retail outlet. The one shovel that, ontologically, has become a work of art remains a snow shovel in all basic respects. One could—and a maintenance person at a museum in Minneapolis apparently did—shovel snow with it. What makes *it* a work of art and its siblings just snow shovels is interpretation. "Interpretation," Danto writes, "is in effect the lever with which an object is lifted out of the real world and into the artworld, where it becomes vested in often unexpected raiment. Only in relationship to an interpretation is a material object an artwork. . . ."[47]

Whatever interpretation may precisely be, that Danto should single it out as a candidate for a (the?) necessary and sufficient condition of art[48] makes a certain amount of sense. The readymades, after all, are supposed to be works of art; and if that is the case, then neither artifactuality nor aesthetic quality could be constitutive of the art work, since the readymade is characterized by neither of them. But something must transform them into art, and if it is not actual work done by the artist, would not interpretation be a likely candidate for the role? But we still have to ask what sort of interpretation, and interpretation by whom?

The Issue of the Kind of Interpretation

To ask about the kind of interpretation involved is really to ask two questions. It is to ask, first, about the level on which the interpretation is supposed to function. Is it interpretation on the familiar level on

46. Arthur C. Danto, *The Philosophical Disenfranchisement of Art* (New York: Columbia University Press, 1986), 26.
47. Ibid., 39.
48. Danto, *Transfiguration*, 131.

which critics regularly offer varied interpretations of a given work of art? Or does it occur at a deeper level, the stratum on which something makes the passage from not being art to being art. Second, it is to ask about the nature of the interpretation: is it, for example, philosophical or theoretical in some other general way, or is it restricted to the nature of the particular work, or is it perhaps both, depending on the level in question? Let us turn to that question of the levels of interpretation first.

Two Levels of Interpretation

Danto can be ambiguous about the level of interpretation he has in mind. In a fairly typical text, he writes: ". . . indiscernible objects become quite different and distinct works of art by dint of distinct and different interpretations, so I shall think of interpretations as functions which transform material objects into works of art."[49] The first part of this statement seems to concern the interpretation of things that are already taken to be works of art. Thus, assuming one of our snow shovels is a work of art, critics might argue over just how it is to be understood, just as critics of various stripes—Marxist, feminist, formalist, etc.—now contend over the proper interpretation of Manet's *A Bar at the Folies-Bergère*. Furthermore, it seems incorrect to say that each different interpretation of this kind generates a distinct work of art. Surely it is reasonable to say that T. J. Clark and Griselda Pollock are interpreting precisely the same work of art: *A Bar at the Folies-Bergère*. The relation of interpretations to a work is an instance of a manifold related to an identity. Each interpretation in this sense does *not* give us an entirely different work, as Danto implies,[50] and each presumes that we already have a work on hand.

The second part of Danto's statement, however, points to a fundamentally different sort of interpretation: a "constitutive" or "transfigurative" sort, one that "transforms objects *into* works of art [emphasis mine]."[51] This would seem to be something quite different from the first kind of interpretation. We might call it primary as opposed to secondary interpretation. Here the question is not what the correct or reasonable interpretation might be, but whether one is confronting a work of art at all. "As a transformative procedure," Danto writes, "interpretation is something like baptism . . . in the sense of giving

49. Danto, *Disenfranchisement*, 39.
50. Ibid.; see also Danto, *Transfiguration*, 119.
51. Ibid., 44.

. . . a new identity, participation in the community of the elect."[52] It would be this "primary" sort of interpretation, then, that would promote one of the three snow shovels to the status of art so that what I will call the secondary interpretations of the critics can get underway. This interpretation would first supply the identity so that the manifold of secondary interpretations could come into play.

These two kinds of interpretation would seem to be quite distinct, but Danto tends to run them together. Even assuming he kept them apart, however, what would be the nature of the primary interpretation, the one that is capable of altering so dramatically the very being of things?

One candidate would be that the interpretation is either a philosophical theory of art or some other kind of general aesthetic theory. This is the way in which George Dickie reads Danto, and I think that Dickie's objection to Danto's position thus interpreted is sound: surely works of art were being created "for a very long time before anyone consciously formulated any art theory."[53] The alternative reading is that this transformative interpretation is just the ordinary and very specific sort of interpretation regularly given by art historians, critics, and other folk in the artworld. But such an identification of what we called primary interpretation with secondary interpretation has its own problems. For one thing, it may beg the question. Secondary interpretation, as we have seen, makes sense only if it is interpretation of something that is already taken to be a work of art. As Danto himself says, one can make two mistakes in interpreting. One is "to interpret something which is not in candidacy for art" and the other is to give "the wrong interpretation to the right sort of thing."[54] The secondary interpretation will not pick out the "right" snow shovel; one may well be brilliant in one's Marxist, feminist, or bourgeois late capitalist reading of the shovel but all the while be committing the gaffe of interpreting the wrong thing—a humiliating fact brought home when the gallery maintenance worker picks up the shovel right in front of one's critical eyes and, without objection from the curatorial staff, takes it outside and begins to shovel snow with it. It remains unclear, then, what kind of interpretation might be able to accomplish the feat of promoting something—the shovel, for example—to the status of art. Neither of the available candidates seems up to the job.

52. Danto, *Transfiguration*, 126.
53. Dickie, *The Art Circle*, 20.
54. Danto, *Disenfranchisement*, 40.

The Issue of the Interpreter

But there is a further question to address to the interpretation theory: *Whose* interpretation is at stake? Is it the artist's or the spectator's?

In the case of secondary interpretation, the spectator would do the interpreting. But the spectator hardly seems to have the capacity to engage in primary interpretation—the interpretation that turns something into a work of art. It is possible that the spectator might interpret the wrong snow shovel, but it is hard to understand how the spectator could account for the "right" snow shovel's having become a work of art. That would be the business of the artist. So we would have to say that it is the artist's interpretation that transports something from the realm of ordinary things into the world of art. But this notion too seems fraught with problems.

A spectator's interpretation of a given work could be mistaken. It seems to be an ingredient of any interpretation that it could be mistaken; things that leave no room for error leave no room for interpretation. But how could Duchamp be mistaken when he chooses one of the three shovels to be *In Advance of the Broken Arm,* that is, to be a work of art, leaving its fellows back in the ordinary universe of the hardware store? Perhaps one might reply that Duchamp's interpretation is constitutive while ordinary interpretation is just interpretive—that is, tries to make sense out of something already constituted as art. But one wonders if interpretations *can* be constitutive in that sense; indeed, whether it is not a contradiction in terms to speak of constitutive interpretation, at least in the case of art. Interpretation is just an effort to make sense out of something already constituted by the artist. So whatever it is the artist does in rendering something art, it is not interpretation.

One might argue in reply that in the artist's case, and only in the artist's case, primary and secondary interpretation do coincide; that is, coincide in the sense that what we have been calling secondary interpretation on the part of the spectator becomes primary interpretation in the hands of the artist. Various spectators can have various interpretations of a work, and the artist can have his interpretation of the work too. The difference between the artist's and spectator's interpretations would consist in the fact that the artist's interpretation, in addition to constituting a particular "reading" of the work, also happens to make it *be* a work in the first place. But to speak of the "artist's own interpretation,"[55] as Danto does, is odd. Would it really

55. Danto, *Disenfranchisement,* 44.

make sense to ask Rembrandt, with regard to one of his own paintings: "Now what is *your* interpretation of this work, Rembrandt?"—as if the artist were just one more spectator or critic among many. It seems to me that the artist could accurately be said to engage in secondary interpretations of his own work, in the same sense as critics do, for example, only if he had forgotten what he had in view when he made the work. In that case, of course, his secondary interpretation would not be constitutive; it would just be one more interpretation of something already recognized as a work of art.[56]

It is unclear, then, just what the nature of the constitutive or primary interpretation that imposes the status of artwork on material objects[57] is supposed to be. It is also unclear just whose interpretation it is supposed to be.

There is one more difficulty with the interpretation theory that deserves mention. An implication of Danto's formulation of the theory is that there is a neutral thing that, thanks to a supervening interpretation, becomes a work of art. Danto sometimes denies that there is a neutral artwork free from any interpretation;[58] that is indeed true: there is no neutral *artwork*. But on Danto's account there are artistically neutral *things* that become works of art when the artist waves his magic wand of interpretation.[59] The three snow shovels in the hardware store are examples of such neutral things. One of them will be interpreted, baptized, as art; the others will remain mere things, although there is no reason why they too could not be interpreted as art if Duchamp chose to do so. The interpretation, it should be observed, does not transform the perceptible qualities in any way: the unbaptized shovel and the baptized shovel look exactly alike. Still, one of them now counts as art while the others do not. This, by the way, is why the title of Danto's book—*The TRANSFIGURATION* [emphasis mine] *of the Commonplace*—does not seem to fit his theory. The title is supposed to apply to things such as the unaided readymades, as well as to Chardin's paintings of pots and pans or to Picasso's sculpture of a bull's head formed by putting together a bicycle seat and handlebars. Chardin and Picasso do transfigure the commonplace, but there is literally no transfiguration in the case of the readymades: no change in figure takes place. There has rather been a kind of trans*portation*: what was not in the house of art has now been moved into the house of art

---

56. None of this is to deny, of course, that there may be much more to a work than what the artist consciously or directly had in mind when he or she created it.

57. Danto, *Disenfranchisement*, 42.

58. Danto, *Transfiguration*, 119, 120, 124.

59. Ibid., 125.

thanks to an interpretation. Or, perhaps coming closer to the actual situation of the readymades, it is as if the pumpkin in Cinderella has indeed become a coach, only it still looks just like a pumpkin. If one wants to use terms with theological overtones to describe this situation, then Duchamp had a more apt one than "transfiguration": "transubstantiation."[60]

The Limits of Interpretation

Now could there be any sort of thing that might refuse an interpretation that would turn it into art? Or is everything neutral material for the imposition of artistic status? Consider the kind of situation Danto takes such pleasure in imagining. Duane Hanson's sculptures of the human figure, made out of synthetic materials, are incredibly lifelike, often deceiving even the most experienced museumgoers. Now suppose that Mr. Hanson becomes tired of laboriously making his figures and instead interprets some real shoppers, construction workers, tourists, etc.—all visually indistinguishable from some of his sculptures—to be works of art, specifically, works of art made by him. The interpretation would involve their appearance in museums and in commercial galleries under Hanson's signature. They could even be sold—these real people—subject to certain conditions. Now intuitively one would object that a living human being resists being interpreted in such a way that it becomes "a contribution to the history of sculpture," which is what Danto thinks Duchamp's snow shovel becomes.[61] But perhaps our intuition is beside the point. Is there any reason why real people could not be interpreted in such a way that they would become works of art of a Hanson-like kind? After all, they are visually indistinguishable from Hanson's polyester and fiberglass sculptures.

Danto claims, correctly, I believe, that of any given work, "the possible interpretations are constrained by the artist's location in the world, by when and where he lived, by what experiences he could have had."[62] Danto means this to apply to secondary interpretations, but he would also say, I think, that primary interpretations—if there are such—are bound by the same restrictions. Not just any work of art can be created at any time.[63] Duchamp's readymades could not have appeared as works of art during the Renaissance, or indeed at any

60. Duchamp, *Essential Writings*, 140.
61. Danto, *Disenfranchisement*, 34.
62. Ibid., 45–46.
63. Danto, *Transfiguration*, 44.

time before they actually did appear. This point certainly seems to be true. But will it help one to avoid the conclusion that anything can be a work if it is properly interpreted? I would argue that it would not. Combined with a theory of interpretation, Danto's views about the artist's situation in time and space imply that the only restrictions on what could be interpreted as art are historical and theoretical. On this reading, if the time is right and the theory is right, then *anything* could become a work of art through an interpretation. A living human being who precisely resembled a Duane Hanson sculpture could be interpreted as a work of art under the right historical and theoretical circumstances. In fact, the theory could well be Danto's and the time could well be now. If one objected that artifactuality would set a limit, the reply would have to be that the pressure of the readymades has forced us to give up artifactuality as a necessary condition of art. The way is open, then, for what Danto explicitly wants to avoid by his interpretation theory: to "be forced into the worst caricatured formulations of the Institutional Theory of Art; that is art which is so designated by the effete snobs of the artworld."[64] And it will be the readymades of Marcel Duchamp that force him there.

III. INTENTION AND ARTIFACTUALITY

I have argued that the readymades unaided have shaped at least some contemporary aesthetic theories in fundamental ways. In the cases we have considered, they have effectively removed the criterion of artifactuality and forced into place an interpretation theory that threatens to allow anything to become art, a position neither Danto nor Dickie wants to accept. Is there any way around these difficulties, or must we simply embrace the theoretical chaos that the fear of Duchamp's readymades has produced?

The first step one might take in this direction, as a kind of thought experiment, is simply to say that the readymades are not works of art. As we suggested earlier, this is a dangerous move, opening one to the most dreadful charge of all in the artworld: that one is a philistine. But philosophers are entitled to their thought experiments, and so let me carry this one through briefly.

One strong objection to tossing the readymades out of the artworld on the grounds, say, that they are not artifacts made by the artist is that art is not a natural but a cultural phenomenon. It makes sense to say that a stone should not be classified among living things. Dif-

64. Ibid., 144.

ferences of that sort seem to be embedded in nature and are not a matter of convention. Art, on the other hand, does seem to be a matter of convention and, on the artist's part, a matter of freedom. Indeed, Clement Greenberg has made the point that the readymades confirm just this distinction: "Duchamp's Readymades . . . showed that the difference between art and non-art was a conventionalized, not a securely experienced difference."[65]

But must it be the case that everything about a cultural practice is conventional? Certainly there seem to be differences among cultural practices, which is to say that there seem to be different kinds of cultural practice. Whatever they have in common, science and art, for example, differ from each other, and each is different from religion. These differences, which are differences in activities and procedures, are not natural differences. But such procedures have a binding force in the sense that if one does not follow them one will not be engaging in the cultural practice in question but in some other practice or in no identifiable practice at all. Now the making of artifacts would seem to be one of the necessary—that is, non-arbitrary, non-conventional—conditions governing participation in the cultural practice we call art. This notion of artifactuality includes the idea that it is the artist who makes the artifact by working in a medium. This is not to say that the artist may not have help or collaboration. It is to say that the artist must do something more than merely say something is art or sign something; he or she must actually engage in a process of making. There may, of course, be total freedom as far as the medium and the manner of crafting are concerned; and there certainly is freedom in what the work will look like when completed. But there is no freedom as far as the fact of actual making or crafting is concerned. Artifactuality is essential to artmaking. If, on the other hand, one insists that the readymades are works of art and that theory must therefore bend to accommodate them, then the criterion of artifactuality has to go. But the price to be paid for that accommodation with its loss of artifactuality is the explosion of art as an identifiable cultural practice.

Bare artifactuality, of course, is not sufficient to account for art. If it were, there is no reason why Duchamp's readymades could not be considered works of art, since they were in fact artifacts, although not artifacts made by Duchamp. Even an artifact made by an artist is not necessarily a work of art: it might just be an easel to be used in the studio, for example. What is required is that the artifact be made by

---

65. Clement Greenberg, "Counter-Avant-Garde," in *Marcel Duchamp in Perspective,* ed. Marshek, 129.

the artist with the intention that it be art. Making and intention are co-necessary. There is a fusion of intention and making in art, with making understood as actual work in a medium. Intention is not interpretation in Danto's sense of the term. The wedding of intention and making in art means that there never is a neutral thing that is changed into art by means of an interpretation. As Danto writes, "Most artworks are objects thrust into the world with the intention that they be works of art."[66] Danto says "most" because he thinks the readymades are works of art, and the objects that form the basis of the readymades, the snow shovels, for example, were certainly not objects originally thrust into the world with the intention that they be art. They were thrust into the world to move snow off of sidewalks and driveways and to make money for their manufacturer and retailer. When such things supposedly become art, no making on the artist's part is involved: it's just a matter of interpreting the neutral thing already there. But adhering to the necessary conditions of intention and artifactuality, we would argue that all, not most, objects that we take to be works of art were thrust into the world with the intention that they be art. What this means is that in the case of Rembrandt, for example, the painting is made from scratch, so to speak, to be art. Rembrandt does not interpret as art something that is already there. He *makes* art by actual work in the medium of paint and canvas. Conceptual interpretation of Danto's sort is not involved. *What is involved is an embodiment through work of the artist's intention*—an embodiment that can be more or less successful, of course, and that, as Danto himself observes, can be the touchstone for the competing interpretations of critics and historians.[67] Duchamp had only to choose a snow shovel to make it a readymade. He uses nothing as a medium in the way in which Rembrandt uses paint as a medium in his painting. Since Duchamp does no making, it is reasonable to say that what he does is to interpret. But there is no transfiguration here, as there is in the case of the painting. The *making* of such objects as Picasso's bull or Rembrandt's *Philosopher* made them *be* works of art from the beginning. There never was a point at which they were neutral objects, and therefore no interpretation was needed to move them from the realm of mere objects into the world of art. (Although I will not pursue it here, this notion of actual making may furnish a way to restore the aesthetic dimension—the visual aspect in the visual work of art, for example—as something necessary rather than incidental to art.)

66. Danto, *Disenfranchisement*, 39.
67. Ibid., 44.

Including the readymades within the realm of art, as we have seen, has the mischievous result of making it very difficult to exclude anything from that realm. Excluding the readymades, on the other hand, and insisting that a work of art must be an artifact made by an artist actually working in a medium with the intention of producing art offer the signal advantage of supplying a way to escape the conclusion that everything can become art. One then does not have to follow the conventional line slavishly; one can avoid the caricature of the institutional theory Danto mentioned that would admit anything and everything as art—surely a considerable boon. But to the extent that it is predicated on the exclusion of the readymades from the artworld, it might be charged that this advantage is gained only at the expense of becoming philosophically disreputable. After all, the philosopher has no business dictating to the artist.

One can reply that the philosopher may be able to say something significant about the essential conditions governing cultural practices. Phenomenologically, it may be the case that artifactuality is precisely an essential feature of art, and this may be established by showing that art as a cultural practice disintegrates in its absence. To accept the readymade uncritically, however, may have its own peculiar philosophical results, of which Danto's theory supplies an example. Interpretation in our time, Danto suggests, has become very much a matter of aesthetic theory. Some artists, particularly those such as Duchamp or Warhol, are really asking the philosophical question "What is art?" when they make their works through interpretation. "Artworks," therefore, "have been transfigured into exercises in the philosophy of art."[68] Indeed, Danto thinks that art has reached such a heightened stage of self-consciousness that it has now become its own philosophy.[69] The distinction between art and philosophy evaporates in the heady atmosphere of what Clement Greenberg called "advanced-advanced art."[70] In that sense, the history of art has come to an end, Danto claims.[71] Now I would suggest that this is another instance in which the readymades have forced the philosopher's hand—in this case leading to a deep confusion between two quite distinct cultural practices: art and philosophy. As George Dickie writes: "It is quite possible that when art takes itself as its own subject that art and philosophy of art address themselves to their subject in quite different ways."[72] So if a philosopher suggests that the readymades might be excluded from

68. Danto, *Transfiguration*, 56.   69. Ibid., viii.
70. Greenberg, 122.   71. Danto, *Transfiguration*, viii.
72. Dickie, *The Art Circle*, 23.

art, he may well be preserving rather than violating the integrity of both art and philosophy.

Still, if it is insisted that the philosopher must listen to the artist— surely wise advice—then let us give Duchamp the last word on the subject of the readymades.

When Pierre Cabanne asked Duchamp: "How did you come to choose a mass produced object, a 'readymade,' to make a work of art?" Duchamp replied: "Please note that I didn't want to make a work of art out of it." He continued: "It was in 1915, especially, in the United States, that I did other objects with inscriptions, like the snow shovel. . . . The word 'readymade' thrust itself on me then. It seemed perfect for these things that weren't works of art, that weren't sketches, and to which no art terms applied. That's why I was tempted to make them."[73] Isn't it about time that we took Duchamp at his word? Who knows, it might have the most sanguine of consequences for the philosopher, and perhaps even for the artist. As Duchamp is reported to have said: "There is no solution because there is no problem."[74]

73. Cabanne, *Dialogues with Marcel Duchamp*, 47–48.
74. Ibid., 9.

8

The Bounds of Art

KENNETH SCHMITZ

Shortly before he was to leave from Toronto for Washington in order to deliver the Mellon Lectures at the National Gallery,[1] Etienne Gilson remarked somewhat mischievously that he had "bad news for our friends to the south." He had to go and tell them that *The Star-spangled Banner* did not exist: there is no such thing. Where would one find it? Surely not on the pages of a score, for that is music without sound. And if it is played, it can never be brought together, each note struggling for breath as its neighbor expires. It lacks even the minimal unity required of the tiniest instantaneous micro-particle. But what then is the being of such an artwork? We talk copiously today about the process by which an artwork comes to be, and we call that process the ontology of the artwork; but is it an *entity* at all? And if it is, in what sense? That is a question that teases the curious taste of a metaphysical mind.

Of course, the *Marseillaise* has no better hold on existence than *The Star-spangled Banner*; nor does *O Canada*. You will be ahead of me, I know, and thinking cleverly that Gilson had chosen his example well; for even when a song is being sung it is never wholly there, as is, for example, Renoir's *Boating Party*, which is *there* in the Phillips—all of it and at once—except, of course, when it isn't there, which is whenever you go there to see it. But then it is hung somewhere else, you hope. And the song, where is it when it isn't being sung? Even if it were hiding in the score, let us suppose against all probability that every score were destroyed. We can take some comfort, perhaps, because songs are older than written scores. For ages now, women have sung babes to sleep, and men have sung in their cups and tuned up for battle with songs that existed surely—where? In the folk memory or in scholarly recollections of past culture? But then, only when actually

---

1. In 1955, subsequently published as *Painting and Reality*, New York: Pantheon (Bollingen Series 35.4), 1957.

being remembered? Or perhaps as long as at least one singer can haltingly recall them? And what of a song beyond recall, the songs of Greeks, say? Presumably they only *have* existed; they exist no longer. To tell the truth, a song is an evanescent, fragile, and fluctuating presence, not unlike a poem, which Wallace Stevens likened to a pheasant in a bush, the feathers of its meaning now glimpsed, now hidden. Let us hurry back, therefore, to more solid ground. Perhaps to the Phillips in the hope that Renoir's painting is still there. And what would we find? For the issue is not peculiar to artworks wedded to the flow of time; it clings to other artworks as well.

Let me turn from the uncertain Renoir to a certain painting that hung on the wall of an apartment I once rented in Freiburg-im-Breisgau. It was a rather good painting, but not what we would call "great." It was done in the mildly sentimental representational style popular in the last century, and there must have been hundreds like it. For that very reason, however, it serves my purpose to recall it, since a great painting might mesmerize my reflection with its singular, commanding presence and its unique quality, whereas I want to put the question in general terms to artworks as such. In the painting a cottage was set upon a hill, past which ran a rutted country road. In the foreground stepped a team of oxen. The right hoof of the ox on the right was lifted—or, should I say, was being lifted? Or rather yet more exactly, had just been lifted and was about to be put down again? For the painting suggested a time flow, a humble plot, a sequence of events of no great dramatic power admittedly, but not without its charm. The perfect past: *had been*; the immediate past: *had just been*; the perfect past: *was being*; the present: *is now*; and the immediate future perfect: *was about to be*. For the action—and in this instance, therefore, the painting—made no sense without some such sequence. Was there not, after all, a memory brushed into the painting and anticipation, too? Even in the still moment of daily country life caught on the canvas? Another painting, from another artist, in another style, would show a different subtexture, perhaps an abstract one; but it too would draw in some way upon our lived experience and would be directed to it in some way. Certainly, the time inherent in the painting on the apartment wall drew upon and was fused with my own—I can surely say, our own—lived experience of time, and it came alive only in tension with that experience.

I have drifted back from musical time into pictorial time: but what of the space of the painting? For while the arts of movement bring time forward in a pronounced way, a portion of space—or more correctly, a spatial portion[2]—allows itself to be depicted in a way that time does not. Now, adjacent to the painted space lay two quite different "unpainted" spaces, one of which belonged to the painting and the other which did not. As my eye ran across the painting, or rather, as it slowly moved along the rutted road, it passed before the little house and up beyond it to the crest of the hill where it met the horizon. It could never pass beyond that crest to the other side of the hill, could never open up the unexplored horizon that lay beyond, tantalizingly beyond that thin brushstroke. What lay beyond, just on the other side? Was there another farm in the distance? Was someone coming home to the small farm house? Or was a band of marauding soldiers about to break upon the quiet rural routine? The painting was silent about all such prospects, its horizon forever fixed and unyielding. Of another, yet similar scene, the poet has sung his word picture:

> What little town by river or sea-shore,
> Or mountain-built with peaceful citadel,
> Is emptied of its fold, this pious morn?
> And, little town, thy streets for evermore
> Will silent be; and not a soul, to tell
> Why thou art desolate, can e'er return.
> (KEATS, *Ode on a Grecian Urn*)

Now, as my eye left the horizon, it came to a second limit—in which the road disappeared in a quite different way, for it vanished into the frame. Here was no ever-receding horizon, nor even a pictorial one, but rather a boundary in which the painting ended and began, and in which my eye passed outside of the painting, over its edge, and was momentarily in transit from the painted space, the space of the painting, to the space of the real-life world. I had encountered and passed over the boundary that both separated the painting from the world of the viewer and at the same time joined it with that world. Here, then, is the question of the singular being of an artwork. How are we to understand the encounter with an individual work of art, when we try to view it not primarily from within the horizon of experience but from the artwork itself, from its mode of being present in the world and in relation to other entities? For I do not mean, of course, in isolation from the viewer or the hearer; as though to say (with another poet):

> All approaches gone, being completely there.
> (WALLACE STEVENS, *Arrival at the Waldorf*)

2. For, strictly speaking, space no more admits of color than does time. We live in a mysterious world of intangibles, which art helps to make manifest.

For the mode of its being in the world is precisely to be for the viewer and for the hearer. And yet, to be *for* something, it must yet *be* something. What, then, is that something?[3]

***

I begin with Hans Georg Gadamer's observations on the German word *Takt*, delicacy of feeling.[4] The observations are made in the context of his discussion of *Bildung*, that is, of educational and cultural formation; but they serve to launch my own reflections on the boundaries of the artwork. For *Takt* manifests a kind of non-observance that is attended by non-mention. The English *tact* also concerns unmentionables, and not only those thrown into the wash. But strictly speaking, tact is not non-observance, though it is non-mention. An admirer remarks: "Did you see how tactful she is? She must have noticed his cigarette ashes dropping into his soup, but you would never have known; she didn't blink an eye or say a word. What tact!" Gadamer tells us that being tactful is passing over something and leaving it unsaid (*etwas taktvoll übergeht und ungesagt läßt*):[5]

Now, to pass over something (*übergehen*) is not to look away from it (*etwas wegsehen*), but to have it in the corner of one's eye (*so im Auge haben*) in such a way that one doesn't stumble against it (*nicht daran stößt*) but rather passes it by (*daran vorbei kommt*).

One neither looks at it nor avoids looking at it, since that too would be obvious: one simply overlooks it. So, too, in our watchful appreciation of works of art, we notice and slip by the very boundaries of the work.

Now, a work of art "leaves out" many things; it neither mentions them nor considers them. One of the oldest entrenched notions of non-consideration in philosophy is no doubt that which the Schoolmen called *abstraction*. In its technical meaning abstraction left out particulars—not by positively excluding them, for that would be excision or "precision"—but by simple non-consideration. And yet, this specific form of negation was not so simple, after all. The abstract universal concept formed in this way was disinterested in the sense of being

<hr>

3. My indebtedness to Paul Weiss's writings on this question is recorded in part in "Art and Existence: Reflections on Paul Weiss's Modal Philosophy of Art," *Review of Metaphysics* (Twenty-fifth Anniversary Supplement), 25 (June 1972), 71–93. Cf. Gilson, op. cit., esp. chaps. 1, 2 and 4.

4. *Wahrheit und Methode* (Tübingen: Mohr, 2d. ed., 1965), 12–16; English translation, *Truth and Method* (New York: Crossroad, 1975), 10–19.

5. My rendering of the German text, p. 13. The English translation renders it well enough (p. 17): "It is tactless to express what one can only pass over. But to pass over something does not mean to avert the gaze from something, but to watch it in such a way that rather than knock against it, one slips by it."

impartial, since it accepted without demur any particular instance of the common sort that fell indifferently within its extension and under its embrace: *A* could be predicated of all *a*'s. No instance of the appropriate kind was to be repudiated by such a process of abstraction or its return reference; and whatever was left out in the formation of the common conception remained available, to be called up again— in theory by appealing to the particulars from which the abstraction was made, and in practice by calling forth the situations or cases in which the rule is potentially present.

In his account of how an evil action first begins to take form, St. Thomas Aquinas appeals to a peculiar fit of abstraction brought about by the moral (or rather, the about-to-be-immoral) agent.[6] The saint traces the genealogy of the evil act to its pre-malicious origins, origins that in themselves are not evil. Prior to the birth of the evil action, the possibility of human evil is lodged in our capacity for abstraction of a peculiar sort: it is willed non-consideration of the specific norm that is relevant to the act and that ought to govern it. We might call this non-consideration the suppression or repression of conscience, though that suggests too positive a process. Of course, no evil would be attributed to an agent if he or she were simply ignorant; nor if he or she were simply forgetful due to forces beyond his or her control and unrelated to the formation of character (for which each person is responsible). Rather, the knowledge of the good must somehow be present to the agent, if he or she is to commit a blameworthy act. What is required is the specific non-consideration that puts the norm out of play, or rather, doesn't let it come into play, that overlooks the norm and does not let it enter into consideration within the agent's deliberation or into the determination of the action. The evil act can emerge initially only insofar as it is grounded in the possibility of an indifference to the relevant norm, an indifference that can eventually be transformed into defiance of the norm. The root of evil, then, takes shape as a non-consideration that, in a way quite different from tact and from abstraction, nonetheless lets something noticed "slip by." This bypass is a curious form of absent-mindedness, a *distraction* or distractedness brought about by the inclination of the agent under the attractive power of the object toward the immediate end sought through the action.

Of course, it would be folly to suggest that the genesis of a work of art is in all respects similar to the commission of a sin or the perpetration of a crime, though some end products may deserve that name.

6. *De malo*, q.1, a.1.

The point of my allusions to non-consideration is to situate our encounter with a work of art within a negative context, implicit or tacit, that is the tell-tale breath of the human spirit. What is suggestive about tact, abstraction, and distraction is the diverse ways in which, as modes of non-consideration, they are partly constitutive of crucial human experiences: of sociality (through tact), of knowledge (through abstraction), of evil (through distraction). To be sure, what the artwork does not consider, what it "leaves out," is of an entirely different character from unmentionables, particulars, and norms. Nevertheless, something analogous to tact, abstraction, and distraction is constitutive of our recognition and appreciation of a work of art. This artistic form of non-consideration provides a key to the outline of the being of an artwork as an entity. Whether that non-consideration should be better left unsaid, and whether it is tactless of me to say it after all, I must leave to you to decide.

What, then, is the being—and not merely the becoming—of an artwork? May we speak of an artwork—a painting, symphony, drama, poem, or novel—as an entity? And if we may, where are we to find its distinctive manner of being? The preceding observations about what is noticed but not considered—unmentionables, particulars, and norms—are meant to direct our reflective attention toward what is overlooked in an artwork, and perhaps must best be. I mean the unexpressed context in which the artwork guards its being by providing for a distinctive sort of non-consideration in our approach to it. As the norm is disregarded in distraction and yet present to the mind, so too are the limits of the artwork not absent from the non-consideration proper to the artwork. As the unconsidered particular instances are available to abstraction, so too the outlines of the being of the work are present in our encounter with it. And as with tact, so too with artistic non-consideration, the proper being of the artwork is noticed but overlooked and unmentioned. The gaze is not averted from the painting, nor is the ear deafened to the music, but something implicit is noticed by way of a penumbra that environs a painting or a statue, and something tacit by the silence out from which a song or poem gives voice to its being. Here, in this noticed yet unmentioned twilight, lie the limits of a work of art—a no-man's land that is neither art nor non-art while yet it is both.

Just such a Janus-like ambiguity is the proper nature of a *boundary*.[7]

7. Cf. Hegel's *Wissenschaft der Logik* (Science of Logic), the so-called "Greater Logic" in contrast to the *Encyclopedia* or "Lesser Logic"; part I, book I, chap. 2: "Limit" (*Grenze*) and "Limitation" (*Schranke*). I have fused both in the concept of "Boundary." I find Hegel's discussion suggestive, without having to endorse his own systematic implications of the term.

The ambiguity is not the mere property of a boundary, but is more deeply and intimately its essential way of being. For a boundary separates one thing from another: a field from the highway, a garden from the neighbor's, one country from another, land from sea, and touching from being touched. Yet the same boundary at the same time also joins together the two things separated by it, throwing them, so to speak, into each other's arms. We pass through such a boundary each time we become involved with a work of art, though the nature of each boundary differs as much as the things differ that are simultaneously divided and united. A musical boundary breathes between silence and song, a painting is space enframed within space, the boundary of a statue or a building includes its ambience, and a play is held together and enclosed by more than its last fading word.

In viewing a work of art, or listening to it, or living with it, we approach its boundary, join with it and pass over . . . hardly noticing and certainly not dwelling in the moment of passage. Yet the boundary plays a role. One usually goes to visit a country, not its border; one passes through—unless there is an incident that blocks the way. If the passage is normal, it is scarcely noticed and goes unmentioned. Or again, the boundary is like a check that has been written but is not yet to be cashed (as with a postdated check for example); its draft—while still outstanding—is for the time withheld. So too, the line between the viewer and the work is drawn up and still stands, but during the viewing it is for that time withheld. It is out of play and usually out of mind, but it still counts in the order of things. Does not the boundary play an unnoticed role in the appreciation felt by an audience, by play-goers or gallery-viewers? And is the boundary not partly constitutive of that appreciation? What used to be called—admittedly with too much emphasis upon the private, psychological aspects of experience—"the willing suspension of belief " points to an inner boundary of the work of art that is drawn within the appreciative and critical consciousness of the viewer or hearer. After all, there is no need to suspend what isn't somehow there in the first place. And when an audience is caught up and drawn together by a performance of an opera, play, or symphony, and in the aftermath formed into a passing company of aesthetic celebration, then the line is drawn not within the individual consciousness alone but, so to speak, out there in the concert hall itself or at the proscenium arch (if there is one).

The language of suspension is echoed in the notion of an *epochē*, a suspension that motivates the aesthete and shapes his expectation. That expectation orients and disposes the hearer, play-goer or gallery-viewer, enframes the space in which he or she encounters the artwork, and announces a kind of *kairos,* a special time. In that space and time the play-goer, hearer, or viewer passes through to, receives and participates in the work of art. The boundary, then, is a sort of threshold into and out of the artwork, both an entrée and an exit.

Not every construction that passes for a work of art or calls itself artistic invites one to enter. This need not be because it is uninviting in the sense of being tasteless; it could be because it has no interior into which to invite anyone. It plays lightly upon one's aesthetic skin, and may mean no more than to please and reassure, or perhaps to crowd out unpleasant sounds or sights, to be a sort of deodorant for the ear or eye. Such a construction does not, properly speaking, exhibit tact, nor does it know its place, since it has none. Background music provides a good example. It seems to be piped in from nowhere and everywhere, and assumes a kind of technological omnipresence. It thinks to attain an anemic success if it does not intrude upon its often involuntary hearers. It smoothes the acoustic boundaries and silences that are natural to a conversation, filling the emptiness and absences with its insinuating and obsequious presence,[8] fusing all sounds into one continuous flow. It pervades the medium like an auditory perfume, as audibly inaudible as the current "state of the art" permits. It is the paragon of technical modesty. A co-host of a morning television wake-up show was asked recently what she thought of the newly installed background music system; to which she replied with creditable candor: "It's pleasant, but it doesn't speak to me." Admittedly, if it did, the show might take on the rhythm of a seance or a dance. But, of course, the very aim of the system is to be an auditory wallflower.

Moreover, given the complex needs of modern life and the many uses to which artificially produced sounds can be put, such a technical triumph is not a crime—not even an aesthetic or artistic one. But if it is no crime, neither does it have sufficient substance and individuality to be an artistic entity. We do not need to bewail a supposed deterioration of cultural standards, however, just because background music is pleasant only to some and by design insignificant to all. After all, the pleasant patterns of flowered wallpaper are rarely aesthetically significant, yet they provide welcome relief from dull walls. Then, too, in many cultures music is used principally as background to or accompaniment of other more-valued activities. Music then remains embedded in the total situation as a humble element among others. Such situatedness is perfectly defensible, of course, but it should not

---

8. Is it not perhaps a technical form of that positivistic presence which Heidegger criticized in his discussions of *Gestell, Anwesenheit* and *Präsenz,* and which is hostile to all negativity?

be confused with the experience that can be offered by a rich musical composition, or even by a moderately good painting, let alone a great one. For some centuries now, the artistic impulse has reached a point in our own culture at which some of its artifacts have come to possess a cultural value *in themselves*. In gaining a certain density of form, content and meaning, an artifact comes to be an entity in its own right as an artwork. Its substance and individuality has appropriated to itself a boundary that encloses it and gives to the work its singular definiteness. The boundary differs particularly with each single artwork, as well as generally with each style, tradition, and genre. Moreover, the way in which and the degree to which the boundary is encountered is determined subjectively by the disposition and preparation of the perceiver. But objectively, it is determined by the constitution of the artwork and by the boundary that defines it and through which the viewer or hearer passes into and out of the work.

In speaking about the implicit status of the boundary I have made it explicit, that is, my reflection has rendered the general notion of an artistic boundary thematic. No boundaries of particular artworks are at stake in the present reflection. That is the task of critical discussion among authors, composers or painters, actors, performers or exhibitors, play-goers, concert-goers, or gallery-viewers, reviewers, critics, and historians. When such discussion flags within a genre, anything and everything comes to be accepted; when the discussion prevails, there quietly in the midst is the unspoken question of the boundary, for what is at issue is whether a particular artifact or trend is or is not a work of art or appropriate to the genre. In this reflection, however, I touch only upon the nature of artistic boundedness as such.

Artworks have physical boundaries, including spatio-temporal ones, but the physical boundaries are not identical with the artistic ones. I look over at my bookshelves and see Shakespeare's *Hamlet* standing between cloth covers; someone else picks up a cassette and plugs the same *Hamlet*—is it or is it not?—into an audiovisual recorder. Obviously, the artistic identity of *Hamlet* is not confined within these physical boundaries. The boundedness proper to an artwork marks off the life of the imagination from other contexts, but the boundary does not lie *within* the imagination alone; for then the artwork would be simply imaginary. That gives too much to aesthetic experience and not enough to the objective existence of an artistic entity. Art dances to its own tune, being neither simply physical nor simply imaginary. The distinctively artistic boundary lies *between* the artwork and other entities, distinguishing and uniting artworks and art lovers, and coexisting with other artworks.

Background music has a certain "artistic" flavor, but its technical aims are so prominent and its artistry so subordinate to those aims that it scarcely possesses much artistic being. It is different with television, however, and we must, in all fairness, admit that it occasionally produces some fine work, entirely appropriate to the visual and mostly subverbal genius of the medium. Unfortunately, all too often it cooks up an impressionless parade of images that are little more than an electronic soup of hi-tech sense data, a stew of comedy, news, and commercials that meanders turgidly across the screen. All that can be asked of the images is that they not intrude upon us, and of us they ask nothing but to tune them in or out, or to turn a casual or blind eye to or from them. Here is no tact, because here is no depth. There is no need to be tactful, for there is nothing to notice, except the occasional sharp shift in volume, tint, or tone that introduces advertisements. And because there is nothing tacit, there is nothing to be silent about. Since television pleads for and even strives to command our attention (if only to sell us something), it counts as failure for it to be so often discussed as mere background to the day's routine.

To be sure, not every glance of the eye or perk of the ear engages an artwork in a serious way—nor should it, nor could it. Easy access to records and tapes tempts us to play music rich in meaning as mere background to our inattention. Of course, such casual listening can become a way by which, through familiarity bred of repetition, we may reach the boundary of a work and enter into its domain. But if the work continues to remain in the background, we are unlikely to encounter its boundary. Contrast a sightseeing trip through a medieval cathedral—better than nothing, to be sure!—with months of living beside it and in it. Or again, contrast a flying first visit to an art gallery—and I confess I wouldn't miss one!—with a prolonged and quiet contemplation of a few paintings. We get an impression from a quick tour, and it is not without its value, but it is usually more of an art-in-general, its styles and genres, than of singular artworks. It is a bit like seeing France from thirty thousand feet. Boundaries that upon closer acquaintance are significant in their own right do not appear or appear only in faded and fleeting outline. If you have never been to France but have flown over it at great height and speed, and are then asked whether you have ever been to France, do you not hesitate, and finally stammer: "Well, really, no; I've seen it sort of, but I haven't *actually* been there"? One has a blurred impression, and perhaps the desire to return at leisure for a real visit. It is much the same with artworks. The visual impressions gleaned from a quick tour may include some striking glances, but they remain mostly on the surface of the works. In like manner, the half-heard strains of background music are muffled in conversation, idle thoughts, or the round of household duties. In such circumstances one is likely to remain removed from the center, heart, and soul of a work and even from its boundary.

For the boundary of an artwork is the entrance into and exit out of it. It constitutes, on the one hand, the finite character of the work itself, and, on the other, the very being of the audience *qua* audience, of viewer as viewer, for they hear it or see it in the mode of not hearing or seeing it. It is the inner outer-limits, the suburbs of the work itself: that intrinsic and proper boundary by which the work detaches itself from the unformed matrix of color, shape, or sound in which it is embedded.

The detachment through which an artwork comes to self-definition and self-realization is not a simple separation. To be sure, some works of painting, music, and drama do approach an asymptote of thin, remote purity, far removed from the indeterminate matrix out of which every physical and partly physical entity arises, including works of art. Such abstract works achieve a purity whose asceticism and deliberate poverty can nonetheless capture a brilliant, single aesthetic quality—one clarion note, one stunning coloration, one piercing theme. One note: Stockhausen's pellucid drops of luscious harmony spread outward into the silence that englobes them, segregating each from the one just heard and the next not yet heard, and still retaining a fragile, luminous unity throughout the whole work. One coloration: Turner's late seascapes, awash in golden light diffused through the water and the sky, light that spills over the canvas and is hardly contained within it. One theme: O'Neill's *Emperor Jones*, which relentlessly presses the trembling nerve of fear. Such works reach an asceticism that lends them intensity, even as it guides that intensity into monophonetic, monochromatic, or monothematic channels. This special mode of purification belongs, however, to specific styles and works of art, and is not the general detachment through which the artistic entity as such exists. Nor is the general detachment merely a re-ordering of the way things are, or a mere clarification or simplification of life's apparent disorder. Art is less like tidy housekeeping, and more like homemaking, for in very diverse ways artworks invite us to enter their view of the sense and shape of things—sometimes celebrating, sometimes troubling or obscuring the sense, or bending the shape in illuminating, puzzling, and even troubling ways.

Lacking its own boundary a work of art would lose its essence and fall back into the mundane. Its artistic mode of being would collapse, and our aesthetic appreciation of it could not be sustained. The boundary, then, must always be in play—even within the play, during the performance, or throughout the viewing. This is to say that the concrete, individual, and entitative definiteness of an artwork must be present, noticed but unmentioned, indeed, too obvious to be anything but taken for granted.

In recent times, however, there have been attempts not merely to enlarge the conventional limits of art but to break the bounds of art itself. Thus, Dadaism sought to dissolve the distinction between art and non-art by placing common and even vulgar items within a specious artistic framework. The intention was to shock the viewer and to strip away what was thought to be the illusory veneer that separated art from non-art. Now that the shock has subsided, however, it is well to ask why we were shocked in the first place. Reflection suggests that the source of the shock lay in the placement of a familiar object (usually encountered in everyday life) in the unfamiliar context of a gallery or concert hall. Traditional gallery-viewers did not expect to encounter tin cans or urinals within frames (or, as I once did in a gallery in Bochum, Germany, one of Josef Beuys's half-melted Nielson chocolate bars with torn wrapper, carefully framed, preserved behind glass, and hung with meticulous care). Nor do concert-goers expect to hear the roar of industrial machines in a concert hall. To be precise, one is not shocked by hearing such a sound in the hall, since we might be surprised, or annoyed, but not shocked to hear the furnace being loudly repaired. The surprise turns to shock—and shock of a specific quality: *aesthetic* indignation—precisely insofar as the context is unfamiliar and judged to be inappropriate. By their very nature such shocks do not have a lasting effect. They either make their argument persuasively and thereby become an integral part of the art form (as have certain disharmonies in music or certain locutions in the novel) or fail to persuade and become at most a historical footnote to the history of art.

But the boundaries of art are by no means static, and art itself can explore the bounds in a thematic way within the work itself. In this regard, it is helpful to distinguish between a horizon and a boundary. The horizon articulates the limiting principle of a work from within it, whereas the boundary defines the being of a work in relation to others: to viewers or hearers, but also to other works of art as well.[9]

9. In a previous essay, and in order to "shake loose" the profile of several mediaeval epics, I carried out an eccentric reading of them that asked and sought to show how evil made its appearance in each epic and gave to it its singular mood and "coloration." ("Shapes of Evil in Medieval Epics: A Philosophical Analysis," in *The Epic in Medieval Society: Aesthetic and Moral Values,* ed. H. Scholler [Tübingen: Max Niemeyer, 1977], 37–63.)

Two recent popular films have explored the "transgression" of boundaries from within the horizon of the films themselves.

In *The Purple Rose of Cairo*, a charming, low-budget sleeper, there is a "film" within the film. A character from the "film" within the film seemingly escapes from the plot and role that holds him within his celluloid prison. He steps out of the "film" within the film into the film. In the "real" world he strikes up a romance with a forlorn young woman of lively phantasy, whose only relief from the tedium of her drab life during the Great Depression is to regularly patronize the local movie house. As the film progresses, however, it seems more likely that the young woman's fancy has put her not into the elegant "film" within the film, where she would like to be but into the cinematic context of the interplay between her hopes and dreams and the "film" within the film. Seen from within the film, the tension that sustains its defining horizon is the tension between the "film" within the film and the character and situation of the woman movie-goer. But the boundary between the purported "real" world of the film and the "film" within the film, by being made thematic, invites us to overlook the implicit boundary that defines the movie itself as an artistic entity, and that distinguishes us who are viewing the film from the woman movie-goer. Both we and she are movie-goers, but in quite different senses, of course.

Another recent movie, *Who Framed Roger Rabbit?*, although quite devoid of dramatic or even of comedic power, is nevertheless of some technical interest, inasmuch as it has attempted an extended interfacing of cartoon figures with "real-life" actors. The interfacing enhances the purported "reality" of the actors in contrast to the unlimited antics of the cartoon characters, and pulls us across the boundary that defines the movie itself as an artistic entity. To the extent that it succeeds as well as it does, it brings about what was wont to be called "the willing suspension of belief."

The boundary proper of an artwork, which divides it from and unites it to the world, must also be addressed in more or less circumspect ways in and by the work itself. And indeed, each work does provide its own devices for entry and exit, devices that join the artwork to the rest of the world. It is interesting that some recent pop rock songs do not, strictly speaking, end; they deliberately simply "peter" out. In formal plays, on the other hand, there are sometimes prologues and epilogues. These do not simply start and stop the play, but carry us into and out of the action. Or again, some poems alert us to their heightened sensibility with the unusual imagery or heightened intensity of their tone. Then, too, there is the frame that bounds a painting, even if in some instances ever so slightly. The rutted country road passes over into the frame, or does it? Does it simply stop? Or does it pass over into the penumbra and disappear? The eye finds itself handed over to the space beyond the painting, to the wall beside it, where it may stop for a thoughtful moment before it passes on to another painting, or return to its prior love or turn to leave the gallery. In music there is the pause before the symphony begins, pregnant with expectation and preparation. Sometimes, as I have said, the audience is on its feet before the music ends, carried there by the force of their own appreciation. The applause, so to speak, preserves the audience in what Husserl would call the transitional phase of retention, the immediate transient memory of a memorable performance not quite yet ended. Or again, the transition may take form at the end of a drama as a fulsome silence before the applause breaks forth. But finally, another painting comes into view, another composition waits to be heard, or the gallery closes, the lights come on in the theater, or the orchestra moves offstage. It is over.

These transitional devices of entrance and exit pass over the boundary, but other devices infuse the horizon with an "atmosphere" or "coloration" that sustains the boundary throughout the duration of the work. The brooding landscape of Hardy's novels, the doom of the sunken treasure of the *Niebelungenlied,* and the sun-drenched countryside of *El Cid*: all bind the plot and characters together into an artistic whole, possessing the integrity of an artistic entity. So, too, the use of symbols in novels, of refrains in poems, and of opening themes that recur in symphonies place a work under a distinctive signature. Undoubtedly, new devices will be found, for the boundaries of individual works of art are fashioned in part by the production of the work itself. As part of that fashioning there is the panoply of artistic techniques that enter into the physical singularity of the work: in poems, meter and accent, for example; in painting, media and brush strokes; in music, rhythm and instrumentation; in theater, lighting and staging; and so on.

It is easy, perhaps, to see how the boundary divides the audience from the play, the viewer from the film, or the listener from the music. It may not be so obvious how the boundary also joins them. What is it, then, in the boundary that provides the energy of juncture and communion? That which joins the artwork to others while yet preserving it as an entity, is *mediation.*[10] Indeed, one might say that me-

10. Here, too, I am indebted to Hegel for his stress on mediation (*Vermittlung*) which has close logical connections with the concept of boundary. Once again, however, I do not accept his systematic resolution, which seems to me to underestimate the discreteness of the boundary.

diation is the very boundary in its dynamic role. Or more exactly, the boundary is the open and closed "place" in and through and across which the artwork is able to preserve its singularity while also being engaged in common relationships with others; for all individuals are integers constituted of singularity and commonalities.[11] Relationships, events, stories, and customs that members of a society or culture hold in common are as much constitutive of the individual human being as his or her singularity. But these commonalities are constitutive of an artwork as well. For artworks, each in its own way, are members of a culture too; they too are enculturated. The mediation by which an artwork attains the status of an entity does not occur simply between a viewer and a painting, or a reader and a poem. It is constituted as an entity through customs, traditions, institutions, and artistic and aesthetic communities.[12] Artworks exist as entities in the context provided by mediating institutions, through which the techniques and themes of artistic genres are handed on and developed, and through which more or less stable communities of artists and aesthetes gather.

Generally speaking, four different kinds of institutions play roles in the mediation through which an artwork is sustained as an artistic entity. First, there are the mediating forces of production, their traditions and communities: authors, poets, painters, sculptors, composers, choreographers, and architects. Secondly, there are the mediating energies of performance: in poetry, readers; in music, musicians; in dance, dancers; in theater and cinema, actors; in architecture, builders. (Editors, producers, directors, exhibitors, and technicians play less direct but essential roles.) Third come the mediating energies of reception, the communities of taste: readership, audience, *aficionados* of dance, theater, cinema, and gallery; and to these should be added patrons, collectors, and participants and continuators of all sorts. Fourth are the mediating energies of interpretation and assessment, the "Senate" or "House of Lords" in the parliament of taste, often irritating and not seldom wrong, but useful nonetheless: literary, music, and art critics, and—with a longer time in mind—the scholars and historians who sift and place and replace each work in a larger context. To each of these four primary institutions of art should be added

11. For a more detailed development see "Community: The Elusive Unity," *Review of Metaphysics*, vol. 37, 2 (Dec. 1983), 245–64; "Metaphysics: Radical, Comprehensive Determinate Discourse," ibid., 39, 4 (June 1986), 675–94; and "Neither With Nor Without Foundations," ibid., 42, 1 (Sept. 1988), 3–25.

12. Other social forms have institutions, too. Thus, modern spectator sports could not exist without their fandoms; and other contemporary social forms, such as antique collecting and various hobbies, without their *aficionados*.

those who teach, guide, coach, and generally promote proficiency and dedication to one or another art form, genre, or tradition.

Each of the institutions relates to the boundary of an artwork and mediates it differently. Yet each provides part of the energy of mediation by which the artwork preserves its integrity even while it engages audience or viewers immediately and eventually finds a place alongside the host of artworks in our culture and its history.[13] In the moment of immediate interpretation and assessment the viewer or audience may participate in a distinctive way: perhaps alone before a painting and caught up in the spirit of the work itself; or in an audience, caught up in a companionate experience of the aesthetic values of the work. Taken in itself, the artwork exists in printed score, in paint or stone, but only habitually.[14] The actuality of its being as an artwork requires mediation by these institutions: by composer, performer, audience, and music critic; by painter, exhibitor, viewer, and art critic; by poet or novelist, reader or hearer, and literary critic. The artwork sustains its habituality and achieves its actuality by a manifold process of mediation in and through the memory and experience of a cultural community. This, then, is the *being* of an artwork. This is the being of *The Star-spangled Banner* and *The Boating Party* and other works of art, each in its own diverse and unique way.

* * *

A last word about boundaries. Only God creates, creates *ex nihilo*: artists mediate *ex aliis*. The manifold mediator by which an artwork receives and possesses its being is the human hand. In some works, however, and at some points, and in some settings, that hand may reach out to grasp the hand of God. To be sure, anything can provide an ascent toward an assent to God in a receptive soul. But a work of art, originally designed for and placed in an architectural or liturgical setting, may bring us more readily to that boundary at which the bounded joins with the Boundless. Such a setting may join the human art worker and art lover to the Supreme Artist. Here, then, is art's ultimate mediation. Here art joins together the issues of life and death,

---

13. "Engages:" more precisely, artworks such as paintings do not, strictly speaking, "engage" their viewers; they are more passive. So too are films. But other works such as theater and dance do. By a distinctive kind of symbiosis, they draw upon the energy of the actors and dancers to "move out" to the viewers and hearers, along a flexible, shifting dynamic boundary.

14. I would concede its *reality*, if that were taken to mean its being as a mere *thing* (*res*) in the modern sense of the term (and not in the broader medieval sense that identified *res* with *ens*). This *res* would express the physical reality of a book, cassette, or canvas, but then it would not name an artistic entity, an art-being in the proper sense.

of time and eternity, and of existence itself. When we turn our eyes
or ears to art that is religiously inspired (and in icon and crucifix we
meet art that is sacramentally empowered), then we encounter the last
boundary: that of the Creator and the creature. For if creation in its
original sense (*brit, creatio ex nihilo*) is the prerogative of God, it is
nonetheless imaged by the human artist, who produces a sort of creature, an artwork.[15] Not every painting, drama, or musical composition
about a religious subject or theme need be religiously inspired. To be
so, it must be able to carry us into that boundary in which Creator
joins with creature, where we encounter the ancient taboo, at once
hidden and manifest: such an artwork is the very mask of God.

15. The Polish art historian Tartakiewicz has noticed what he thinks is the first
transference of the term "creation" to designate human artistic activity, prompted (it
seems) by the wonder inspired by Michelangelo's work in the Sistine Chapel. This is
surprisingly late, and shows the force of the taboo.

9

Creativity and Beauty[1]

PAUL WEISS

1. EXCELLENCES AND CREATIONS

A creator must get himself into a position where he is relatively free of established constraints and from tendencies pointing him toward what he daily does, confronts, and needs. As he progresses in the course of his creative venture, the prospect he faces is made more and more determinate, and thereupon becomes more and more effective. Whether noticed or not, from the beginning to the end of his venture, it will control and guide his activity, thereby distinguishing it from all others. Because of it, even flawed created works have to be sharply distinguished from those which, even if more valuable, are produced in other ways and for other reasons. An excellence is realized to some extent in every creation, even those with serious defects.

An ideal excellence differs from a possibility, both in its radical indeterminacy at the beginning, and in its controlling operative presence at the end, of a successful creative venture. Possibilities have no power and must await what will possess them in order to have both roles and content. A prospective excellence, by contrast, receives determinations from what is outside it, and is thereby empowered. It also enables what it embraces to have interlocked functions. Because of it the work is able to contain pivots, climaxes, thrusts, and rests which bear on one another and on other parts.

An excellence becomes integral to what makes it determinate, until it finally becomes an operative, singular unification of functioning items in a single work; a possibility is parasitical on what gives it determinations. An excellence is changed; a possibility is unaffected on being realized. One may commit oneself to realizing the prospective excellence; no one is committed to actualize a possibility, unless he has already obligated himself by what he had already done. Both

---

1. Selections from my *Creative Ventures,* a work in progress.

are due to the meeting of conditions and the Dunamis,[2] but a possibility lacks a backing of its own, and is therefore unable to affect what makes use of it.

A creator must move back into himself in order to be free enough to be occupied with the realization of a prospective excellence, and thereupon be able so to act that what this requires is provided. While controlled and guided by the prospect, he must be sufficiently independent of it so as to be able to realize it through the production of parts for it to connect with what else is produced under its aegis. There is no knowing in advance exactly what contribution the sought excellence or the produced parts will make to the final outcome, their actual contributions being mainly determined by what was produced and by the excellence sought. That excellence, together with all the produced parts, is satisfied only in a completed work to which all contributed.

Humans alone have privacies able to possess, express themselves through, and partly control their bodies, so as to realize what may have no bodily value. That is one reason why humans (even those whose desires, fears, and expectation dictate what they do) are superior to all other living things. They and humans are superior to what is not alive, even when this is well formed. Those humans who are corrupt, mutilated, sick, seriously defective in mind, body, morals, and ways of acting are still superior to the greatest of created works, since they are individuals with at least a latent ability to assume accountability or to become responsible. They alone are able to reach the stage where they freely act, and are therefore able to create. Those humans who have been denied the opportunity to develop or to realize their potentialities differ from other kinds of beings by having those potentialities.

Although the beauties that some create have an incomparable nature and may be more attractive and satisfying than are those humans who are radically incapacitated, they are without distinctive privacies and, despite their singularity, lack individuality. Humans are individuals who maintain themselves in contradistinction to ultimate factors just so far as they continue into and possess privacies and bodies—and conversely, just so far as they maintain themselves in contradistinction to their privacies and bodies, they continue into and can make use of the ultimate factors.

A created work is self-limited, but cannot hold itself off from all

2. For further discussion of the Dunamis, see my *Philosophy in Process* (State University of New York Press), vols. 9 (1986), 10 (1987), 11 (1988), especially pp. 160ff; also, *Toward a Perfected State* (SUNY, 1986), 22ff; and *The Review of Metaphysics* 40 (June 1987), 657–74.

else. It is unable to impose boundaries on anything; it has neither desires nor appetites; it cannot maintain itself against all else. The beauty of a created work is its own, making singular demands on one's attention. This it does through its appeal, not through the exertion of force, or by limiting one's actions.

Created works stand midway between the outcomes of the adventitious joinings of ultimate factors in every actuality and what men might be able to do with those factors in other ventures. The use of materials brings one face to face with obduracies that cannot be entirely overcome. When those materials are utilized in a creation, they are made to contribute to the nature of what is done, while continuing to exist outside this. So far, they are unlike the ultimate factors used in a creation, since these are unaffected by that use, and both continue to be and to act on one another. Actively contributing to the constitution of what is achieved, the use of them is one with their insistent presence. Material, instead, supplements the private use of the ultimates.

Not a predicate or a category, not necessarily confined to created works, able to be present in individuals and in groups of them, beauty and other excellences lack individuality, substantiality, productive power. Not themselves unified, they are not excellent. A 'beautiful' soul is presumably splendid throughout. It is so, though, only if it has a plurality of subdivisions which the beauty presupposes and connects. Like other realized excellences, beauty exhausts itself in its active unification of distinguishable functioning units.

An actuality has an individuality contrasting with and possessing bodily parts and private powers. Could the parts of it be wholly unified, it would be excellent in and of itself. It would then also deny them a separate status, unless it could use the excellence to enable them to be unified in contradistinction to their possessor.

Excellence presupposes realities existing apart from it in order to be able to be realized. An individual, in contrast, is a singular to begin with, already possessing what he might enhance. Creative work requires a production of what a realizable excellence is to enhance and turn into a singularity.

2. 'NATURAL' BEAUTIES AND THE BEAUTY OF CREATED WORKS

The excellence pertinent to the creation of a work of art is distinctive. Commonly designated as 'beauty,' it is usually set alongside truth and goodness. There are sound reasons for adding glory and justice to that list. None of them holds the attention of creators explicitly;

instead, as radically indeterminate prospects, they guide and control, and eventually are realized in what the creator produces with the help of needed material and the Dunamis. Although beauty makes an enormous difference to whatever is done and achieved, no one but a stray philosopher seems to be interested in its nature. This does not prevent it from being inescapable, operative, and needed. Without it, creative works of art would not be properly carried out, or ever come to a proper close.

From beginning to end, whether noticed or not, a creative venture in the arts is controlled and guided by a prospective beauty, and thereby distinguished from non-creative endeavors, and other kinds of creations. Since that prospect is to be converted finally into a unification of all that is produced, it can be identified as a distinct entity only as long as it is not fully determinate, and therefore only as long as it is not fully realized.

Beauty is one of a number of specializations of a primal excellence. Like truth, goodness, glory, and justice, it is realized as a single inter-involvement of a plurality of functions. So-called 'natural' beauties, unlike the beauties a man might realize, do not do this. They do not transform and unify a plurality of separately produced parts. Cloud formations, sunsets, mountains, and oceans have no well-defined, internally constituted limits, nor do they depend on a privately maintained subjugation to the guiding, controlling presence of a gradually realized excellence. They exhibit no evidence of commitments, accepted and fulfilled, or of any work having to be done to produce them. As just present for appreciation, their excellence is primarily contrastive, setting them over against the commonplace. Creative works, on the other hand, are loci of commitments fulfilled, not just regions that excite or exhilarate.

Natural beauties, which are well marked off from other objects, are to be set in contrast with sunsets, storms, and similar occurrences, since these have to be arbitrarily credited with separations from all else. Pebbles, twigs, ponds, 'found' beauties, precious stones, the songs and plumage of birds, a tree, a flower, a persian cat, a dalmatian, a young horse, humans, some of whom are young, others old, male, female, strong, or supple, are all unduplicable and outstanding, with appearances that partly express what they individually are. Were a work of art like them, it would not make a prospective excellence be present, and it would not signify a condition of which it had made specialized use, together with other factors.

Works of art open appreciators of them up to what can have a plurality of different instantiations. Natural objects and occurrences have appearances enabling those who appreciate them to grasp what those objects and occurrences are. The seamed face of a sage can be classed with natural beauties, for it is uncreated, leading one into him. Created beauties, instead, lead to an ultimate beyond themselves and all other particulars.

Not dependent for its presence on a privacy attending to a prospect and carrying out a plurality of acts, a natural beauty is the product of unguided expressions of natural forces, sometimes characterized as awesome. It does not provide a sign of what is primal, nor help one reach this. It is more like a created work suddenly come upon, not yet read, and therefore neither articulated nor able to signify anything. No foreshadowed excellence is realized in it. Did one try to read it as one reads a created work, one would surely begin to lose it.

The reading of a created work enables one to become acquainted with its beauty in its full concreteness; a 'natural beauty' is to be yielded to. If, on first entering a great cathedral, one is overwhelmed, one has then taken the first step toward the achievement of an adequate appreciation of it. A natural beauty, in contrast, is to be accepted as it appears, dissection of it being one with its dissolution. To call a natural beauty 'sublime' or 'awesome' is but to point up the fact that it is to be accepted as it presents itself. A work of art, instead, asks to be lived in and lived with, thereby enabling one to be directed beyond it toward an ever-present condition affecting everything.

3. COPIES, FORGERIES, AND THE TIGHT UNITY OF ORIGINALS

Machines have been made that work faster and more accurately than any human can. They can be programmed to bring about results no human, on his own, has been able to produce. To suppose that mankind is now edging closer and closer to the stage where machines will be able to create—or even to think, imagine, hope, or fear—is to suppose that creations, or even thinking, willing, desiring, etc., provide only comparatively better ways for items to be brought together than they otherwise would.

Unifications are not tight unities. Unlike these, they do not allow the units they encompass to continue to be just units. Machines do, and must. They cannot duplicate what some things in nature do, for these are able to produce more than aggregations. They need no one to overlay separated parts with interpretations. When the outcome of a machine's activity is taken to be beautiful, or even to be true, one adds to what it in fact presents. Where the excellence of a created work is ingredient in it, the product of a machine needs someone to add a unification to the aggregate it provides. A created work is itself unified, the outcome of a machine's activity is not. Since what the machine produces is unified in the act of accepting its aggregated results, the outcome is comparable to a copy mistakenly identified with an original.

Montages, collages, and assemblages seem to add part to part, and to invite a spectator's unifying act. Yet they do not really differ in principle from other kinds of painting or sculpture, for their parts, too, are subjected to a single unifying prospect, able to turn their units into focal points, transitions, pauses, climactic turns, and intermediaries. Unifying excellences are operative in them just as they are in works produced in other ways.

Although a complete understanding of what had been created requires a reference to other works that had an effect on it, and perhaps even a reference to what might have been produced later, and, although a creation depends for its existence on the use of ultimates having their own integrity and power, each created work can be appreciated as a unique singular. The appreciation, though, must be directed at what is already unified.

Copies, no matter how splendid, differ in kind from what they copy. It is not always possible to tell the difference between the two, mainly because it is not always possible to distinguish an appreciative judgment from an interpretation. An appreciation of a created work, while inseparable from it, has a subjective side; an interpretation that ends with an appreciation, because inseparable from the interpreter, of course, also has one. In the first, however, the work finally takes over; in the other, the subject. The difference can be best seen if, in addition to comparing copies and originals and the products of machines and creations from the side of one who judges, they are viewed from the side of what is judged. A slave does not cease to be a man because he is viewed as property or a tool. Indeed, as Hegel saw, he must be allowed to work as a man in order to be able to have incomparable value as either. Similarly, a created work must be unified to be worthy of the judgment that it deserves appreciation. Crediting the excellence to one who appreciates, treats a created work as something that could be produced non-creatively.

When it is supposed that the product of a machine could be excellent, one either takes the machine to be able to produce what is excellent, or takes the excellence to be the outcome of a judgment. The first of these alternatives makes no provision for the functioning of parts within a single unification. The second takes the unification to be externally imposed. The first reductionistically takes unifications to be unities; the second subjectivistically takes unifications to be the products of judgment. The second, while usually more sensitive than the first to the nature of an excellent work, also ends by denying that anything is created. Both overlook the gradual achievement of the completed work. Since one may not be sure whether or not some particular object is a creation, a copy, an aggregate, or something wrongly identified as one of these, in the end there can be only one recourse—seeing if the object is able to be understood as an inter-locked set of functions, imbued with feeling, in which an excellence was gradually achieved by one who accepted a commitment to it, to what he had done, and to what was required in the course of the production.

The difference between an original and a copy might remain un-detected for an indefinite time. That does not mean that it is not present. Usually, we need some clue, perhaps even a confession or some betraying improper use of paper, canvas, notation, language, paint, or the like, before the distinction is suspected and firmly made. This is but to say that judgments and appreciations are not without their prejudgements and dangers. Whatever excellence a copy is judged to have is, like the product of a machine, due to the tacit intrusion of the supposition that there is a unification operative there. The discovery that it is a copy or the work of a machine makes man-ifest that a unification was wrongly attributed to it.

Forgeries differ from copies, for they are original works, offered as belonging together with other acknowledged originals. They require some creativity, but not enough to produce genuine excellences. Made to fit into an established canon of the works of a creator or of a particular period, they are unduly limited, precluded from being guided and controlled by a gradually realized, prospective excellence. Whatever unifications their makers might make possible can never be more than partial, here and there, not present throughout, since they are subordinated to the need to make them compatible with some already accepted completed work.

The unifications due to creators are complete and inherent in their finished works. Forgeries insinuate themselves among them. Since they are not unified apart from the established canon, they cannot be completed just by realizing an accepted prospective excellence as that which makes its own demands on what is being produced. They de-pend on the existence of other works, the context in which these are, and accepted ideas of what some figure or period accomplished; some-times they depend on an ignorance of the way works of a certain kind had been produced. Usually, they make use of partial unifications to lull one into accepting them as being unified. Where creators allow their works to be bounded, forgers produce boundaries designed to mislead one into taking their works to be self-contained. Theirs is original work carried out, not to produce something excellent, but to fit in with what had already been accepted as being so. Sometimes their works closely approximate what is excellent, exhibiting a common style, and stressing various obtrusive functioning items; created works nevertheless radically contrast with them in not depending for an acceptance on the supposition that they fit in with other creations.

4. NOVELTY, BOUNDARIES, AND MATERIALS

Some painters do not seem to produce interlocked, functioning units within the compass of a gradually realized beauty. Their works are apparently begun without preliminaries, and apparently end with new ways of exhibiting paints in relation to one another. "What you see," some minimalists maintain, "is what you get." No feeling is supposedly present, no excellence is supposed to affect either the course of the production or the outcome. Traditionalists reject their works as debased, perverse, anarchistic. That, of course, is the reaction to expect from those who reject deviations from accepted standards, procedures, or conventional topics. Such rejections are to be avoided as at least question-begging; new genres deserve to be accorded the same consideration that more traditional works receive, particularly if an initial appreciation of them is supported when one reads them with care.

What is radically new may not be properly approached or characterized even by those who favor those novelties. It is hard to know how to work through them, since their materials, techniques, topics, and themes are so novel. It is not surprising to find that the terms and categories used to explain or to justify them are primarily negatives of those which have been long used. Innovators rightly demand that traditional techniques, ways of assessing, established canons of good taste, and traditional themes and topics not be treated as sacrosanct. Nothing should be allowed to keep creators from using different units, combinations, and materials. The new, of course, does not deserve acclaim just because it is new. One does it more justice in fact if one takes time to learn how to read it, even if the reading results in a rejection of it as not well enough unified to merit being accepted as excellent. Fortunately, the works are rarely as radically different from the old as their programs claim them to be, in good part because their novelty and the ingenuity of their makers are not essential parts of them. Innovators may be creative. By freeing one from unnecessary restraints or ways of realizing beauty they also promote ways to read old works in new ways. What had once seemed to be auxiliary, mediocre, incidental, may then be revealed to be crucial and illuminating.

Some painters do something similar to what photographers do. Having decided to depict a battle or a waterfall, they provide boundaries for their works, deciding that they are to be of such and such a size, with such and such subdivisions, scenes, and combinations. As a consequence, they focus on certain particulars rather than others as mutually supportive. They differ from other creators mainly in using the imposed boundaries to confine whatever they create. When natural occurrences are taken to be beautiful, something similar is done, but crudely.

A distinction must be made between those who deliberately set about to realize an ideal prospect and those who occupy themselves with working over material until they are able to discern that prospect. An exclusive occupation with the task of satisfying an ideal overlooks the demands each achieved part makes on others, while an exclusive occupation with these or with materials overlooks the demand made by the prospective excellence. Both are needed.

Beauty is an ideal. Like other ideals, it specializes a more general excellence. In different fields of art, creations are occupied with distinctive versions of it, to be realized by carrying out distinctive acts. In the absence of a common, more indeterminate beauty that they diversely focus on and attempt to realize, they would have to exhibit the kind of beauty realized in another kind of art—or would have to produce what could be called 'beauty' only by analogy. It is only a matter of ingenuity, though, to find an analogy between any items. There are analogies between a brook and a computer. A brook runs on without supervision, a computer has a location in a public world; a brook and a computer receive what is put into them, and change it, sometimes into what is better. Similar analogies can be made between any other arbitrarily selected objects, since all are constituted of the same ultimates.

Beauty, like other excellent prospects, is able to function as a guiding ideal because it has a status of its own. It may not be acknowledged until a work has been completed. That does not mean that it was not used as a guide and control for what is done; nor will it affect a creator's commitment to realize it, or to produce the parts that promote the realization of it as their unification.

A prospective excellence guides and controls so far as it is accepted as a guide and control, affecting the nature of particular acts and their outcomes. In its absence, there would be only stimuli, provocations, arousals, able to terminate in a miscellany of items which may well get in one another's way, unable to sustain, modify, or enhance one another.

There is no way to demonstrate that, in the absence of humans, what they create will continue to be excellent, or even that what is appreciated is not constituted by the act of appreciation—unless what is known, made, created, or perceived is related to or grounded in what is able to possess the termini of the relations men have to it. Created works, since they have no depth or interiorities of their own, must, in contrast with actualities, depend for their continuance, when not attended to, on the materials used and the works' relation to what they will signify for a creator, appreciator, or attentive reader.

When creations are completed, they are bounded off from and bound off other items, most which are not created, at once making use of externally maintained materials and being effectively resisted by them. Within the externally determined boundaries that the creations acquire from the objects external to them, the creations intimately interrelate what is within them. Just as more loosely joined objects can carry out functions in the absence of human observers, the roof stopping the rain, the floor holding up the table, roots feeding a tree, so the functions acquired in a creation continue to be exercised within the unification that a creator achieved.

5. HUMANS AND CREATED BEAUTIES

Anthropologists have long struggled with odd marks, trying to determine whether they were due to the weather or were deliberately set down. The Turing experiment, which asks one to determine whether or not some presented set of items form a message sent out by a human, could have been formulated by them well before the age of computers. It is not always possible to know that something is a message any more than that it is a copy. Just what kind of functions distinguishable items actually exercise may be hard to discern. Poor readers of great works miss most of the functions that the distinguishable items carry out. The failure to determine what is well unified in this or that case does not, of course, preclude its being present, or show what must be known if other attitudes were assumed and other clues followed. If the question whether or not something is unified cannot be definitely settled, one still has no right to conclude that there is no difference involved, or that we cannot possibly know what the difference is. If we had additional data the issue could conceivably be resolved.

The Turing experiment depended on the suppositions that there was a well-bounded computer existing and functioning independently of any human, though apart from humans it would not be more than an accentuated item in a public world; that a string of units could be mistaken by humans for a message; and that failure by humans to make a correct decision means that there might be no difference between humans and computers. Without humans able to do what computers cannot, there would, though, be no presumed messages, no questions asked and answered, and no computers able to be set apart from all else and do more than make marks or noises in a public world where they interplay with all else.

If we cannot determine whether or not the units in a work are well unified we cannot know whether or not it is beautiful. Sometimes, though, we can see that they are. At those times, there can be no question but that the work is excellent. To be sure, one might wrongly suppose that the distinguished items were unified, but that supposition can be tested by beginning at other places, following other routes, and emphasizing different distinguished functions. We know we are reading a great poem when we see how the words reverberate throughout, making a great difference to some, little differences to others, and hardly detectable differences to the rest. In the end, we must be content to settle for a recognition of reverberations greater than those to be found in most other poems, and with a final sign of a primal effective condition.

Were one to hold that language is a communitarian matter, and that all truth claims reflect common uses and acceptances of some established language, one would still be faced with the fact that a painting or a sculpture is able to be appreciated, be well 'read' without using that language. That, it might be contended, is exactly why there is no agreement on what is or is not beautiful. There are, though, other ways in which humans agree besides those which involve a common language—as rowers, the participants in a car wash, and relay runners make evident. It is also possible to make sound judgments about works which no others accept. If all else but language is subjectified, we would, at the end, be left with no one to speak to, or able to understand what was said; a history would be lived by no one; a society would contain no one—or, all these would be produced when men begin to speak.

A created beauty continues to be present and encompassing, both when the work is externally related to others and when it is made part of another. Without losing the excellence it already possesses, the work will then be subjected to new determinations, as the heart is when one begins to run. Necessarily, without affecting the excellence, the work will then differ from others in influence, economic value, political role, and in multiple other ways and areas which have no necessary pertinence to its excellence.

Creators realize most of their objectives by making use of different techniques, employing different materials, following different routes, and meeting their commitments with different degrees of fidelity. Today, as surely as yesterday, there must be a completeness produced, a unification in which disparate items are interlocked, adding to one another's import, without precluding conflicts, incompletenesses, cross purposes, and mistakes in multiple areas. Their creators will have to learn from experience; all will have to try to be in control of their work. This is best done if they first retreat deep into themselves before they begin the hard work of creating what is excellent. Yeats's "The Circus Animals' Desertion,"[3] as great poems do, speaks opaquely and clearly, thematically and unthematically, illuminatingly and darkly about this, while making one aware of the nature of time—here, the locus of origins—and making evident the basic problem every poet must solve.

I

I sought a theme and sought for it in vain,
I sought it daily for six weeks or so.
Maybe at last, being but a broken man,
I must be satisfied with my heart, although
Winter and summer till old age began
My circus animals were all on show,
Those stilted boys, that burnished chariot,
Lion and woman and the Lord knows what.

II

What can I but enumerate old themes?
First that sea-rider Oisin led by the nose
Through three enchanted islands, allegorical dreams
Vain gaiety, vain battle, vain repose,
Themes of the embittered heart, or so it seems,
That might adorn old songs or courtly shows;
But what cared I that set him on to ride,
I, starved for the bosom of his faery bride?

And then a counter-truth filled out its play,
The Countess Cathleen was the name I gave it;
She, pity-crazed, had given her soul away,
But masterful Heaven had intervened to save it.

---

3. Reprinted with permission of Macmillan Publishing Company from *The Poems of W. B. Yeats: A New Edition*, edited by Richard J. Finneran. Copyright 1940 by Georgie Yeats, renewed 1968 by Bertha Georgie Yeats, Michael Butler Yeats, and Anne Yeats.

I thought my dear must her own soul destroy,
So did fanaticism and hate enslave it,
And this brought forth a dream and soon enough
This dream itself had all my thought and love.

And when the Fool and Blind Man stole the bread
Cuchulain fought the ungovernable sea;
Heart-mysteries there, and yet when all is said
It was the dream itself enchanted me:
Character isolated by a deed
To engross the present and dominate memory.
Players and painted stage took all my love,
And not those things that they were emblems of.

III
Those masterful images because complete
Grew in pure mind, but out of what began?
A mound of refuse or the sweepings of a street.
Old kettles, old bottles, and a broken can,
Old iron, old bones, old rags, that raving slut
Who keeps the till. Now that my ladder's gone,
I must lie down where all the ladders start,
In the foul rag-and-bone shop of the heart.

A creator, over the course of his work, is also appreciative, while an appreciator, from beginning to the end of his reading of a created work, is also pulled into and directed beyond it. The entire enterprise is accompanied by multiple tensions and various degrees of relief, absorptions and satisfactions. At the end, the work remains between what it signifies and what is privately undergone, enabling each to bear on the other. As a consequence, what is signified will not only be privately reached, but will have an affect on the reader. The work, while still present, will have vanished so far as it allows the creator and appreciative readers to face directly what is correlative with them as individuals. At the same time, the work will provide a way by which the past and future are enabled to affect each other. As one item in a larger world, the work will also be subject to and instantiate all the ultimates, thereby becoming part of a single totality with all other occurrences, created or not.

The mastery of one kind of art makes evident what in other kinds might otherwise be overlooked. Nothing less than a detailed study of all the arts will expose all the aspects that a sound, adequate account of any should consider. No less important is the fact that other creative ventures emphasize what none of the arts do. Each is occupied with realizing a different kind of excellence and, thereupon, makes use of a privacy in a different way, specializes and makes emphatic uses of a different ultimate condition, joins this to the Dunamis in distinctive kinds of acts, texturizes and stabilizes it by using different kinds of materials, and realizes a distinctive kind of unification. What one knows about art should make one alert to otherwise slighted aspects in other kinds of creation. The result should make more evident what is present in every art, though there slighted and sometimes misconstrued. By contrast, but also by bringing new issues to the fore, other kinds of creation should illuminate what has now been said about art—and conversely.

10

Aesthetics in the Kantian Project

ROBERT WOOD

1. INTRODUCTION: THE CRITICAL PROJECT

Immanuel Kant's mature aesthetics appears in the context of a project aimed at a critical assessment of the nature and limits of the basic human faculties of knowing, willing and feeling.[1] The assessment of knowledge in the *Critique of Pure Reason* pivoted around a distinction between the phenomenal and the noumenal, between things as they make their appearance in terms of the peculiar temporal finitude of human faculties and things as they are in themselves; or between things as they are displayed to a spatially and temporally perspectival and receptive mode of knowing that must constitute the appearance of its objects, and things as they would appear to a wholistically intuitive intellect whose thinking constitutes the being of its projects. The phenomenally bound knower is tied to sensory givenness, to streams of impressions arising from without and from within. That such impressions pass from successive personal experiences to objective knowledge, that is, to an awareness of that which stands over against awareness as *ob-jectum*, basic principles of sorting are involved. Following the presuppositions of Newtonian science that likened the movements here on earth to the regularities of the starry skies above, Kant's analysis leaves us with a completely deterministic world of objectively sorted sensory presentations, but it also leaves open the status of the supersensuous noumenal ground.[2]

The analysis of willing in the *Critique of Practical Reason* attends to that opening. It introduces, as the ground of moral action, the notion of free self-determination allied with the moral law within over against

---

1. Immanuel Kant, *First Introduction to the Critique of Judgment*, trans. J. Haden (New York: Bobbs-Merrill, 1965), 45ff. This Introduction was not published by Kant, but in many ways it provides a more helpful statement than his published Introduction (henceforth *FI*).

2. Immanuel Kant, *Critique of Pure Reason*, Preface to the Second Edition, trans. N. K. Smith (New York: St. Martin's, 1965), Bxviii–Bxxxi, 23–30 (henceforth *CPuR*).

the non-free, law-governed character of our appetites that make their appearance in the phenomenal world. The analysis once again points in the direction of the supersensuous noumenal ground, but now as the ground of our personhood in distinction from the ground of nature.[3] The fundamental concepts that support moral freedom, like the fundamental concepts by which we sort out the objective from the subjective in experience, are a priori forms, given with the structure of experience. Judgment in their respect consists in subsuming the particulars of experience under those forms. Kant calls this function that of *determinant judgment*. There is another function: what he calls *reflective judgment*. The first critique analyzed the conditions of objectivity but told us nothing of the *kinds* of things that might appear objectively. Reflective judgment begins with individual objects and goes in search of the concepts that allow us to make sense of them. The third critique deals with this reflective type of judgment.[4]

The analysis of the faculty of willing led to the freedom of moral self-determination in the practical order. The analysis of knowing led to the determinism of the world of appearance for cognition. This leaves us with two unrelated and seemingly unrelatable regions. The *Critique of Aesthetic and Teleological Judgment* not only analyzes the third faculty, namely *feeling*, but also aims to bridge the two regions of knowledge and moral activity.[5]

It seems odd that a work dedicated to the analysis of feeling should focus upon *judgment* and that it should include teleological as well as aesthetic judgment. But what links them is the central concept of the work: *nature viewed as art*.[6] The comprehensive notion involved in that is the notion of finality or purposiveness (*Zweckmässigkeit*). Kant divides the notion into subjective and objective forms and subdivides these in various ways. These divisions constitute the conceptual substructure (though not the actual outline) of the work. (See the accompanying diagram.)

3. Immanuel Kant, *Critique of Practical Reason*, trans. L. Beck (New York: Bobbs-Merrill, c. 1956), 137ff (henceforth *CPrR*).

4. Immanuel Kant, *Critique of Judgment*, trans. J. Bernard (New York: Hafner, 1951), Introduction, IV, 15–17 and no. 69, 232–33. Since our references will be largely to this work, we will henceforth refer to it by division number (or Introduction followed by a section) and page(s).

5. Introduction IX, 32–34.   6. *FI*, 16ff.

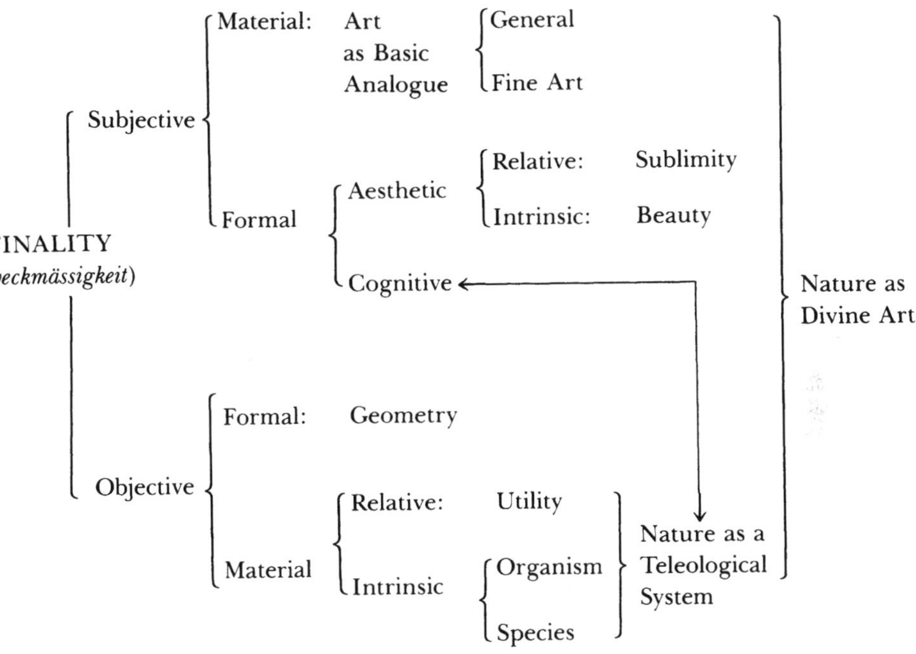

Kant's *Critique of Judgment*: Basic Conceptual Structure

2. PURPOSIVENESS AS THE ORGANIZING PRINCIPLE OF THE THIRD CRITIQUE

Purpose involves causality through concepts and is exhibited immediately and unequivocally in artefaction in general: in the light of a basic idea or concept, I transform the shape of a given natural material. Art here is the prime analogate for all other types of purposiveness treated in the work. Kant calls this original type of purposeness *material subjective purposiveness*: the human subject shapes material in the light of a preconceived end.[7] Kant uses that idea as a concept of reflective judgment to pull together various regions of phenomena—indeed, to pull together the whole field of human experience and its multitudinous object-types.

7. No. 61, 206–7; no. 65, 222.

Its first and most obvious application is to living forms whose structures suggest the notion of objective material purposiveness or natural teleology. It is a notion created by reflective judgment as a projection of material subjective purposiveness (our own artefaction) onto the world of living things as the only way we can make sense out of them. Knowingly or not, Kant here follows Aristotle's analysis in Book II of the *Physics*. There Aristotle derives the notions of form and matter from the shape given to material in artefaction, and the notions of efficiency and finality from the activity of the artisan imposing form upon the material at hand by reason of an end in view. Aristotle then synthesizes these four notions and projects them onto the natural character of the material and of the agent: nature is a self-formative principle that organizes the material elements for the sake of the realization of the ends of a species.[8] Kant recognized this to be a projection. Affected deeply by the notion of the infinite and mysterious beyond of noumenal being, he considered the projection of the notion of teleology upon nature to be a non-divine, all-too-human way of making sense out of things *for us*, not as the way things must be *in themselves*. However, he underscored the necessity of the projection as the only way we can make complete sense of things.[9]

Fine art, whose objects are the special province of aesthetics, is, of course, a subdivision of artefaction as such and will provide us with a way of thinking about what might be involved in the creation of natural species. Aesthetic appreciation, on the other hand, is rooted in the perception of the beautiful which Kant describes as being "purposive without a purpose." This is an example of what he calls *formal subjective purposiveness*. Particularly in the case of natural aesthetic forms, the object presents itself as if it were made for the purpose of bringing about aesthetic appreciation.[10] This is an aspect of a deeper formal subjective purposiveness which concerns nature's self-presentation to us as systematically suitable, even in its myriad empirical forms, for our capacity to judge.[11] Here is where judgment and aesthetics have a special tie, and we will have more to say about that later.

Like subjective purposiveness, objective purposiveness involves a formal as well as a material type. Formal objective purposiveness characterizes geometry, which parallels the formal subjective purposiveness involved in aesthetic perception.[12] The two types of material purposiveness are most readily identifiable: the subjective type involves our subjectively originated transformation of material things

8. Aristotle, *Physics* II, iii, 194b ff.
9. No. 75, 245.
10. No. 17, 73.
11. *FI*, 18ff.
12. No. 62, 208–12.

through artefaction; the objective type is found in the natural teleology of living things. The formal types are more difficult to identify clearly. Aquinas's use of the expression *abstractio formae* to describe the founding act of the mathematical order as the isolation of the form of quantity might offer some illumination here.[13] The Kantian twist is that geometry abstracts the a priori form of space from its function in providing the subjective frame within which things appear objectively.[14] The form that is abstracted in aesthetic perception is the link between two forms: (1) *the general form of the judgment* as the play between imagination and understanding[15] brought about by (2) *the aesthetic form*, as distinguished from the sensory features, of sensorily given things.[16] We will explore that further on.

But to return to material objective purposiveness: in the case of living beings, the very term *organ*, in the proper sense of the term, means instrument, a notion derived from the products of human technology. The intelligibility of the system of organs we call an organism appears geared up to fulfill its own intrinsic purposes: nourishment, growth, and organic articulation as ultimately providing instruments for the manifestness of things.[17] The reproductive systems involve an external teleology of male to female within the species, and the multiplicity of species appear as if they are made for each other in those reciprocal relations we now call an ecosystem.[18] Humanness is the only thing given in experience which, in the form of the fundamental moral imperative, is an end and not simply a means. It appears as the final end of the whole of nature viewed as a teleological system. And humanness in turn, by reason of its moral destiny, has itself a final end.[19] In the present context, the imperative to treat humanity as an end and not simply a means links up with the aesthetic region in a special way. It involves the imperative to cultivate our distinctively human faculties in creating works of art and in cultivating appreciation of art, beauty, and sublimity; it involves creating a community around aesthetic matters which, as an aspect of the explicitly moral community, respects the autonomy of the judging subject.[20]

What finally puts together all of these notions of purposiveness—subjective and objective, formal and material, intrinsic and relative—is the notion of nature as divine art, where the divine is the artist

---

13. Thomas Aquinas, *Division and Methods of the Sciences*, trans. A. Maurer (Toronto: Pontifical Institute of Mediaeval Studies, 1958), 29ff.

14. *CPuR*, B37/A23–B45/A30, 67–74.

15. No. 9, 51–54.

16. No. 13–14, 64–68.

17. No. 65, 22off.

18. No. 82, 274–279.

19. No. 84, 284–286; no. 86, 292–294; no. 60, 200–202.

20. No. 83, 279–284.

constructing species through the intuition of aesthetic ideas, but is also, in this very activity, the ultimate moral agent.[21] Art is the basic analogue for drawing together the whole of experience and bringing reason into harmony with itself. The formal subjective purposiveness suggested by art and inducing the play of cognitive faculties as the form of judgment is linked to the more encompassing formal subjective purposiveness of nature as a whole, in the multiplicity of its empirically given forms, as suited to our capacity to judge. And the encompassing notion that judgment necessarily arrives at is the notion of nature as divine art.

Having set forth this underlying conceptual framework in the various types of purposiveness, I want to explore further the notion of the beautiful (section 3), the descriptive relations between nature and art (section 4), the notion of the sublime (section 5), the relation between art and morality (section 6), and the final, encompassing notion of nature as divine art (section 7).

3. THE NOTION OF THE BEAUTIFUL

Within the general framework of these different types of purposiveness arrived at by reflective judgment projecting the literal purposiveness involved in human artefaction unto various regions of experience, Kant does not, as his original project seemed to intend, provide an inventory of the various types of feeling. Instead, he focuses upon and distinguishes three basically different states of feeling: the feeling of the agreeable, the feeling of the beautiful and the feeling of the sublime.[22] The former two are set off from the latter in that the beautiful and the agreeable operate within the limits of imagination and sensory experience respectively, while the sublime involves the transgression of such limits.[23] We will return to the sublime in a later section of this paper.

Both the agreeable and the beautiful are based upon a feeling, and the very character of feeling is to be a subjective state.[24] But the feeling of the agreeable is what we might call a private subjective state, whereas the feeling of the beautiful is, by contrast at least, public, that is, universalizable. It is not that its object is universal. Quite the contrary, its object is a uniquely arresting individual. But, like a universal and necessary truth, its very uniqueness makes a universal claim upon the assent of all humans. To say "I like it" is to report on private

21. No. 86, 292ff. Cf. section 7 *infra*.
22. No. 7, 46–48.   23. No. 23, 82–85.
24. No. 1, 37.

satisfaction; to say "It is beautiful" is to make a public claim. (Kant here distinguishes two very different claims, although, since one might be mistaken in particular cases, it is quite another thing to cash in on the claims.)

The agreeable is tied in with the effect of the *sensa qua sensa*, that is, as organically based effects. Kant holds to the typical modern empiricist notion of the sensory features of things as *secondary qualities*, as subjective effects of things. The beautiful, by contrast, is tied in with the *form* of the *sensa*, their peculiar togetherness in space and/or in time that leads us to call an object beautiful.[25]

One might see better what is involved here if we considered the same melody played by a pipe organ and by a tuba. The melody is the same, the timbre of the instruments different. Because of personal proclivities one might prefer the timbre of the tuba to that of the organ. What is agreeable to one might not be so to others, even though most might prefer the organ. The distinctively aesthetic judgment has to do with the form of the melody, not with the timbre of its carrier. However, Kant does admit that the sensuousness of a certain kind of timbre might better serve to focus one kind of form than another.[26] Consider Gregorian chant played on an organ and the same chant played on the tuba.

The agreeable evokes a response of the animal appetite; the beautiful involves a detachment from that appetite. In Kant's terms, the agreeable provides *interested* satisfaction, the beautiful *disinterested* satisfaction.[27] Consider here the distinction between an aesthetic and an erotic response to nude statuary. The latter involves an organic reaction, the former something more detached.

Schopenhauer understood the disinterested character to involve a kind of escape from life and provoked Nietzsche's passionate attack.[28] Kant rather sees the aesthetic experience as referred to the feeling of life. Indeed, what is involved in aesthetic experience for Kant is a quickening, an enlivening of precisely the play of imagination and understanding as the subjective form of the judgment.[29] The work of art stems from the spirit of the artist as an animating principle. Quickened by an aesthetic idea, the genius gives birth to a form that subsumes and transcends the technical mechanisms involved in its pro-

25. No. 14, 65–68.   26. No. 14, 60.
27. No. 2, 38–39.
28. Arthur Schopenhauer, *The World as Will and Representation*, III, no. 38, trans. E. Payne (New York: Dover, 1969), vol. I, 196ff (henceforth *WWR*); Friedrich Nietzsche, *The Will to Power*, trans. W. Kaufmann and R. Hollingdale (New York: Vintage, 1967), nos. 802, 804, and 812.
29. No. 1, 38; no. 12, 58; no. 23, 83.

duction.[30] Such a work of art is characterized by being alive, organic, vital, as distinguished from work that is dead and mechanical.[31]

In the case of the agreeable there is a direct relation of the object to the appetite; in the case of the beautiful, disinterest is made possible because the relation is mediated by judgment and thus distanced from the appetite. The agreeable involves the taste of sensation; the beautiful the taste of reflection.[32] Here we must distinguish a judgment immanent in the experience of the beautiful from a critical judgment reflecting upon the experience after the fact. Kant claims that what we have called the immanent judgment involves the operation of that which is involved in all judgment, namely a harmonious relation between the cognitive faculties of understanding and imagination. Only, in the case of the judgment of the beautiful, what is crucially involved is the relation of the faculties rather than the conceptual content provided by the understanding.[33]

Kant seems to move to this position for at least two reasons. The first is that judgment in general involves a certain distance from the sensory and thus from animal immediacy, drawing upon our sense of the whole as we are, as it were, brought from it to the present. The second reason is his claim that genuine aesthetic experience facilitates and enlivens the general capacity for communication and thus for judgment.[34]

Just as he strives to set off the beautiful from that which merely agrees with our animal appetite, Kant also strives to set it off from the conceptual. The beautiful is a peculiar zone of human experience in which neither animals nor angels (hypothetical separate minds) could participate. Perception of the beautiful attends to no intellectual criteria but to direct though detached perception of sensory form.[35]

In this regard Kant makes another basic distinction: that between free beauty and dependent beauty.[36] Free beauty is independent of concepts. Kant refers to arabesque drawings on the one hand and flowers or bird plumage on the other: free beauties of art and free beauties of nature. In these cases it is not the classificatory dimension that is crucial but the aesthetic form, that is, the relation between the parts. Dependent beauty involves aesthetic form linked to conceptual content in such a way that conceptual recognition enters into the character of the aesthetic experience. In this area falls Kant's ideal of beauty (the human being acting under moral laws) to which we will

<hr>

30. No. 47, 153.
32. No. 4, 41; no. 8, 48; no. 59, 199.
33. No. 9, 51–54.
35. No. 5, 43–45; no. 8, 50.

31. No. 49, 156–57.

34. No. 60, 200–202.
36. No. 16, 65–66.

return later. The distinction between free and dependent beauty is made in order to move from what Gadamer calls the *normative* notion of beauty to the *ideal* of beauty.[37] The normative notion isolates the presence of beauty independently of concepts so as not to confuse the aesthetic judgment of beauty with a cognitive judgment. It also detaches beauty from sensory appetite and thus from the agreeable. It focuses attention upon the aesthetic form of the object, the peculiar togetherness of all the factors that enter into the immediate appearance of the object. Once the essential, normative character of beauty has been isolated and analyzed, we can observe it as it interplays with the conceptual and reaches toward the ideal of beauty.

At the end of the analytic of the beautiful, Kant points to the ground of the judgment of taste in the *sensus communis*.[38] In this context it is neither the scholastic notion of the common faculty of sensation, possessed by humans and animals alike, in which the proper senses are rooted;[39] nor is it the fund of rules of thumb common to a historic community by which members of the community commonly find their way in that community. However, like the common sense of a community, the Kantian aesthetic *sensus communis* is developed over time. *Sensus communis* is the ground of the public claim made by the judgment of the beautiful; it involves the universal communicability of the claim, as distinguished from the privacy of merely organic satisfaction. *Sensus communis* is the general form of the judgment as the togetherness of the faculties of imagination and understanding affected by the beautiful. The beautiful is characterized by its peculiar capacity to affect the *sensus communis* as if the object were made purposely to bring about such an effect. Reflective judgment in its cognitive form brings about the togetherness of understanding and imagination in the notion of the purposiveness of nature as a whole, in its concrete types, as a teleological system, on an analogy with the activity involved in artistic activity.

4. ART AND NATURE

In the case of beautiful forms and in the case of living forms, nature presents herself in a purposive way, as if she were geared up to bring about the free play of the cognitive faculties. Even in the case of fine

37. Hans-Georg Gadamer, *Truth and Method*, trans. G. Barden and J. Cumming (New York: Crossroad, 1982), 44.
38. Nos. 21–22, 74–77; no. 40, 135–138.
39. Thomas Aquinas, *Summa theologiae*, I, 78, 4. The notion is derived from Aristotle, *On the Soul*, III, i, 425a, 15ff.

art where the purposiveness is arranged by a human being—the artist—his genius is the basis for distinguishing the genuine work of art from mere fabrication; and in genius it is nature that gives the rule.[40] Though technical recipes are involved in artistic production, the mastery of technique remains a strictly subordinate dimension in the work of fine art. Genius is the capacity for originality which, as it is original, also terminates in *exemplary* products. Such exemplary originality is a gift of nature. Consequently, in the experience of the beautiful, it is as if the supersensuous ground of all appearance, outside in nature and inside in the operation of genius, arranged things for our cognitive faculties.

Kant claims that a certain reciprocity is involved in our perception of the beautiful in nature and in art. Nature itself, he says, is beautiful insofar as it looks like art.[41] The hackneyed expression "pretty as a picture" picks that up. This means that we need art in order to become sensitized to the beauty of nature. Art itself is linked to communicability and thus to the *sensus communis* and is one way in which a community is built up. Kant goes so far as to say that, as a matter of empirical fact, it is only in society that men take an interest in the beauty of nature.[42] At least part of the reason is that it requires artists to help us learn aesthetic appreciation. Kant also says that art, in its turn, is beautiful only insofar as it looks like nature even as we recognize it to be art. So we have to be sensitive to the beauty of nature in order to be sensitive to the beauty of art and vice-versa. There is an obvious circle here. But it requires the initial breakthrough of genius that, sensitive to nature, gives birth to art. And this, in turn, sensitizes the community to the beauties of nature. Giving oneself over to the exemplarity of the works of genius, one learns to cultivate that detached perception that allows one to recognize the pure aesthetic form of things, whether in nature or in art.[43] Attention to the works of genius throughout the ages cultivates the *sensus communis* and establishes a community involved in the beautiful. Beginning the analytic of the beautiful with the isolation of aspects of the judgment of pure beauty not only abstracts from the conceptual dimension involved in dependent beauty; it also abstracts initially from the process of historical sedimentation that made the perception of beauty concretely possible in the first place.

The genius works through *aesthetic ideas*, which Kant describes as intuitions to which no concept is adequate. They are the very reverse

40. No. 46, 150.　　41. No. 45, 149.
42. No. 41, 139.　　43. No. 60, 200–202.

of a *rational idea* as a concept to which no intuition is adequate. The aesthetic idea suggests much thought but cannot be captured in a single concept. Its source lies in *Geist*, spirit, as the animating principle in the mind that sets the cognitive powers in motion.[44]

There are several types of aesthetic ideas. First are the ideas that are the source of pure beauty in the realm of art. Music unaccompanied by text (and that means also music untitled except for a formal indicator, for example, Brahms's Symphony No. 2)—music apart from what we usually call language—furnishes perhaps the best example of pure beauty in the region of art. Harmony and melody provide another kind of language, "a language of the affections," and give expression to "the aesthetic idea of an integral whole of an unutterable wealth of thought."[45] That whole is being, the correlate to reason as the drive toward absolute totality, translated into its relation to our affections. This aesthetic idea is the general form for those other aesthetic ideas without relation to concepts that are appropriate to the various affections as they interplay with the variety of things within the whole. Thus music is happy or sad, vigorous or languid, restrained or unbridled, and so forth. Linked to verbal language through descriptive title and/or text, it provides an example of dependent beauty in the order of art.

These notions formed the basis for the views of Schopenhauer and Nietzsche on music as the mirror of the underlying noumenal Will expressing itself in the phenomenal forms of species and individuals and on verbal language as a deficient translation generated out of the spirit of music.[46] However, contrary to these successors, music for Kant was not the highest but the lowest of the art forms.[47] The pure beauty it expresses parallels the free beauties of nature and presents us with an aesthetic minimum which threatens to sink into the vanity, triviality, and superficiality often associated with the effete snob.[48] For Kant the beautiful must be brought from its minimal pure state into relation with the serious conceptual work of the mind. Hence Kant, at the height of dependent beauty, posits an ideal of beauty in the human being acting under moral law.[49] Here we have an example of depen-

---

44. No. 49, 157.   45. No. 53, 173.
46. Schopenhauer, *WWR*, IV, no. 54, I, 274ff; Nietzsche, *The Birth of Tragedy*, trans. F. Golffing (Garden City, New York: Doubleday, c. 1956), 32ff (henceforth *BT*).
47. No. 53, 174.   48. No. 42, 140–41.
49. No. 17, 68–73. Kant speaks here "an der menschlichen Gestalt." It is, he says, "der sichtbare Ausdruck sittlicher Ideen. . . ." It seems to me that the human form as visible expression of moral ideas could be considered literally, and then it would be found in painting and in sculpture; or it can be taken figuratively as the Gestalt of a human life in which we intellectually "see" the expression of moral ideas. Since Kant

dent beauty involving a concept and a moral interest. What makes it beautiful is neither the conceptual content nor the moral interest, but only the aesthetic form. There is still the disinterest in relation to animal appetite, but there must be an aesthetic fusion here between the sensuous form and the conceptual referent. Poetry is the art form most able to bring about this fusion. Poetry reaches its height when its object is sublime. Here the harmony of the faculties in the experience of the beauty of presentation fuses with the experience of the disproportion of the faculties in the experience of the sublime.[50] And when poetry focuses upon the human being acting sublimely, the ideal of beauty is realized in a double mode. We will return to that in the next section when we look more closely at the sublime.

There are, we said, several levels where aesthetic ideas operate. Kant speaks also of the intuition of the *normative idea* (*die Normalidee*) of a species.[51] This is the origin of Goethe's *Typus* and of Schopenhauer's *Platonic Ideas* of the various natural species.[52] The normative idea is "the image that, as it were, forms an intentional basis underlying the technic of nature."[53] It is an aesthetic idea, one to which no concept is adequate. As Schopenhauer expressed it, the genius says through his work that which nature stammeringly tried to say in the multiple members of each species.[54] Through the work of the artist, not only are we more sensitized to the beauties of nature, but we learn to view nature as the product of artistic activity.

There are also aesthetic ideas that function as symbols of rational ideas. An aesthetic idea fused with a rational idea provides a kind of schematization, a metaphorical equivalent that involves a kind of surrogate presence of that which lies beyond strict knowledge: heaven, hell, eternity, creation. It removes the rational ideas from their natural distance and brings them into concrete presence. Even in the case of concepts available within experience—such notions as death, envy, vice, love, fame—their fusion with an aesthetic idea gives them a fuller embodiment than they would otherwise possess.[55]

------

argues that poetry is the highest of the art forms, I have tried in my interpretation here to locate the ideal more fully in poetry.

50. No. 52, 170.   51. No. 17, 70–73.

52. Johann Wolfgang Goethe, *Zur Naturwissenschaft in Allgemeinen,* 31 and *Morphologie,* 171ff, in *Werke,* vol. XIII (Hamburg: Wegner, 1958); Schopenhauer, *WWR,* III, no. 30, I, 169ff.

53. No. 17, 70.

54. Schopenhauer, *WWR,* III, no. 36, I, 186.

55. No. 49, 157–58.

5. THE SUBLIME

For Kant, the sublime is an aesthetic state that concerns the use we make of certain aspects of nature to gain a deeper sense of our moral destiny. For Kant it is not nature that is sublime: it is our moral destiny that is so.[56] Nature as overwhelming might presents us with the occasion for conceiving of the dynamically sublime; nature as immense magnitude, the mathematically sublime. The power and size of nature dwarf us into material insignificance. If the beautiful world and the agreeable make us feel at home in the world, the measureless size and power of nature suggest the opposite. But in the feeling of the sublime, we are rather uplifted than crushed, as we gain a sense of the collusion between the absolutely great and our own moral action.

On Kant's tombstone are written the words "The starry skies above, the moral law within."[57] The epitaph is taken from the last pages of the *Critique of Practical Reason,* the fuller text of which reads: "Two things fill me with awe: the starry skies above, the moral law within."[58] The starry skies are occasions for the experience of the mathematically sublime and at the same time prototypes of the basic analogue for conceiving of the deterministic universe of Newtonian physics. Their phenomenal presentation guides the analysis in the first critique. The moral law is, of course, the object of the second critique. Kant's response to both the starry skies and the moral law is the state of awe, the aesthetic modality characterizing the feeling of the sublime. Awe involves two simultaneously felt factors: that of attraction and that of repulsion. The negative pole is response to the sense of our own insignificance as material entities, the positive to our destiny as moral agents. Such a compound feeling Kant describes as a *spiritual feeling* (*Geistesgefühl*).[59] It sets the mind in motion by the sense of limits it poses to our imaginative powers and the breaking of limits by reason as the demand for totality. It is in the space of that demand that the idea of God arises.

There is another type of spiritual feeling, that for the moral law, which Kant terms respect. But awe is much more than respect. Respect is more reserved; awe is clearly an emotional response, a being moved.[60] Encounter with the presentations of nature that occasion the

---

56. No. 23, 83–84.
57. Friedrich Paulsen, *Immanuel Kant: His Life and Doctrine,* trans. J. Creighton and A. Lefevre (New York: Ungar, 1972), 53.
58. *CPrR,* 166.   59. Introduction VII, 29.
60. No. 29, 109; cf. *CPrR,* 40, 79ff.

sense of the sublime stands in the relation of mutual causality with respect for the moral law. The sense of the immensity and overwhelming power of nature heightens the sense of the greatness involved in moral activity.

In the experience of the sublime we find "the straining of the imagination to use nature as a schema for ideas."[61] Nature's threat to our organic being schematizes the opposition to our appetites that is inevitable in following the moral call. But the notion of the sublime also involves reason using imagination to look "into the infinite, which for it is an abyss," and thus to link our moral call to the infinite beyond.[62]

In the experience of the sublime, the starry skies and the moral law call out to one another: the sense of the moral law (and thus of the sublimity of our moral calling) saves us from being crushed by the sense of our own insignificance in the experience of the immensity of the starry skies. The Psalmist, looking at the skies with no knowledge of modern astronomy, exclaimed: "When I consider the heavens, the work of your hands, what is man that You are mindful of him?"[63] Of course astronomical knowledge can deepen that.[64]

Kant's whole approach to things in the third critique suggests that "we are meant" by what underlies nature. The starry skies above and the moral law within are ciphers of the supersensuous ground that one is led to think of as having arranged things for our moral destiny.[65] The moral sense is what allows us to hold our ground by reason of an awareness of our own moral righteousness in relation to the supersensuous. Without that, the experience of the immeasurable magnitude or the overwhelming power of nature would crush us. When it is linked to the notion of a personal ground, it appears as the wrath of God.[66]

A higher cultural development is required for the experience of the sublime than for the experience of the beautiful. The former requires

61. No. 29, 104.   62. Ibid.
63. Psalm 8:4.
64. Kant's reading of the aesthetic situation here returns to the Psalmist's condition. It involves explicit abstraction from all that we know about the stars in terms of scientific knowledge. It deals with just what we immediately experience. That is a loss, for experience is always invaded by what we know. And the experience of insignificance is enhanced by what we know through astronomy. The pious Pascal's horror at the thought of the infinity of empty space was brought about by the new realization of the immensity of the starry skies introduced by the Copernican view (Blaise Pascal, *Pensées*, no. 206). Given the size of the orbit of the earth (186,000,000 miles) and the lack of observable shift in the so-called fixed stars as we are carried seasonally from one side of the diameter of earth's orbit to its opposite, the distance of those stars is revealed as staggeringly more than the Psalmist could ever have dreamed.
65. No. 86, 292–98.   66. No. 28, 102–3.

taste, the latter, moral or spiritual feeling.[67] Both "are final in reference to the moral feeling,"[68] the beautiful preparing us to love something apart from interest, the sublime to esteem something in opposition to sensory interest.

6. THE MORAL DIMENSION

It is the moral sense, turned into awe when linked to the immensity of size and power in nature, that ultimately rescues aesthetic sensibility from the danger of a fall into triviality and vanity. Both the experience of the sublime and the experience of the beautiful are read by Kant ultimately in terms of their relation to the moral. The moral sense rescues taste from its constant temptation to fall into a wallowing in the merely agreeable or to lose itself in the trivially beautiful.[69] The moral sense gains its ultimate deepening through the experience of the sublime, in which the moral is intrinsically involved, for there we feel most deeply the collusion between the immensity of the super-sensuous ground of things and our moral calling.

But even apart from its ultimate affective grounding in the sense of the sublime, moral sensibility is fostered by the perception of the beautiful, insofar as both moral sensibility and the perception of the beautiful involve detachment from appetite and attachment to the normative. In this way beauty becomes the symbol of the moral.[70] For Kant the relation is reciprocal: moral interest is likewise the ground of attention to beauty.[71] Indeed, the interplay of the perception of beauty and moral perception brings about the projective sense of moral qualities in nature: the majesty and stateliness of mountains, the innocent, modest or soft character of colors.

We said before that Kant finds the ideal of beauty in the human being acting morally. The notion of *ideal* in Kant is idiosyncratic: it is "the representation of an individual existence as adequate to an idea," where 'idea' involves a surplus intention beyond what can be adequately filled.[72] But a human being is just such an idea, moved by the intention of totality that founds reason. For Kant the ideas of reason are only filled morally and hence the ideal of beauty is the human

---

67. No. 29, 104ff.   68. No. 29, 108.
69. No. 53, 170.
70. No. 59, 196–200; no. 29, 108. See Donald Crawford, *Kant's Aesthetic Theory* (Madison: University of Wisconsin Press, 1974), 66–69 and 142–59, on the grounding of aesthetics in morality. For a critique of Crawford, see Paul Guyer, *Kant and the Claims of Taste* (Cambridge: Harvard University Press, 1979), 351–94.
71. No. 88, 310.
72. No. 17, 69; *CPuR*, A568/B596ff.

being acting morally.[73] How that is the ideal of beauty is difficult to see in any other realm than art. Assuming Quasimodo to be a real and not a fictitious character, his saving the heroine, though morally edifying, is scarcely aesthetic. However, one could speak of Victor Hugo's literary rendering of the action as indeed aesthetic. The ideal of beauty would seem to be fulfilled in the artistic presentation of sublime action. Along these lines, but with the claim to a speculative and not simply a moral filling of the drive for totality, Hegel will present the ideal of beauty in the human form as the adequate expression of the supersensuous beyond viewed as finite mind.[74]

The moral dimension is involved more deeply in the aesthetic, in that Kant claims that the universality and necessity of aesthetic judgment place a *duty* upon us to cultivate aesthetic judgment. That duty translates both the duty to develop our talents and the duty to communicate to others our sensibility in the perception of beauty and thus to enter into an aesthetic community. In this way we learn one manner of concretizing what it means to treat humanity in ourselves and others as an end and not simply as a means.[75]

7. NATURE AS DIVINE ART

As I said earlier, what gathers the whole Kantian enterprise together is the notion of nature as the creation of divine art. The position has several steps. First of all, there is the antinomy of taste generated both by Horace's claim, *De gustibus non disputandum est*, "There ought to be no disputing about tastes," and by the fact of continual dispute.[76] Dispute involves conceptual claims, but the judgment of taste as such is without a concept (though it may be accompanied by one). Kant distinguishes here between a determinate and an indeterminate concept. The latter has no specified content other than that of a supersensuous ground that makes the universality of the claims possible.[77] He links the concept of the supersensuous to the supersensuous ground involved in the presentation of nature in the first critique, of freedom in the second, and of subjective purposiveness in the third.[78] In a second step, following the development of the third critique, the supersensuous ground underlying both nature without and freedom

73. No. 17, 77.
74. G. W. F. Hegel, *The Philosophy of Fine Art*, trans. F. Osmaston (London: Bell, 1920), I, 209ff.
75. No. 59, 199. See Salim Kemal, *Kant and Fine Art* (Oxford: Clarendon, 1986), 9, on treating humanity as an end through the development of aesthetic community.
76. No. 56, 183.   77. No. 57, 184ff.
78. No. 57, Remark II, 190–91.

within is further filled in by the notion of a divine artist as author of creation. The supersensuous ground of things is viewed as an archetypal intellect constructing things of nature according to normative ideas that are the natural equivalent of aesthetic ideas. As the genius's subsumption of the mechanisms of his craft under the inspiration of aesthetic ideas produces an artwork that is live, organic, charged with vital energy, so the divine artist subsumes the determinable mechanisms of nature in the production of the various species of life.[79] But unless, in a third step, such a notion is also linked up with the moral dimension, such a ground can be also thought of as an artistic demon—just as Schopenhauer and Nietzsche viewed it: a demonic Will or Will to Power generating, in the vastness of its creative power, not only beauty and satisfaction, but also ugliness and suffering.[80]

For Kant the divine artist is the source of the inspiration of genius that affects the sensibility of the community, weaning it from the dominance of appetite and aiding in the transition to the moral dimension. The moral community draws nature into the constitution of the community viewed as a kingdom of ends through the cultivation of aesthetic sensibility.[81] But the whole aesthetic realm is given its greatest deepening through the experience of the sublime, which is the emotional ground of Kant's critical enterprise. The starry skies above and the moral law within call out to one another. Both afford us a sense of the vaster, more powerful character of the supersensuous ground that gives us our moral end.

The somewhat surprising discovery of an emotional state at the ground of the apparent coolness of the Kantian enterprise places Kant's constant warning against religious enthusiasm and fanaticism in a significant light.[82] His basic admonition that speculative knowledge has definite limits that do not extend into the supersensuous is a bridle made to rein in his own enthusiasm. The third critique comes perilously close to transcending the limits. But just when we think that he has surpassed them, Kant reminds us that this is all in the mode of "as if." The starry skies, in their vastness newly discovered through modern astronomy, schematize the infinity of the noumenal to which we are directed, but which we can never reach in this life. The perception of the sublime and of the beautiful, taken together, support the moral project in this life; the sublime suggests—but only suggests—its fulfillment hereafter.

79. *FI*, 18–20; no. 23, 84; no. 51, 164; no. 57, 184ff; no. 86, 292ff.
80. Schopenhauer, *WWR*, IV, no. 54, I, 272ff; Nietzsche, *BT*, 29ff.
81. No. 60, 200–202.
82. No. 29, 115–16. Cf. also Immanuel Kant, *Religion within the Limits of Reason Alone*, trans. T. Greene and H. Hudson (New York: Harper, 1960), 48 and 162–63.

8. CONCLUSION

Kant's *Critique of Judgment* is neither a complete theory of judgment, being restricted to an analysis of reflective judgment, nor a complete inventory of the modes of reflective judgment. It purports to present the analysis of judgment as at least parallel to the analysis of feeling, but it presents little convincing parallel; nor does it do a systematic inventory of the forms of feeling. Rather, it focuses upon two modes of reflective judgment: the aesthetic and the teleological. It unites them under the general concept of purposiveness and thereby draws the critical enterprise into unity. And it does so finally by giving a certain primacy to the aesthetic realm when art is considered as the basic cosmic analogue.

The treatment of the aesthetic provides many incisive analyses. In particular, Kant presents a significant description of the differences between three major aesthetic modalities in the feeling of the agreeable, of the beautiful, and of the sublime. The distinction and relation between disinterest and interest, conceptlessness and conceptuality, distills the particular features of the experience of the beautiful from their ordinary concomitants and links them back to those concomitants. The care Kant takes in distinguishing the positions along the spectrum of types of epistemological stringency that attach to them is admirable. Overall, the *Critique of Judgment* leads the way from the mechanical, value-free view of the universe characteristic of the Enlightenment to an organic, value-laden view promoted by early nineteenth-century thinkers in the age of Romanticism. Kant's third critique provides penetrating insights into significant structures in the field of experience and into modes of construal for the whole suggested in experience. It also helps us to understand a historical transition of major proportions.

WALTER HINDERER

In 1794, the intellectual, dramatist, historian, essayist, and philosopher Friedrich Schiller wrote to the world-renowned poet and statesman of Weimar, Johann Wolfgang von Goethe, whose friendship he had recently won with diplomatic skill. In this intentionally self-critical letter, Schiller contends that "my reason really functions more in a symbolizing way and so I vacillate like some sort of hermaphrodite between the abstract concept and the visual perception, the set rule and the sensibility, between the technical mind and the genius. Especially in my early years, this gave me a rather awkward reputation, both in the field of speculation and in poetry. Usually, the poet overcame me when I should have philosophized and the philosophical spirit dominated when I should have been writing poetry."[1] Yet German drama is so indebted to this amphibiousness for its intelligent theater idiom that it has been difficult ever since, as Thomas Mann wrote in his Schiller speech, "to speak of the stage without schillerizing."[2] Goethe never ceased to admire Schiller's drama *Wallenstein,* but he remarked to Eckermann on July 23, 1827, with friendly regret that, with Schiller, "those two great aids, history and philosophy, get in the way of parts of the work and prevent its purely poetic success."[3] Schiller's philosophical writings met with a similar ambivalent reaction. One fervent admirer of Schiller's saw only "hieroglyphs" in the *On the Aesthetic Education of Man* (*Ueber die ästhetische Erziehung des Menschen in einer Reihe von Briefen,* 1795),[4] while a reviewer thought it an adventurous whim "to want to depict Kantian ideas," as if in a

1. Johann Wolfgang von Goethe, *Briefwechsel mit Friedrich Schiller* (Zürich: Artemis, 1964), 19–20.

2. Thomas Mann, "Versuch über Schiller." T. M., *Schriften und Reden zur Literatur, Kunst und Philosophie,* 3 (Frankfurt a.M.: S. Fischer, 1960), 331.

3. Johann Peter Eckermann, *Gespräche mit Goethe* (Zürich: Artemis³, 1976), 267.

4. Carl Ludwig Fernow. See *Schillers Werke. Nationalausgabe,* 27 (Weimar: Hermann Böhlaus Nachfolger, 1962), 239.

drama.[5] Even the duke of Augustenburg, to whom Schiller had dedicated his *On the Aesthetic Education of Man,* believed that "good old Schiller was really not meant to be a philosopher. He needs a translator to develop with philosophical precision what he had written in beautiful poetry, to translate him [in other words] from poetic into philosophical language."[6] Fichte even criticized Schiller for putting the image in the place of the concept and wrote discouragingly: "*Your* way . . . is completely new and I know among the ancient and the modern writers no one who could be compared to you in this regard. You bind the powers of imagination, which can only be free, and want to force them to think. But they cannot. This is the cause, I believe, for the fatiguing effort it costs me to read your philosophical writings. . . . I have to translate everything you write before I can understand it; and others have the same experience."[7]

Fichte's polemic is, of course, his answer to Schiller's fundamental criticism of Fichte's own abstract style of writing and lecturing. Rather arrogantly, Schiller countered Fichte, with whom he had from time to time been friendly enough to play cards: "It is my ongoing tendency to employ an ensemble of emotional powers, in addition to the treatise itself, and to the greatest extent possible, to affect them all at the same time. I do not simply desire to make my thoughts clear to another but to give him my entire soul and to affect his sensuous and intellectual powers."[8]

In his essay *On the Necessary Limitations in the Use of Beauty of Form Particularly When Expounding on Philosophical Truths (Ueber die nothwendigen Grenzen beim Gebrauch schöner Formen,* 1795), Schiller developed this idea further. He differentiated between scientific and popular exposition, whereby the former deals only with principles and the latter appeals solely to the imagination, and then combined both literary or lecture styles in a synthesis of "beautiful literary manner."[9] Thus Schiller articulated the unity of reason and imagination, concept and image, thereby approaching the idea of the totality of man, a notion fundamental not only to his philosophy and aesthetic, but to

5. Jakob, "Annalen der Philosophie und des philosophischen Geistes," Halle 1795. Julius W. Braun, ed., *Schiller und Goethe im Urtheile ihrer Zeitgenossen. Schiller,* 2 (Leipzig: Bernhard Schlicke, 1882), 32.

6. In: *Schiller und der Herzog von Augustenburg in Briefen.* Hans Schulz, ed. (Jena: Dietrich, 1905), 153.

7. *J. G. Fichtes Briefwechsel.* Hans Schulz, ed. (Leipzig: H. Haessel, 1925), 473.

8. Letter of August 3, 1795 in *Schillers Briefe,* 4. Fritz Jonas, ed. (Stuttgart/Leipzig/Berlin/Vienna: Deutsche Verlagsanstalt, 1892/96), 221.

9. *Schillers Werke. Nationalausgabe,* 21 (Weimar: Hermann Böhlau Nachfolger, 1963), 3–27.

the educational program of the eighteenth century from Lessing, Wieland, and Herder to Goethe and on to Jean Paul and Hölderlin.[10] In his *Letters in Promotion of Humanity* (*Briefe zur Beförderung der Humanität*, 1772), for example, Herder defined the concept of "humanity" as the "character of our species" and elaborated: "We are born only with a predisposition towards [humanity], which really has to be taught us. We do not come into the world with it complete, yet, in the world, it should be our goal, the sum of our efforts, our value."[11] In 1770, Christoph Martin Wieland, a novelist, poet, journalist, essayist, and translator famous throughout Europe in the eighteenth century, made the following statement that had many repercussions: "Man, as he slips from the formative hand of nature, is practically nothing but potential. He has to develop and expand himself, give himself the final polish that covers him with splendor and grace—in short, man in a way must be his own second creator."[12] In this context, "poetic art" has a very specific purpose that Wieland calls "the beautification and ennobling of human nature."[13] Schiller's aesthetic program prescribes a similar role to art as a means to self-completion. In the programmatic formulation of his twenty-first *Letter On the Aesthetic Education of Man* he wrote that "it is, then, not just poetic licence but philosophical truth when we call beauty our second creator."[14]

Whereas not only are animals and plants endowed by nature "with their destiny" but this destiny is fulfilled by nature alone, Schiller explains in his essay *On Grace and Dignity* (*Ueber Anmut und Würde*, 1793) that nature gives man "only his destiny," and leaves up to him "its fulfillment."[15] Man in his quality of person therefore has "alone of all beings the privilege to break the chain of necessity by his will," that is, by free action.[16] Art, understood in this way, is the teaching of humanity; Herder explained in his *Letters in Promotion of Humanity*: "For the nature of man is art. Everything for which there is a predisposition in his existence can and must in time become art."[17]

10. For the context, see also my essay, "Beiträge Wielands zur deutschen Klassik." W. H., *Über deutsche Literatur und Rede* (Munich: Wilhelm Fink, 1964), 9–38.

11. "Über das Wort und den Begriff der Humanität." *Herders Werke in fünf Bänden*, 5 (Berlin/Weimar: Augbau, 1964), 103.

12. *Wielands Werke*, 3. Fritz Martini and Hans Werner Seiffert, eds. (Munich: Carl Hanser, 1965/68), 231.

13. Ibid., 271.

14. *Schillers Werke. Nationalausgabe*, 20, op. cit., 378.

15. Ibid., 272. See also Friedrich Schiller, *On the Aesthetic Education of Man in a Series of Letters*. Elisabeth Wilkinson and L. A. Willoughby, eds. (Oxford: Clarendon Publication, 1967), 147.

16. *Schillers Werke. Nationalausgabe.* loc. cit.

17. *Herders Werke*, op. cit., p. 96.

Existentially expressed, yet in adherence to Schiller's thought processes, we could summarize that, although nature supplies the condition of the possibility of existence, the expansion and fulfillment of this possibility are within the power of the individual. The artists' duty thus includes the cultivation, ennoblement, and humanization of human nature (*natura*) through art (*ars*). "Mankind's dignity," wrote Schiller in his philosophical poem *The Artists* (*Die Künstler,* 1789), is put into the artist's own hands.[18] The foregoing already may have made clear that Schiller's philosophy of art actually represents a set of instructions for aesthetic education and contains a program that is at the same time didactic and anthropological.

However, Schiller's philosophy of art or, as I would prefer to say, his anthropological aesthetics, has historical-philosophical, cultural-historical, political, and socio-critical aspects and ramifications. Schiller's writing style, through which he intended to allow the reader to sense with his imagination what the author had been thinking, appears to reduce the accessibility of his philosophical writings, as does his irritating tendency to jump from one context to another without giving any warning of his intention to do so. There is a continuous alternation among a variety of subjects. No sooner has Schiller defined the fundamental aspects of individual human history than these same aspects are identified as the foundations of universal history. Similarly, the theory of cultural-philosophical triads immediately is transformed into a political, sociological, aesthetic, or individual-psychological three-step experiment. The frequent change of ordered subject areas, this *metabasis eis allo genos,* does not lead in Schiller to a poeticization or aestheticization of all aspects of life, as it does in German Romanticism. Instead, it may be explained by the specific method of the aesthetic or poetic spirit. It is that *mode utopique,* a utopian method that combines analysis and criticism of social and political reality with the intellectual experiment "of new possibilities" that make better offers.[19] Indirectly, the failures of society and of the contemporary context in which Schiller was writing may be discerned from the dream, the ideal anticipation of that which should be.

In the following, I will attempt to clarify Schiller's aesthetic-anthropological program with the help of a number of pertinent examples. In other words, I will try to translate—to use Augustenburg's and

<hr>

18. *Friedrich Schiller: Sämtliche Werke.* Gerhard Fricke and Herbert G. Göpfert, eds. (Munich: Carl Hanser, 1962), 173–87, esp. 186.

19. See my essay, "Utopische Elemente in Schillers ästhetischer Anthropologie." *Literarische Utopie-Entwürfe.* Hiltrud Gnüg, ed. (Frankfurt a.M.: Suhrkamp, 1982), 173–86.

Fichte's phrase—his philosophy of art on the basis of his youthful writings, the two dissertations, the *Philosophical Letters* (*Philosophische Briefe*, 1786) and their central piece, the *Theosophy of Julius*, as well as the three great philosophical essays, *Grace and Dignity*, *On the Aesthetic Education of Man*, and *On Naive and Sentimental Poetry* (*Ueber naive und sentimentalische Dichtung*, 1795/96).

I

In the eighteenth century there was a close relationship between philosophy and physiology and between philosophy and medicine. Schiller's training and his own tendency led him to align himself with the "philosophizing physicians" who propagated unity of psyche and soma. Schiller accordingly entitled his first dissertation, presented in a Stuttgart military academy, the so-called "Karlsschule," *Philosophy of Physiology* (*Philosophie der Physiologie*, 1779), and his second bore the revealing title *Essay on the Connection between the Animal and Spiritual Nature of Man* (*Versuch über den Zusammenhang der thierischen Natur des Menschen mit seiner geistigen*, 1780). Both essays reveal that Schiller's philosophical program was oriented from its inception toward a psycho-physiological approach to mankind—in other words, toward what has been called since the end of the eighteenth century anthropology. The fundamentals of his philosophy of art are to be found in his youthful writings. In the nineties, when he was intensively involved with the study of Immanuel Kant, they needed only to be modified and, above all, conceptually differentiated.

Already in his first dissertation the young Schiller defined "the destiny of man" as "to be God's peer."[20] At the same time, he pointed out the utopian aspect of such a demand. His formulation is so characteristic of later writings that we should remember it here: "Man's ideal [to be God's peer] is infinite: but the spirit is eternal. Eternity is the measure of infinity. In other words, the spirit will develop infinitely but will never attain its ideal."[21] Here Schiller formulates his basic, dualistic, anthropological concept, which he transforms in nearly existential terminology in his eleventh *Letter On the Aesthetic Education of Man* into a dialectic between person and condition. This dissertation is furthermore the first of his many attempts to create a synthesis from the dichotomy of human existence.

20. "Philosophie der Physiologie." *Schillers Werke. Nationalausgabe*, 20, op. cit., 10.
21. Ibid. See also Friedrich Schiller, *Medicine, Psychology and Literature*. Kenneth Dewhurst and Nigel Reeves, eds. (Oxford: Sandford Publications, 1978), 150. The "spirit" in my translation is rendered here as "mind."

Schiller introduces the concept of "transmutative force" in order to heal the "rift between the world and the spirit" of which he speaks in his dissertation. In his lecture entitled *What Can a Good Permanent Stage Really Achieve* (*Was kann eine gute stehende Schaubühne eigentlich wirken*, 1784) he finds this possibility in "aesthetic sense," in a "mediating condition," which he then defines more specifically in *On the Aesthetic Education of Man* as an "aesthetic condition." But even this state, implying aesthetic mediation between existence and time, life and ideal, formal and material impulse, is no more than a way to correct a deficit that society has incurred. This correction at least has the potential to set free man's lost human totality. In Schiller's lecture, "aesthetic sense" or the "feeling for the beautiful" already has the function of recreating human potential that had been reduced or suppressed by the demands of business and profession.[22]

The way to higher humanity leads, like the way to politics, through art. In his second letter *On the Aesthetic Education of Man*, Schiller pronounced the familiar conviction "that in order to solve that problem of politics in practice, [man] must approach it through the problem of the aesthetic, because it is only through Beauty that man makes his way to Freedom."[23] The principle of beauty not only leads to freedom, however, but is also the prerequisite for the autonomy of the person. In his essay *On Grace and Dignity*, Schiller defines the three conditions under which man can exist: 1. man suppresses the demands of his sensuous (physical) nature; 2. man fulfills the demands of sensuous (physical) nature, to which he subjects his reason; 3. sensuous (physical) and rational nature are in harmony one with the other.[24] The first condition, or the first existential situation, is equally displeasing to beauty and to grace and thus to the entire aesthetic sphere. Politically, this condition approximates that of a monarchy in which the ruler disallows any free initiative. The second condition, too, in which man succumbs to materialism, has a negative effect on the aesthetic and political spheres, according to Schiller.[25] In this case, material concern determines aesthetics and political anarchy reigns. The third condition, in which the senses and reason are in harmony, unites in a "beautiful" bond grace and dignity, predilection and obligation, and ideally, in the political sphere, law and anarchy.[26]

In *On the Aesthetic Education of Man*, individual-psychologically the

22. *Schillers Werke*, op. cit., 90.
23. Ibid., p. 312. See also Friedrich Schiller, *On the Aesthetic Education of Man in a Series of Letters*, 9.
24. *Schillers Werke*, op. cit., 280.
25. Ibid., 281–84.   26. Ibid., 282.

aesthetic condition and politically the *aesthetic state* correspond to this condition. On this level, the state reflects the "totality of human potential" which is reduced or eliminated under other conditions. A prerequisite for the "state of freedom" is the "aesthetic condition," which itself can be achieved only through art, for it is art that frees men from the opposing drives of material and form, nature and culture, body and soul, and leads them to experience their own freedom and to realize all their abilities and possibilities. While in Schiller's anthropological program the physical quality of a thing can directly relate to "our sensual condition," the logical quality "to our reason," and the moral quality "to our will," the aesthetic quality relates to "the totality of our different abilities."[27] In other words, only aesthetic experience is able "to cultivate the totality of our sensuous and intellectual abilities in the greatest possible harmony."[28]

A quotation from Schiller's letter of July 13, 1793, to the duke of Augustenburg serves to illustrate the extent to which this program from the *On the Aesthetic Education of Man* was directed against the events of the French Revolution, which Schiller initially had supported: "Any durable reform," he writes, "must emanate from a way of thinking, and where the principle is rotten, nothing healthy or benign can grow. Alone the character of its citizens creates and upholds the state and makes political and civilian freedom possible."[29] Only the "art of idealization," the purposes of which Schiller detailed in 1791 in a sharp criticism of the then-popular poet Gottfried August Bürger, can lift "mankind's character from its deep decay."[30] This "art of idealization" equally implies an aesthetic, educational, moral, and political demand;[31] it provides an answer to the quality of contemporary conditions and of society. Thus, in his consideration of Bürger's poems, Schiller defines the poet's "first and most important duty" as the "greatest possible" ennoblement of his own "individuality" and its purification "to the purest, most glorious humanity."[32] The level of education of the poet himself is obviously the prerequisite for such an idealization. Thus, according to Schiller, deficits in literary works can and should be attributed to the person who created them. Values missing in the person cannot be contained in the artistic production.

As we have seen, the idea of mankind begins already in Schiller's first dissertation with the concept of "being a peer of God."[33] This

---

27. Ibid., 375–76. See also Schiller, *Aesthetic Education*, 141–43.
28. *Schillers Werke*, 376. See also Schiller, *Aesthetic Education*, 143.
29. *Schillers Briefe*, 3, op. cit., 335.
30. "Über Bürgers Gedichte," *Schiller. Sämtliche Werke*, 5, op. cit., 970–85, esp. 979.
31. Ibid.   32. Ibid., 972.
33. Schiller, "Philosophie der Physiologie," op. cit., 10.

idea as an "eternal ideal" that cannot be reached is the orientation point for Schiller's anthropology and aesthetic. Behind this ideal, or, more specifically, behind the need to approach this ideal, is Schiller's intention that can be traced throughout his philosophical writings: to stimulate man to the optimal expansion of his potential. For this reason, Schiller opposes anything that threatens this expansion: repressive political institutions and one-sided cultural development in which either feelings dominate principles or principles dominate feelings. Because man's actions are often unilaterally determined by one of the two basic directions, either the physical or the intellectual power, art plays a decisive role as a correcting mediator between the two powers.

That which holds true individual-historically for the primacy of the powers, whether of feelings or of principles, also holds true universal-historically. As Schiller demonstrates in *On the Aesthetic Education of Man*, the condition of the "savage when feeling predominates over principle" is the opposite of that of the "barbarian when principle destroys feeling."[34] Specific forms of government also correspond to these individual conditions, the natural state and the legal or rational state, but the shortcomings of the two political institutions are obvious. Particularly the legal or rational state of his time inspired Schiller to make his famous criticism in the sixth letter *On the Aesthetic Education of Man*, where he writes: "Eternally chained to a single, tiny fragment of the Whole, man himself develops into nothing but a fragment; eternally hearing only the monotonous sound of the wheel that turns, he never develops the harmony of his being, and instead of imprinting humanity on his nature, he becomes nothing more than the imprint of his occupation, of his specialized knowledge."[35]

The natural state and the rational state are equally far removed from the goal of a state of freedom that represents the "totality of human potential." To create such a state and provide it with an adequate constitution, a corresponding elaboration of the human character is necessary. Schiller writes in this context that "totality of character must be found in a people that is capable and worthy of exchanging the state of necessity for the state of freedom."[36] It is self-evident that this idea of an aesthetic state based on aesthetic condition was expressed, too, against the terror regime of the French revolutionary government.

Just as the aesthetic state in Schiller's thought experiment represents

---

34. *Schillers Werke. Nationalausgabe*, 20, op. cit., 318. See also Schiller, *Aesthetic Education*, 21.

35. *Schillers Werke*, 20, op. cit., 323. See also Schiller, *Aesthetic Education*, 35.

36. *Schillers Werke*, 20, op. cit., 318. See also Schiller, *Aesthetic Education*, 23.

an improvement in the contrasting dynamic and ethical states of his twenty-seventh *Letter on the Aesthetic Education of Man,* the play-impulse, or play-drive, another expression for the *aesthetic condition,* reconciles the two conditions or drives of material and form.[37] Expressed in modern terms, the play-impulse is the aesthetic action of the aesthetic condition. To the extent that the play-impulse—even only temporarily—enables man "to abolish time within time, to reconcile becoming with absolute being and change with identity," he experiences through and with it the highest concept of humanity.[38] Schiller thus writes in his fifteenth letter *On the Aesthetic Education of Man:* "Man plays only when he is a human being in the fullest sense of the word and *he is fully a human being only when he plays.*"[39]

Play, in the rhetorical formula of chiasmus that illuminates the law of mutual effect, is only possible for the man who is on a higher level and who can experience "fulfillment" in the instant in which he plays. In Schiller's view, "beauty" is the "consummation of [man's] humanity" and therefore the "object common to both impulses or drives."[40] Contemplating the beautiful, the spirit is "at a happy mid-point between law and necessity," as he writes in his fifteenth *Letter.*[41] Only the play of art develops the nature of man at once, only play makes man complete. Understood in this way, the ideally beautiful and the ideally human are, for Schiller, two names for the same concept. He stresses, however, that the place where man can be completely himself is limited to the "world of semblance,"[42] to the aesthetic condition as "the highest of all bounties, as the gift of humanity itself."[43] The scope of the beautiful frees man from the reigning laws of absolute formality and of absolute reality, but Schiller stresses the playful character of this action and elaborates: "With beauty man shall *only play,* and it is *with beauty only* that he shall play."[44]

II

If in his critical essays of 1782 Schiller appears to consider painting in poetry to be dangerous and to prefer, as in drama, a manipulation of affects, in 1794 in a positive assessment of the poetry of Friedrich

37. *Schillers Werke,* 20, op. cit., 410.
38. Ibid., 353. See also Schiller, *Aesthetic Education,* 97.
39. *Schillers Werke,* 20, op. cit., 359. See also Schiller, *Aesthetic Education,* 107.
40. *Schillers Werke,* 20, op. cit., 356. See also Schiller, *Aesthetic Education,* 103.
41. *Schillers Werke,* 20, op. cit., 357. See also Schiller, *Aesthetic Education,* 105.
42. *Schillers Werke,* 20, op. cit., 401. See also Schiller, *Aesthetic Education,* 197.
43. *Schillers Werke,* 20, op. cit., 378. See also Schiller, *Aesthetic Education,* 147.
44. *Schillers Werke,* 20, op. cit., 359. See also Schiller, *Aesthetic Education,* 107.

Matthisson he put greater value on the painterly depictive form in poetry. Here he claims that we actually view "every painterly and poetic composition as a piece of music" and apply "to a certain extent the same laws to them."[45] This argumentation also places the modern propinquity of poetry and music in an anthropological connection, for the poet should not just "affect the heart," but should also *determine* the state of our sensibility." In the assessment of Matthisson's poems as in other writings of the nineties, Schiller speaks of the necessity of a mutation of the individual into the species as an aesthetic as well as an anthropological principle. Here he demands two qualities from a work of art: first, the "necessary relationship to its object (objective truth)," and secondly, the "necessary relationship of this object ... to the human abilities of feeling (subjective generality)."[46] Thus Schiller first intimates the sentimental operation that he describes extensively in *On Naive and Sentimental Poetry* (*Über naive und Sentimentalische Dichtung*) and that he claims is the prerequisite for aesthetic and conscious progress. He stresses here as he had in his review of Bürger that every aesthetic progress requires individual progress on the part of man.

Since at our level of culture the totality of man is no longer expressed in the reality that surrounds him, as had been the case for the Greeks, the modern artist must recreate in and from himself through the "depiction of the ideal" that which he can no longer achieve by "imitating reality." Whereas the ancient—that is, the naive—poets moved us through nature, the modern—that is, the sentimental—poets touch us with ideas. The central thesis of Schiller's work is that "nature brings [man] to unity with himself, art separates and divides him, through the ideal he returns to unity."[47] Schiller demands of the sentimental poet that he spiritualize "from the inside out [the] raw material through the subject," that he recover "through reflexion the poetic content that the exterior sensibility had lacked," and that he supplement "nature through the idea."[48] In other words, the poet should transform a limited objective into an infinite one by means of a sentimental operation. Of course, this operation is possible for us only if the poet has cultivated and educated himself correspondingly.

Schiller wrote to Wilhelm von Humboldt on December 25, 1795, that the relationship between "naive and sentimental *poetry* . . . [is the same as that of] naive and sentimental *humanity*,"[49] so the obligation

<hr>

45. "Über Matthissons Gedichte." *Friedrich Schiller. Sämtliche Werke,* 5, op. cit., 999.
46. Ibid., p. 996.
47. "Über naive und sentimentalische Dichtung." *Schillers Werke,* 20, op. cit., 438.
48. Ibid., 478.
49. *Schillers Briefe,* 4, op. cit., 366.

of art is bound to the development of mankind. In the argumentation of the essay *On Naive and Sentimental Poetry* he writes that the path the modern poets are taking is the same that man both as an individual and as a species must take. However, since the ideal is infinite and can never be reached by man, the "cultured man," that is, the idealist, can never achieve perfection in his way, although "natural man," the realist, is quite able to do so. Yet Schiller confronts this measure with two goals: a) the goal "that man reaches for through culture" and b) the one "that he *achieves* through nature."[50] This comparison leads him to the characteristic conclusion that the goal of modern man, or of the idealist, is "immensely preferable" to that of natural man, the realist. Whereas the realist or naive poet achieves "merit because of the absolute achievement of infinite greatness," the idealist or sentimental poet achieves merit "by approximation to infinite greatness."[51] Man's progress is thus possible only if man "cultivates" himself, that is, if he moves from the naive to the sentimental stage.

The concept of idealization and of sentimental operation represents a reaction to the cultural conditions of Schiller's time, the social and human deficits of which, according to him, could be corrected or neutralized only by the intervention of the aesthetic. According to Schiller's essay *On Naive and Sentimental Poetry*, art and poetry are defined by the fact that, in the aesthetic sphere, they anticipate intended anthropological and social progress and give "mankind the most perfect and complete expression possible."[52] Schiller demands from the artist nothing more and nothing less than the development of the individual to culture. Modern art as opposed to ancient art has a unique opportunity to lead back on a higher level to lost nature and to unity by means of the ideal. Whereas ancient art (which Schiller in his essay calls naive poetry) "depicts the *object with all its limitations, individualizes* it," modern art (which he calls sentimental poetry) removes "*all limitations* from its object, *idealizes* it."[53]

Schiller characterizes the differences between naive and sentimental poetry with the two fundamental concepts of "individualization" and "idealization." If the former by virtue of its very form can be "infinite," the latter can be "infinite because of its material."[54] There are two different sources of error in the character of the two types of art and their level of development in human consciousness. Naive poetry produces an "object without thought or reflection" and sentimental poetry

50. *Schillers Werke,* 20, loc. cit.
51. Ibid.
53. Ibid., 470.
52. Ibid., 437.
54. Ibid.

produces "a play of thought and reflection without object."[55] There can be no question but that Schiller prefers, for both aesthetic and historical-political reasons, the "depiction of the absolute," that is, the operation of sentimental poetry, to "absolute depiction,"[56] or the operation of naive poetry. Only in this way does his requirement of a "sentimental operation" make sense, that spiritualizes "through the subject material that is too rough on the exterior from the interior," supplements "nature through the idea," and makes "a limited and finite object an infinite one."[57]

For Schiller, the artist's present position renders the sentimental operation absolutely necessary. In *Naive and Sentimental Poetry,* the modes of the expression of feeling as well as the process of idealization are both part of the equipment of the sentimental, modern poet. In Schiller, the three basic modes of the expression of feeling correspond to the three basic types of poetry: satire, elegy, and idyll. Sentimental poetry differs from naive poetry primarily in that the former applies ideas to reality or to the real state or condition, while the latter "remains in the real state or condition."[58] The sentimental poet thus is confronted with two contrary objects: the ideal and experience. In this context, three conditions are conceivable:

1. contradiction between the real state (or condition) and the ideal (satire);

2. harmony with the real state (or condition) and the ideal (idyll);

3. alternating states of contradiction and harmony, stillness and movement (elegy).

Yet when Schiller in the course of his essay speaks of the impossibility of naive poetry in his time and defends his opinion with cultural-historical arguments against Rousseau, one wonders why he goes on to criticize the sentimental poet and to claim: "Every true genius must be naive, or he is none."[59] Furthermore, Schiller believes that the "naive poet-genius" still needs "support from the outside, since the sentimental nourishes and cleans itself."[60] The naive poet is dependent on experience and on the reality that surrounds him. What happens, however, if the naive poet does not find these prerequisites fulfilled in the reality of his time? In that case, reasons Schiller, he must step out "of his manner" or stage and become a sentimental poet—he must progress from the naive to the sentimental operation. Goethe represents for Schiller the naive poet-genius who no longer finds an ade-

55. Ibid., 482.   56. Ibid., 470.
57. Ibid., 478.   58. Ibid., 466.
59. Ibid., 424.   60. Ibid., 476.

quate context and thus must escape into the sentimental operation. Schiller explains the process to Goethe in a letter of August 23, 1794, as follows: "Now, since you were born a German, since your Grecian spirit was contained in a Nordic creation, you had no other choice but either to become a Nordic artist or, according to your imagination and with the help of your ability to think and to reflect, to replace that which reality denied you and thus from the interior and in a rational manner, to give birth to a Greece." Lost nature or reality thus is recreated here through the sentimental operation "with the extra help of the ability to think and to reflect, from the interior and in a rational manner."[61]

The dichotomy of north/south, modern/ancient may be interpreted both as the anticipation of romantic aesthetic theories and as the placement of the concept of eternity within the context of sentimental poetry, which in fact could be defined as a progressive universal poetry.[62] The fact that Schiller at once critically separates and brings together the two poetic concepts of the naive and the sentimental has to do with his ongoing tendency always to change his perspective and finally to achieve a synthesis of contradictory concepts. He first analyzes the respective advantages and disadvantages with regard to the species and then brings them together under the point of view of the "absolute poetic concept." Schiller believes that only both poetic concepts include the necessary content and form to give *"mankind its completest possible expression"* and unify "the idea of mankind in one."[63] For the "ideal of human nature," as Schiller notes towards the end of his essay, is divided between both types of poet, although it is not "completely achieved . . . by either."[64]

The sentimental phase in poetry and in the development of humanity can thus, for Schiller, not be the last phase. This is an aspect of his argument that is frequently overlooked. In a letter to Humboldt dated December 25, 1795, Schiller explains that if sentimental culture or humanity is *"complete* . . . it is no longer sentimental, but ideal. . . . I present the sentimental as only *striving after* the ideal."[65] This also demonstrates that the sentimental operation is not only an aesthetic concept, but also an anthropological and cultural-historical one. Naive poetry is followed by sentimental and finally by ideal poetry, just as

61. Goethe, op. cit., 14.
62. See Peter Szondi, "Das Naive ist das Sentimentalische. Zur Begriffsdialektik in Schillers Abhandlung." P.S., *Lektüren und Lektionen* (Frankfurt a.M.: Suhrkamp, 1973), 88.
63. *Schillers Werke*, 20, op. cit., 437.
64. Ibid., 500.
65. *Schillers Briefe*, 4, op. cit., 366.

naive humanity is followed by sentimental and finally by ideal humanity. The latter—ideal—phase actually leads back "to nature on the
path of reason and of freedom,"[66] which Schiller defined as the goal
at the beginning of his last great essay. Culturally-historically, Schiller
explains the progression in 1793 within the context of his discussion
of a work by Wilhelm von Humboldt: "During the first phase there
were the Greeks," he writes. "We are in the second phase. We can
only hope for the third, and then one won't want to wish the Greeks
back either."[67] Thus Schiller first defined his own standpoint on which
he expanded two years later in *Naive and Sentimental Poetry.*

III

To summarize the most vital points: already in his youthful writings,
Schiller demonstrates a high concept of man whose destiny he identified with being "a peer of God" on the one hand and with the realization of the idea of totality on the other. Even in his early writings,
Schiller indicates how the negative elements in political and social
development have their corollaries in individual psychological history.
Aspects of feeling such as love and hate not only mean either psychic
expansion of the ego (that is, approachment to the ideal of totality)
or reduction of the ego (that is, removal from the ideal of totality),
but also socio-politically mean either a "flowering state of freedom"
or "despotism." For example, Schiller writes in his *Philosophical Letters*
(*Philosophische Briefe*): "Egoism and love divide mankind into two very
dissimilar classes, whose limits never interfere. Egoism erects its center
in itself; Love plants it beyond itself, in the axis of the eternal All.
Love intends unity: egoism is solitude. Love is the co-ruling citizen of
a flourishing republic; egoism, a despot in a desolate creation."[68]
This application of psychological processes to political phenomena
is contained particularly in the central piece of the *Philosophical Letters*,
the "Theosophy of Julius." But already as a pupil in the Karlsschule,
Schiller held a model speech on January 10, 1779, in which he attempted to delve into the hidden motives of history and disclose the
veiled intentions of Augustus as well as the "masked vices" of the lust
for power of Absalom, Ravaillac, and Catiline.[69] In the perspective of
the young Schiller, desire for power and despotism in ideologies and
political-social systems endanger mankind's destiny to be "a peer of
God" and prevent the free development of man's personality. For this

---

66. *Schillers Werke*, 20, op. cit., 414.
67. Ibid., 21, 63.   68. Ibid., 20, 122–23.
69. Ibid., 5.

reason Schiller believes that freedom is the condition that creates the possibility of every self-determination.

Over the years, Schiller formulated in his anthropological speculations three fundamental laws that had pronounced aesthetic implications. The first of these emerged from his dissertation, and he called it, with reference to the "philosophy of physicians,"[70] the "fundamental law of mixed nature." He described it as: "the activities of the body correspond[ing] to the activities of the mind, i.e. any overexertion of the mind will always result in an overexertion of certain bodily functions, just as the equilibrium of the former or the harmonious activity of our spiritual faculties is associated with the most perfect balance of the latter."[71] Schiller also derives from this law of psychosomatic interdependence, as we would call it today, his poetological definition of pathetic depiction, which applies particularly to his youthful dramas, that is, "the two fundamental laws of all tragic art."[72]

Schiller expands on this second fundamental law above all in his writings *On the Sublime* (*Vom Erhabenen*, 1793) and *On Pathos* (*Ueber das Pathetische*, 1793; first published in 1801), which originally belonged together. He defines these "fundamental laws" as follows: "They are *first*: depiction of suffering nature; *second*: depiction of moral independence in suffering."[73] This independence clearly indicates the autonomy of the personality, the "God in us," as Schiller calls the principle in *Grace and Dignity* (*Ueber Anmuth und Würde*, 1793), the suprasensuous in man.[74]

Schiller then expands on the third of his fundamental laws under the aspect of the existential destiny of the "mixed nature" of man in his eleventh letter *On the Aesthetic Education of Man*,[75] and on the dialectic of person and condition and the mutual effect of existence and time. "Two fundamental laws of sensuo-rational nature" are involved that he explains as follows: the first fundamental law "insists upon absolute *reality*": man should "turn everything which is mere form into world, and make all his potentialities fully manifest." The second fundamental law "insists upon absolute *formality*": man should "eradicate everything in himself which is mere world and bring harmony into all his changes; in other words: he is to externalize all that is within him,

---

70. Wolfgang Riedel's study, *Die Anthropologie des jungen Schiller. Zur Ideengeschichte der medizinischen Schriften und der "Philosophischen Briefe."* (Würzburg: Königshausen und Neumann, 1985), esp. 11–37 and 61–151, provides valuable information. See also *Friedrich Schiller, Medicine, Psychology and Literature*, Kenneth Dewhurst and Nigel Reeves, esp. 89–141 and 307–72.

71. *Schillers Werke*, 20, op. cit., 57.

72. Ibid., 195.

73. Ibid.

74. Ibid., 303.

75. Ibid., 344.

and give form to all that is outside him."[76] Both these tasks, conceived "in their highest fulfillment," Schiller goes on to say, "lead us back to that concept of divinity from which I started."[77] In the last of his great writings, *On Naive and Sentimental Poetry*, Schiller discloses this "concept of divinity," the "ideal of human nature" through the dualistic typology of the "inner spiritual form," the "noteworthy psychological antagonism among men,"[78] and the division into the basic types of realists and idealists, to the extent that the elimination of this dualism or these antagonisms would mean the appearance of this ideal.

At the end of Schiller's aesthetic reflections comes the insight that really only a synthesis of naive and sentimental poetry can create the state of being "a peer of God" sought in the first dissertation (*Philosophy of Physiology*), the totality of all human potential, and thus "give human nature its complete expression."[79] The arts of idealizing and of naturalizing thus approach one another more closely, at least in theory, in his last consideration of this theme. "Nature and art, they seem to flee each other" are the relevant first lines of Goethe's well-known sonnet, *Nature and Art,* "And before one notices it, they have found each other."[80] Schiller expressed this new insight in a letter to Goethe dated September 14, 1797: "Two things have to be part of the poet and the artist: that he lifts himself above reality and that he remains within the sensuous. Where these two are joined, there is aesthetic art."[81]

This quote from a letter seems to me to be, *in nuce*, a relatively good summary of Schiller's thoughts on the philosophy of art. It is of course inseparable from his anthropological conception, which also includes specific suggestions for solving the political and social problems of his time. Just as the speculations and ideas about art in his essays always lead into political, cultural-historical, and anthropological questions, so too do his discourses on politics, cultural history, and anthropology always lead back directly to art—the most important aid in the consideration of human concerns. On November 4, 1795, Schiller explained his overlapping thought processes to a friend, Charlotte von Schimmelmann, with the following revealing words: "The highest philosophy ends in a poetic idea, so do the highest morality, and the highest politics. It is the poetic spirit that indicates the ideal to all three, and to approach it is their greatest perfection."[82]

76. Ibid.   77. Ibid.
78. Ibid., 491.   79. Ibid., 473.
80. Johann Wolfgang von Goethe, *Sämtliche Werke*, 2: *Sämtliche Gedichte* (Zurich: Artemis, 1977), 141.
81. Goethe, *Briefwechsel mit Schiller,* op. cit., 422.
82. *Schillers Briefe*, 4, op. cit., 315.

<table><tr><td>12</td><td><h1>Art, Origins, Otherness:
Hegel and Aesthetic Self-Mediation</h1></td></tr></table>

<h2>WILLIAM DESMOND</h2>

I

A currently fashionable theme for which Hegel's aesthetics is known is the so-called "death" of art. This is an extremely complicated issue in Hegel himself, with religious, political, historical and ontological dimensions. It has been called to our attention in our century by thinkers as diverse as Heidegger and Danto. For the first, the "death" is related to the oblivion of the origin in *Seinsvergessenheit*—in the evening of the West we must await the dawn of a new origin. For the second, one wonders if a secularized world spirit has at last found a comfortable post-Hegelian resting home in some New York art circles. Hegel himself never uses the term "death," though he does talk of art's dissolution (*Auflösung*).[1] I will not focus directly on the "death" of art but will ask about the sense of the *origin* implicit in Hegel's aesthetics and continuous with a pervasive feature of his entire system. For the issue of the end is really a result of a certain sense of the origin. This should not surprise any close reader of Hegel, since for him origin and end are not two radically separated extremes. In a sense they are one, since both are two mutually implied moments of a circle that traverses only its own circumference to constitute itself as a self-articulated whole.

The issue has an aesthetic importance, since in post-Kantian aes-

---

1. G. W. F. Hegel, *Vorlesungen über die Ästhetik*, vols. 13–15 of *Werke*, ed. E. Moldenhauer and K. M. Michel (Frankfurt: Suhrkamp, 1969–71), vol. 14, 220ff. where Hegel speaks of *die Auflösung* (dissolution) and *das Ende* of the Romantic art form; *Hegel's Aesthetics*, trans. T. M. Knox (Oxford: Oxford University Press, 1975), vol. I, 593ff. Hereafter I cite the German as VA, and the English as HA. Arthur Danto speaks of the end of art in *The Philosophical Disenfranchisement of Art* (New York: Columbia University Press, 1986); M. Heidegger in "The Origin of the Art Work," in *Poetry, Language, Thought*, trans. and ed. A. Hofstadter (New York: Harper and Row, 1971) notes the still unmet challenge of Hegel's remarks about the end of art.

thetics the sense of origin predominantly gets articulated in terms of notions like "originality" and "creativity." This sense is already implicit in Shaftesbury's utterance that, suitably modified, might be seen as a manifesto for aesthetic modernity: "We have undoubtedly the honour of being originals." I say modified, since Shaftesbury also calls the artist "a Just Prometheus under Jove." The qualification is essential, since it places human originality in relation to a more ultimate power and hence hearkens back to the Platonism that Shaftesbury also maintained.[2] Later aesthetic modernity will hold that the honor of being an original demands that the creative self image or imitate *nothing other than itself,* that it image, indeed originate, itself alone. As Emerson famously said, "Imitation is suicide."[3] Prometheus will refuse to be under Jove, indeed will claim to be self-creative. I think of Marx and Nietzsche as two such modern Prometheans. Marx stresses man's social self-creation through historical production; Nietzsche's artistic *Übermensch* is the individualistic hyperbole of Promethean self-creation.[4]

What is at stake here is the relation of the "creative" self to otherness. The original that the modern aesthetic self claims to be is often associated with Romantic genius. The latter, in turn, can be understood as the aesthetic counterpart to the active constitutive subject of Kantian transcendental epistemology. Here the significance of what is other to the subject is not intrinsic to otherness as such but is constituted by the self as actively originative. Of course, such a subjectification[5] of origination has met with much criticism in the wake of Romanticism. What passes under the protean banner of "postmodernism" is perhaps only the most recent expression of this criticism, one that tries to deconstruct the notion of self entirely. Hegel's sense of origin, articulated *within* the context of Romanticism, is already beyond any such subjectification. Many aspects of Hegel's aesthetics make him contemporary to these issues,[6] but his sense of origin evidences a powerful dialectical interplay between selfness and otherness. In the end Hegel is a modern in that this dialectic comes to rest in a complex self-mediation in which otherness is included as one of its

2. For Shaftesbury's remarks, see *Philosophies of Art and Beauty,* A. Hofstadter and R. Kuhns, eds. (Chicago: University of Chicago Press, 1976), 252, 240.

3. *Emerson's Essays* (New York: Thomas Corwell, 1961), 32.

4. See my "Paul Weiss and Creativity," paper read to the Society for the Study of Creativity, to be published, along with other contributions, by this Society.

5. I use the term "subjectification" as the subjective counterpart to "objectification": just as objectification is the process of turning something into an object, subjectification is the process by which something is turned into subjectivity.

6. On Hegel and postmodernism, see my *Art and the Absolute: A Study of Hegel's Aesthetics* (Albany: SUNY, 1986), esp. chaps. 5 and 6.

necessary moments. Otherness is necessary to self-mediation, yet within dialectical self-mediation there is no radical otherness that is recalcitrant to incorporation.

This may seem very abstract, and perhaps irrelevant to aesthetics. But one must be extremely cautious in saying this in Hegel's case, where the underlying logical and dialectical structure of his thought percolates into his most challenging statements about art's importance and vocation. For what I have called dialectical self-mediation points toward a sense of both aesthetic origination and ending, each of which, as many now recognize, have extremely important consequences for how one hermeneutically views the history of art and interprets its present dilemmas, for whether one envisages its present state as an exhaustion or as a prelude to a future of renewal.

In the following I will first make some relevant remarks on the issue of origins and otherness in the aesthetic tradition. Then I will turn to Hegel's sense of origin, both at the individual level in terms of genius and at the historical level in terms of the three forms of art—the Symbolic, Classical and Romantic. At both levels we will see that Hegel conceives of the relation of self and other in terms of dialectical self-mediation. Finally, I will note a crucial difficulty at the end with Romantic art when all otherness seems for Hegel to have been aesthetically overcome. Dialectical self-mediation fits perfectly with Hegel's view that the radical turn to inwardness of Romantic art produces art's dissolution and transcendence of sensuous otherness. But the issue of otherness reappears in an even more recalcitrant form *within* the context of inwardness. At the so-called end of art, an inward otherness, inwardness as itself other and recalcitrant to dialectical encapsulation, makes a claim, signalling a sense of origin in excess of dialectical self-mediation. This sense of the origin helps us understand certain post-Hegelian thinkers who treat art with proper philosophical seriousness.

II

Let me broadly consider the question of origins as aesthetically manifested in the contrast between ancient and modern strategies. This will help us understand the impossibility of separating the question of origins from the issue of otherness. It will also help situate Hegel's complex response.

The question of origins cannot be confined to aesthetics, conceived of in the more modern way as a separate philosophical discipline. It obviously has metaphysical overtones. Indeed, these very overtones indicate that the questions of aesthetics themselves are inseparable from one's sense of being as a whole, and hence ineradicably metaphysical. This is especially evident in Hegel, in that art is said to evidence (as do religion and philosophy) a dimension of *absoluteness*. The extremely important place of art in the metaphysical economy of the human spirit is also evident in Schelling, Schopenhauer, Nietzsche, and Heidegger, all thinkers for whom the metaphysical question of origins intertwines with the issue of artistic origination. Indeed origination in art serves to exemplify a deeper sense of original being that cannot be confined to art considered as some special domain. The great artwork serves to tell us something significant about the deepest sense of being in relation to the meaning of being as such. It articulates a sense of being at its deepest and ultimate. Hence the philosopher must give weight to what it reveals. If necessary, he may even have to acknowledge the *breakdown* of his categories in the face of its resistant otherness.

Thus if we consider Plato as a chief representative of an ancient philosophical response, we must never think of his "aesthetics" in terms of any putative self-sufficiency of *"l'art pour l'art."* This would be to superimpose on his concerns an essentially modern, hence foreign and misleading conception. His "aesthetics" are concerned with art's metaphysical significance, more particularly with the relation of aesthetic image to original being, considered as *eidos*. Often Plato is treated as a moralistic denouncer of the powerful, seductive passion to which art is said to pander. But the ethical is itself grounded in a sense of original being—the good human being is a *mimēsis* of the good. As aesthetics and metaphysics cannot be divorced, neither can ethics and metaphysics. As itself a *mimēsis*, the artwork is grounded in a relation to original being, here identified with the *eidē*. That the metaphysical distance between artistic image and ontological original is one of thrice removal may yield a negative evaluation of art, but it cannot undercut the fact that there is a *relatedness* of aesthetic image to ontological original. Though it is an image, the artwork nevertheless is a sensuous mediation of intelligible being, considered as original and other, a mediation that paradoxically keeps us metaphysically distant from that intelligible otherness.

I emphasize the fact that Plato's metaphysics of image and original is informed with a sense of the irreducible *otherness* of the *eidē* as original being. The aesthetic (*to aisthētikon*) concerns what is sensuously presented to us, but this sensuous presence is an image of what is not directly presented, an image of an intelligible otherness that cannot be reduced without remainder to sensuous manifestation. This sense of otherness is very important because it serves to suggest a limit relative to which our lack of mastery of original being is brought home to us. An otherness remains unmastered.

This seems very clear with aesthetic mediation, but even in philosophical mediation, where we might anticipate a more complete, conceptual overcoming of this otherness, we come across a limit. At this limit of *logos* Plato will perforce resort to *muthos*: then the most infamous denouncer of the image gives us the most famous, powerful philosophical images (the divided line, the Cave, the Sun . . .). Similarly, while his aesthetics of imitation easily sets up an incompletely bridged dualism of image and original, this aesthetics of imitation is itself incomplete without the complementary relations of eros and beauty, as well as the disruptive power of mania. Eros serves to mediate the gap between image and original in terms of the drive beyond present partiality of human desire, a movement from the present to the "beyond." Mania serves to mediate the gap between image and original by the ingression from beyond of a powerful inspiration that is itself beyond our complete rational control. What cannot be doubted is that the question of origin in Platonic "aesthetics" is tied up with a metaphysics of original being whose transcendence is precisely its otherness to human mastery.[7]

Modern thought turns away from the attempted Platonic mediation between ourselves and the otherness of the transcendent. It turns toward the inwardness of the self as trying to mediate from itself its own dualistic opposition to nature, which has now been reduced to an ensemble of objective things or a homogeneous *res extensa* (Descartes). Eternity as transcendent otherness is bracketed by philosophical reason or offered to religious faith for its safekeeping. No eternal Ideas mediate our relations to things (nominalism); things are just things, neutrally there. The upwardly directed motion of Platonic eros is redirected toward inwardness, since the search for original being finds no ultimacy in the external ensemble of soul-less objects. The modern epoch originates, as it were, with the *epochē* of Platonic eternity and ends with its Nietzschean eclipse. Hegel stands somewhere between, as does his sense of origin and end, as we shall see.

In post-Kantian aesthetics the sense of origin is consonant with the turn toward the self in modern philosophy generally, and elevated to highest form in transcendental philosophy in particular. Large tracts of post-Kantian aesthetics depend on aesthetic reformulations (some

7. Plato's negative evaluation of imitation is most pronounced in the *Republic*; see my *Art and the Absolute*, chap. 1, on imitation in relation to dualism; on beauty and eros in Plato, see *Symposium*; also *Art and the Absolute*, 120–29; on mania see *Ion* and *Phaedrus*.

covert, some overt) of Kant's doctrine of transcendental imagination. This is especially clear when the epistemological origin as the active constituting self becomes the aesthetic genius as the exemplary creative self who serves as the standard for less concentrated forms of human creativity. I will below show how Hegel breaks with this subjectification of the origin, while retaining a crucial emphasis on self-mediation. But I first want to say that this emphasis on the originative self serves to put the accent on art as itself a form of self-mediation.

As is well known, a fundamental issue of transcendental philosophy is whether its emphasis on the active constituting subject makes impossible, or at least attenuates, a rich concept of otherness as other, of being in its otherness to the mediating self. Does the mediating self so dominate the relation of self and other as to strongly redefine otherness as nothing but a mediating detour to its own self-appropriation? If so, otherness is significant only in so far as it is *for* a self.

This little word "for" hides a host of fundamental questions. The main one here is: Even if the "for" acknowledges a relativity, even co-relativity, of self and other, does the "for the self " inevitably place the other in an ultimately subordinate position in the mediating relation as a whole? The "for" then signals the will of the self to stamp its own self on the relation as a whole, vis-à-vis not only the origination of the relation but also its final determination or consummation. Aesthetically this would mean that art becomes a form of self-mediation in which the human being always mediates only with itself, even while seeming to mediate with otherness. The image of the artwork becomes a mirror in which we see only our own face. At best art becomes a mediated, if sensuous form of *self*-knowledge. There is no irreducible otherness. If otherness now remains, it too will be mediated, and the human being will see only *itself* again in that mediated otherness. No mystery, no enigma, no riddle will remain, or be allowed to remain, to mock our mastery.

Hegel's ambiguous answer points in this direction. But the question is metaphysically and aesthetically important in the wake of Kant in a number of ways. Let me mention some significant responses at odds with Hegel's to indicate the importance of the issue. I return to these again in my conclusion. Thus, Schelling broke with subjective idealism to preserve a sense of otherness that the great artwork concretizes in a way that resists complete conceptualization. Similarly, in Schopenhauer's understanding of will as primal being one finds a sense of what elsewhere I called a dark origin. In relation to this dark origin the source of art is on the *other* side of reason and any logicist determination of the character of primal being. This other to logicization is also invoked by Nietzsche when—and in ambiguous tension with his apotheosis of the Promethean, creative *self*—he speaks of the ultimate origin or original being as Dionysian will to power. Finally, Heidegger offers a sense of the origin's otherness both to the inherent will to power of modern subjectivism and to the putative "logocentric" mastery of the metaphysical tradition.[8]

In sum, the issue of aesthetic origins is inseparable from the metaphysical nature of original and primal being. The ancient response (taking Plato as representative) tends to see the matter as bound up with a sense of original being in its transcendent otherness, requiring acknowledgment of this ineradicable otherness and strategies that enable our mediation with it. The modern strategy situates the issue relative to the active self as original. The question of transcendent otherness seems attenuated and we wonder if all otherness is to be subordinated to the immanent mediations of the active self. But the issue of otherness resurfaces in relation to the closure of self-mediation in total self-sufficiency. Is self-mediation exploded from within by an inward otherness and a sense of original being deeper than any and every subjective mastering?

III

Let me preface my remarks on Hegel with a reminder that, as a concern with origins permeates his whole system, so it also informs his aesthetic philosophy at a very deep level, though it is not made there the object of thematic attention. Hegel's obsession with beginnings is linked to the issue of philosophy as presuppositionless science. Of course, this concern with origins is pervasive in modern philosophy, extending from Descartes's view that philosophy requires a radical new beginning to Husserl's claim that phenomenology was an unprecedented philosophy of transcendental subjectivity. Hegel's concern is very clear from his *Logic*, concerning which the most debated question is probably the legitimacy of Hegel's starting point. In his *Logic* Hegel dwells on the question "With what must science begin?" yet a remarkable fact is that, at least in one interpretation of the entire

8. See F. W. J. Schelling, *System of Transcendental Idealism*, trans. P. Heath (Charlottesville: University Press of Virginia, 1978); see my "Schopenhauer, Art and the Dark Origin," in *Schopenhauer*, ed. Eric von der Luft (Lewiston, NY: Edwin Mellen Press, 1988), 101–22; this paper also discusses the aesthetic legacy of Kant regarding transcendental imagination and genius; F. Nietzsche, *The Birth of Tragedy*, trans. F. Golffing (Garden City, NY: Doubleday, 1956) is concerned with what we might call the Dionysian origin and the tension, often conflict, between philosophy and the tragic vision; on Heidegger see, "The Origin of the Art Work," cited note 1 above.

system, it is the task of the *Phenomenology* to provide the beginning for genuine philosophical science. The task is to provide natural consciousness with the ladder to absolute knowing, which allows us to *begin* to philosophize, properly speaking. It is to articulate the dialectical unfolding of consciousness from the immediacy of the natural standpoint to the entirely mediated self-knowing of philosophical science. Any genuine beginning, it seems, cannot be simple but must be inherently complex or mediated. We cannot simply begin or begin simply; to begin is already to be under way, to already have begun.

Unfortunately we cannot pursue these issues further, except to reiterate that the issue of otherness is bound up with origins. The telos of Hegel's entire thought is implicit in his thought of beginnings. The telos is that thought become absolutely self-mediating, and so fulfill philosophy's *desideratum* as Hegel saw it, namely, that it be self-grounding, self-determining knowing. This means that the origin is known as origin only in so far as it mediates with itself. Thus the development or unfolding of the origin is simply its own self-mediation. Moreover, since what is implicit in the origin is known only in and through this self-developing mediation, the full nature of the origin is known only in the completed end. The end is the origin, in so far as the end is the completed self-mediation of the immediacy of the putative first.

Thus for Hegel there is no radical origin as an *absolutely immediate* first; rather, the immediate first is always the undeveloped. Though in a sense we are always beyond the first immediacy, nevertheless the process of continuation, hence ongoing origination, does have a determinate character. For Hegel this recurring dynamic structure is again dialectical self-mediation in which the end of the process fully realizes what was only implicit in the beginning, and in which the beginning is impoverished if asserted in its simple immediacy. All otherness is progressively appropriated by the process of dialectical development.

Lest the non-Hegelian reader think we have become lost in a labyrinth of Hegelian abstractions, let me turn to the *aesthetic* manifestation of this sense of the origin. Since Hegel is committed to the view that the structure of the logical concept is the structure of being, the law of dialectical self-mediation that marks the logic will also appear in the unfolding of the logic of the aesthetic, and this will be so not only in concept, but also in reality, which means in human history.

Concerning aesthetic origins and a concept of "creativity," Hegel certainly breaks with the subjectivism that was taken, rightly or wrongly, to follow the Kantian sense of transcendental origin. Hegel does emphasize dialectical self-mediation in art, and a certain relation to otherness, but origin in the truest and fullest sense means the self-generating Idea, self-articulating *Geist*. Thus the Hegelian Idea as original being tries to unite the Platonic *eidos* and Kant's transcendental ego: with the Platonic *eidos* it shares an ontological character and an emphasis on determinate structure; with the transcendental ego it emphasizes the active subject as self-articulating and self-relating. But there are differences also with Plato and Kant. For Hegel's Idea articulates itself in *time*, hence breaking with the Platonic dualism of time and eternity. History tells of the emergence of *Geist* which becomes free in its dialectical overcoming of otherness: spirit becomes at home with otherness by recognizing *itself* in otherness. This also involves a break with Kantian aestheticism as attempting to demarcate the aesthetic as a self-contained realm. For Hegel reasserts the dialectical *porosity* of art, religion, philosophy, history. Gadamer rightly praises Hegel for this.[9]

First let me dwell on origination as individual to illustrate the stress on dialectical self-mediation. An artwork is the production of an artist and as such it is something other to and external to its maker. We might here be tempted to insist on a *dualism* of creator and creation, but Hegel's dialectical way of thinking will undermine any such dualism. Creator and creation cannot be abstracted from each other and frozen into rigid poles of an opposition. Rather both participate in a larger process of origination and articulation in which each plays an indispensable role, a role that indicates their mutual implication rather than separation.

Suppose, on the one hand, one were to understand the creative artist as an original power sufficient unto itself, as in some versions of Romantic genius. Then the genius is a godlike being in himself; he has to do nothing but be himself, for it is simply his being that establishes him as an original (Picasso said as much about himself). In the preciousness of his self-sufficient inwardness, he feels his status as creator. This reminds us of the beautiful soul (*die schöne Seele*) that

9. As uniting Platonic and Kantian emphases, consider the remark in the aesthetics (VA 13, 110; HA I, 78) that the original concept (*der ursprüngliche Begriff*) itself must *invent* the shape of concrete spirit, so that the *subjective* concept (in this case the spirit of art) merely *finds* this shape and makes it appropriate to free spiritual individuality. This shape which the Idea as spirit assumes in proceeding out into temporal manifestation is the human form. For further discussion of Hegel's aesthetics in relation to Plato's and Kant's, see *Art and the Absolute*, chap. 6. H.-G. Gadamer praises Hegel's break with Kantian aestheticism in *Truth and Method*, translation edited by G. Barden and J. Cumming (New York: Seabury Press, 1975), 87–88; see my "Hermeneutics and Hegel's Aesthetics," in *Irish Philosophical Journal* 2 (1985), 94–104.

knows its aesthetic and ontological superiority, no matter what it does. Indeed it might be better not to do anything, for this would be to become entangled in the soiling otherness, and hence to compromise one's purity. The genius floats in condescending superiority over all otherness, but remains a god within himself.

Hegel is vicious in his attacks on this understanding of creative genius. It is the abstraction of supercilious subjectivity. Far from being originative, it is impotent. It will not adventure in the world of otherness and so give real expression to itself. Apart from its smirk of divine condescension, it is as nothing; it is not original. It is the smile of the Cheshire cat that has vanished into its subjectivistic self-satisfaction. But the self must *other itself* to be properly itself. This is one of Hegel's great insights: the self articulates itself in the objects it originates, but those objects are the mirrors in which it knows its own power. Hence the object, seemly other, is simply the self in its otherness. Hence the work is the mediation, the middle by which the self comes to itself and its own self-knowledge.[10]

The same point can be made if we try to assert the artwork as something subsistent apart from any reference to self or spirit. Hegel will deny this. The work is not exhausted by being a mere thing that is there. Rather, even as such a thing, it is already an invitation to thought or mind. The work as worked is the objectification of active mind and hence the concretization of original activity. It is the call of this objectified origination to a responding activity in the beholder that actualizes the promise of the work. The work in itself is a mediation of its originating self, and as self-mediating calls for a corresponding self-mediation on the part of the beholder. In its seeming thereness, its very otherness as there is a call to the other.[11] The other as beholder, in responding to the call of what is there, comes to mediate not only with the work as a given externality, but with *itself*, as finding itself at home in this externality. The otherness of the work becomes appropriated as the beholder's own otherness, and hence the medium or middle in which the opposition of work and beholder is dialectically overcome. The inescapability of dialectical self-mediation reasserts itself again.

So whether we take the matter from the side of creator or work,

10. On individual dialectical self-mediation, see for instance VA 13, 50–51, 60–61; HA I, 31–32, 38–39.

11. In relation to the call to the other, Hegel speaks of the artwork as displaying the subjective for the subject and says that the spectator is as it were in the artwork from the beginning. VA 15, 28; HA II, 802. Danto quotes this passage from Hegel (op. cit., 135).

Hegel will claim that the entire process is this dialectical self-mediation in which the spirit comes through otherness to its own self-knowledge. Here this is not philosophy's conceptual self-knowledge, but the sensuous self-knowledge of art. In that art affords such knowledge, it offers us a dialectical circularity that is the aesthetic counterpart to the conceptual self-knowledge of philosophy.

Still it would be quite wrong to think that this process of aesthetic self-mediation is adequately conceived in terms of an individual creator or beholder. This is to be trapped by a misleading abstract individualism, of which indeed the cult of the godlike genius or beautiful soul is itself an expression. It is absolutely essential to place the individual creator in a more enveloping context. In turning now to this, my claim will still be: the otherness of the social and historical context to the isolated individual does not mean that Hegel abandons the view of aesthetic origins as self-mediation in favor of an original otherness that resists our mastery. Far from it, the development of the aesthetic in its rich historical unfolding, indeed at the level of the absolute or whole where Hegel places it, evidences the same story of dialectical self-mediation. The genuine origin is bound up with a process of historical emergence, but the law of its unfolding and completion is dialectical self-mediation.

IV

The inseparability of the artistic creator and the concrete historical world is especially evident in Hegel's three forms of art, the Symbolic, Classical, and Romantic. Hegel rightly rescues the idea of origination from a merely subjective form: the genius (if we retain the idea) is originative in terms of gifts given by nature, but more importantly in terms of his rootedness in a rich *Sittlichkeit*. This is very clear with premodern artists who did not have to imagine from nothing a distinctive aesthetic content; their content was often the already rich mythological tradition, for this was a spontaneous formation of *Geist* in its social, ethical, religious embodiment. The genius as individual was the exemplary voice of this already operative historical and cultural formation of *Geist*. Origin has to be thought of in more than subjectivist terms.[12]

Only in modernity, with its unparalleled stress on the individual, does there emerge the idea of the individual creator as a unique orig-

12. On genius, VA 13, 363–73; HA I, 281–88; on the Greek artist and mythology, VA 14, 27ff.; HA I, 438–40. The stress on myth in the "Earliest System-Program of German Idealism" is not denied, even if perhaps qualified, by the *Aesthetics*.

inal in its radical difference from the social ground. Indeed a great problem in modernity is just that the individual is uprooted from such a *sittlich* ground, with the result that he has the subjective freedom to make *any* content his concern, but also the difficulty of imagining from himself a content that he must thereafter invest with appropriate aesthetic power. Art in premodern times serves to articulate the origin in a more than individualistic sense; for the aesthetic was the sensuous manifestation of the character of *Geist* as concretized in a particular epochal formation; hence the religious, the ethical, the political were not differentiated from the aesthetic. There is here an interesting affinity with the Platonic notion of the "aesthetic" as bound up with the ethical, religious, political formation of a society. The "aesthetic" is musical, in the more encompassing sense of the Greek *mousikē*.

Hence Hegel's three art-formations are not just "aesthetic" categories: they are names for *Weltanschauungen* (Hegel's word), that is, names for different formations of the power of being or *Geist* at its most originary and ultimate.[13] A consideration of these three will tell us about Hegel's epochal theory of art and his sense of the origin as instituting, mediating, consolidating itself in different cultural, historical formations of *Geist*. Again the entire historical process of aesthetic formation is characterized entirely in terms of a dialectically self-mediating origin. This process begins with an unmastered otherness, but in the long run, coming to our time, it ends in the aesthetic mastery of the first otherness. Everything is aesthetically brought out of the initial hiddenness or mystery.

The first formation, the Symbolic, is dominated by nature's otherness and mystery. Here we find an indeterminate beginning, an aesthetic origin closest to the immediacy of sensuous nature. Such immediate beginnings are hardly beginnings at all. One thinks of Adorno's identification of origins and immediacy and his rejection of philosophical concern with either.[14] But Hegel rejects any simple identification of immediacy with origin: the origin is always mediated. Hegel does not deny entirely a moment of immediacy, but concern with pure immediacy only displaces the problem of beginning. Instead of regressing along a temporal series to an immediate, pristine first, we are always in the middle, which is a mediation of the immediate. The origin as a mediated origin always appears in the middle. The really crucial issue is not Adorno's rejection of origins as immediacy

---

13. VA 13, 107ff.; HA I, 76ff.
14. T. Adorno, in *Against Epistemology*, trans. W. Domingo (Cambridge: MIT, 1983), 20, seems to identify fascism, immediacy and the search for origins.

but whether that mediated origin is to be exhaustively described as dialectical self-mediation.

With Symbolic art the sense of beginning found in Hegel's *Logic* crops up again. The undeveloped and indeterminate character that Hegel here stresses is found in the arts of oriental pantheisms, in Jewish sublimity, in Egyptian enigma. All art for Hegel expresses the Ideal, which is the Idea in sensuous manifestation. The Idea manifests itself historically in the different epochal formations of *Geist,* but in these self-formations, the Ideal evidences a unification of form and content, a unification susceptible of different configurations, depending on the state of development of either the content or the form. The content ultimately is the Idea, but the Idea can lack its full self-mediation. Likewise, the sensuous form in which it tries to manifest itself can possess the character of an other that stands in opposition to the content's inherent requirement to be self-mediating.

This is the case with the Symbolic beginning: the sensuous stands as an external otherness that overwhelms the spirit in its rudimentary state of development. Thus to bring together the content and form involves *struggle* rather than harmonious unity; hence Hegel calls this art the aspiration of the Ideal. It is an art of yearning, one in which the spirit throws itself repeatedly into bizarre shapes because it does not really know itself and because nature's overwhelming presence affords it the only occasion of self-expression. It is an art of discord, of not-being-at-home with being. Spirit is not first at home with itself, because the natural form has not been subdued as a proper other for spirit's own self-articulation and mediation. It is an alienating other. If any harmony and peace is attained at all, it is either provisional or else one such as to diminish the promise of spirit.[15]

Surrounded by the otherness of nature, spirit subordinates itself to the engulfing whole. External otherness is infinite and inexhaustible, while inwardness is frail and finite. This disproportion between external otherness and inwardness is nowhere more clear than in Hegel's example of the pyramids (Egypt for Hegel is "the land of symbols" and the Sphinx is the "symbol of symbols"). The purpose of the pyramid is spiritual—to be the burial chamber of the divine pharaoh, a vessel to safely carry the god-king to eternity. But the very massiveness of the physical structure swamps, engulfs, encases the soul of the dead god-king. Spirit is entombed in a lifeless externality. The very tinyness of entombed soul is eloquent testimony that spirit has not yet properly asserted its superiority to matter. Spirit is drowned in sensuousness,

15. See VA 13, 107–9; HA I, 76–77.

though its aspiration expresses its yearning for self-mediation. It tries to mediate with itself in otherness, but it cannot adequately do it because the otherness of nature and the sensuous medium of its own self-expression is not yet subdued to its spiritual shape. Thus the Sphinx, "symbol of symbols," is half-animal below, half-human above, imaging the emergence of the human from nature while being still immersed in it. Indeed only by struggling with the otherness will it develop its own power sufficiently to stamp itself on the otherness with greater mastery, and only then will its proper self-mediation be possible.[16]

For Hegel spirit emerges from and wrests itself free from nature with Jewish religion, as is reflected in their sublime poetry (e.g., the Psalms). God as spirit is elevated absolutely above nature. Through God's otherness as a radical "beyond," nature as an external otherness is dedivinized. Hence the human being, as the bearer of a higher spiritual destiny, itself promised by the transcendent God, can assert its superiority to nature. If Jewish sublimity allows the human self to assert its superiority to nature as an otherness, still for Hegel, *God's otherness* is such as to diminish human spirit to a subordinate role. Not nature's transcendence but God's prevents the more complete self-mediation of the human spirit. Dualism is necessary for Hegel to develop our difference, but if we remain at the level of opposition to the otherness, then the mediation of self in the otherness is itself stopped. The human being becomes a servile, alienated thing confronted with a godless nature over against it, and threatened above by the towering and majestic transcendence of God.[17]

I am not endorsing these views of Hegel. Far from it; it is not at all clear that every form of otherness can be subordinated to Hegel's dialectical self-mediation. I am concerned here to show how Hegel sees the historical working out of dialectical self-mediation with a powerful, almost appalling consistency. Thus, not surprisingly, it is with Classical art, epitomized by Greek art and religion, that we move beyond the above dualisms and beyond the striving of Symbolic art generally. Art arrives with Classical art. Hegel says the Ideal is attained, for here is dialectical self-mediation in the most consummate aesthetic form.[18] But even the acme of Greek art in the classical period is a mediated result—it has a history of struggle behind it where what

16. On Egypt see VA 13, 448ff.; HA I, 347ff.
17. On Jewish sublimity see VA 13, 478ff.; HA I, 371ff.
18. On the classical attainment of the Ideal see VA 13, 109ff., 114 [there he says of the three forms: "*Sie bestehen im Erstreben, Erreichen und Überschreiten des Ideals als der wahren Idee der Schönheit.*"]; HA I, 77ff., 81.

precedes harmony has strong symbolic overtones.[19] The indeterminate symbolic origin is dialectically self-mediated and, as aesthetically articulated, here receives its greatest manifestation. Nature, and especially the human body,[20] become the body of the gods, themselves seen as personal powers, not subpersonal savage forces (captured in the Titans). Spirit emerges from nature, comes into its difference as other to spiritless nature, yet retains its continuity with the sensuous symbolic beginning out of which it emerges. This is the aesthetic *Aufhebung*. For instance, the battle of the chthonic and Olympian gods (and the latter's victory, which preserves something of the former) yields an *Aufhebung* in *myth* of the Symbolic into the Classical.[21]

Hölderlin called the Greek world *ein Reich der Kunst,* and Hegel agrees. Yet he had a complex attitude to the Greek world, mixing enthusiasm and skepticism, respect for its achievement but cold awareness that no simple return to it was possible.[22] His enthusiasm and reservation center precisely on the Greeks as *the aesthetic people.* That is, their way of being exhibits the logical structure of the concept as dialectical self-mediation, but this self-mediation predominantly takes an aesthetic form. Hegel even calls their religion the religion of art (*Kunstreligion*).[23] Their gods are beautiful gods, expressing a union of nature and spirit, a union that itself is spiritual and not still sunk in the otherness of nature as is the symbolic beginning. Spirit comes into its own as other to nature; and though it still is bound to nature as a sensuous other, it knows itself to be fundamentally dealing with *itself* in its dealing with nature. Thus it epitomizes the sensuous self-knowledge that we discovered above in aesthetic self-mediation.

It is because self-mediation attained the full promise of its aesthetic form in the Greek world that Hegel sees art as the fundamental mode of expressing the *absolute* here. What is salient is the *anthropomorphic* self-mediation of original *Geist.* With their "logocentric" predilections, philosophers tend to think of the Greek world in terms of its great thinkers. One would expect this especially of the "panlogist" Hegel. But in his philosophy of history, the Greeks are not the people of philosophy but the aesthetic people. In this, Plato is an *anomaly* in his relation to Greek aesthetic being, as Nietzsche claimed about Socrates.

---

19. See VA 14, 64ff.; HA I, 468–75.

20. On the body as organ of spirit see VA 13, 194–95; HA I, 146–47; also *Enzyklopädie der philosophischen Wissenschaften im Grundrisse (1830)* (Hamburg: Meiner, 1959), nos. 411, 558.

21. See VA 14, 46ff.; HA I, 453ff.

22. See *Art and the Absolute,* 106–14.

23. See G. W. F. Hegel, *Phenomenology of Mind,* trans. A. V. Miller (Oxford: Clarendon Press, 1977), 424ff.

And in a sense Hegel agrees with Nietzsche. As a people the ancient Greeks were artists, not philosophers, whose sense of the ultimate is expressed in threefold fashion: as the subjective, the objective and the political work of art.

First, it is expressed in the care and cultivation devoted to the human body, the only truly proper vehicle of spirit in nature for Hegel. Hegel speaks of the subjective work of art: the bodied subject shapes itself as a living organic work of art, imbued with reverence for the body that is not opposed to religious reverence. Second, the Greek people objectified their sense of the ultimate powers in the statues of the gods that are beautiful spiritual individualities: again the artistic idealization of the human body is essential. Here also in opposition to the formless indeterminacy of the Symbolic, we are confronted with defined, determinate, indeed radiant individual wholes. As the aesthetic people the Greeks are the people of the Ideal, for in the attained Ideal every indeterminacy has been overcome. Hegel calls these statues, which are religious as well as aesthetic figures, the objective works of art. (An interesting conjecture is to what extent Plato's Ideas are the philosophical counterparts to such determinate aesthetic wholes.)

Third, Hegel refers to the Greek polis itself as the political work of art. Here we find the ethical, legal, and political self-mediation of the Greek people that articulates itself in aesthetic shape. The polis was like an ethical, religious whole, shaped by its citizens as if by a community of artists. It is self-mediating, not at the level of some solitary individuality, but at the level of the community as a whole; for in the assembly, the customs and laws, in the games and festivals, the people came to recognize themselves in the social otherness. The polis in fact overcomes the otherness of the social world for the citizen and so, like a communal work of art, was a dialectical whole wherein the people found themselves again.[24]

Nevertheless Greek absoluteness is an *aesthetic absoluteness*, a balance of mediated spirit and immediate sensuousness. Just because of the otherness of the aesthetic immediacy, the limit of this mediation of absoluteness appears. Dialectical self-mediation can never be complete for Hegel if it remains tied to a sensuous other that remains a sensuous other. But there will *always* be some such a remainder in the aesthetic. The third form of art for Hegel, the Romantic, testifies to this more thoroughgoing self-mediation. For here we find the most radical turn to inwardness.

---

24. On the subjective, objective, political work of art, see *The Philosophy of History*, trans. J. Sibree (New York: Dover, 1956), 241–74.

Thus philosophy itself comes on the scene and in its elevation of *thought* marks a break with the sensuous otherness of Greek aesthetic being (again see Plato). Hegel singles out Socrates as the beginning of the end of the Greek world and hence as marking a break with Classical art. Hegel actually has some sympathy for Aristophanes' attack on Socrates, a sympathy that should astonish those who charge Hegel with simple "logocentrism."[25] Yet for Hegel philosophical thought does insist more uncompromisingly on dialectical self-mediation, the constitution of a self-grounding knowing. Still philosophy mediates for the few, not the many. For the latter, the Christian religion (passing through the Roman world) articulates and historically consolidates a sense of spirit as an infinite inwardness that can never be adequately mediated in an aesthetic way. Spirit overreaches all sensuous otherness, because it knows itself to be always and in principle in excess of sensuous mediation. This means that dialectical self-mediation must now take place in inwardness. Here for Hegel both conceptual thought and religious representation are more adequate than art.

If, in Symbolic art, the infinitude of sensuous otherness exceeds the finiteness of spirit, with Romantic art the infinitude of spirit as inward is always in excess of sensuous otherness as finite. Hence, where Symbolic art was the aspiration for the Ideal, and Classical art its attainment, Romantic art is the transcendence of the Ideal. We move beyond art as an *aesthetic* self-mediation. The opening of the depth of inwardness gives rise to a sense of the transcendence, one might say, excess of inwardness, to any sensuous manifestation. This is reflected in the Christian emphasis on the infinite worth of the individual. Not unrelated to the Romantic notion of original genius, individuality as individuality is emphasized. The sense of original individuality will of course only be developed further by the secularization of the Christian standpoint in modern Romanticism. But it is already contained in the Christian view of God as an individual human being—Christ. Romantic art does not present the idealized human body of classical, Greek art. We see the concrete body racked by the particularity of suffering, torment, and death; Christ's agony and crucifixion cannot be idealized in an Apollonian way. What is at stake is not a beautiful sensuous other but a deeper appreciation of inwardness, including inwardness as alone capable of giving meaning to suffering.

For Hegel, human selfhood as thus individual is the concrete embodiment of infinite inwardness. From the end of the Greek world to

25. "Can Philosophy Laugh at Itself? On Hegel and Aristophanes," *The Owl of Minerva* 20, 2 (Spring 1989), 131–49.

our own time, the formation of spirit is dominated by this sense of infinite inwardness and the working out of its implications. It is not that otherness vanishes but that its overcoming takes place in this new context. Hegel details a long process of this overcoming. The Roman emphasis on the legal person's universality contributes, as does the anguish of a godless world driving the self into itself. Then Medieval dualism projects this "beyondness" of the self to sensuous externality into a supersensuous "beyond." The Reformation emphasis on the individual, the subsequent secularization of selfhood that transforms worldly life—Hegel sees all these as helping the final reconciliation in his own time: the completed mediation of an unsurpassable return to self.[26]

This compressed summary of Hegel's view of historical development was necessary, for at the end of this development what we normally called Romantic art appears, though obviously for Hegel the term has a wider connotation. Now the development reaches an end in the full articulation of all the essential aesthetic possibilities. Note how this telos reiterates the structure of origination, namely, dialectical self-mediation. Romantic art is the art of infinite inwardness, hence its self-mediation cannot be simply aesthetic—no sensuous otherness will ever serve as the absolute mirror in which inwardness can completely recognize itself. This is one reason why Hegel sees Romantic art as art transcending itself. What was implicit in the beginning has at last come out of its hiddenness. The indefinite, symbolic beginning, with its enigma, mystery, yearning for elusive "beyondness," has now been entirely mediated, aesthetically speaking. Art has fulfilled its task of entirely mediating the dialectical origin. The new disproportion between sensuous otherness and spiritual inwardness signals the completion and exhaustion of the power of the aesthetic as an absolute mode of self-mediation. This is why I said at the outset that Hegel's view of the end of art can be fully understood only if we understand his sense of origin. For this end is the entire self-mediation of what was implicit in the aesthetic origin and its being brought out into the light of spirit. The end is the origin again, in the sense of a return to symbolic disproportion, but in an entirely new context demanding both religion and philosophy for the self-mediation of inwardness.

I underscore here that this result, while necessary for Hegel, is also fraught with ambiguity. For this end may be a completion, but it also produces the *subjectification* of origination that I spoke of earlier. Thus

---

26. See "Hegel, Legal Status and Otherness" *Cardozo Law Review* 10 (Mar./Apr. 1989), nos. 5–6, 1713–26.

Hegel speaks of an overcoming of the content of art in its otherness. The modern Romantic artist is no longer tied to the substantial ground of a rich *Sittlichkeit*. He is a subjective creator, no longer rooted in one of the essential *Weltanschauungen*. I cite the most important passage where Hegel implies that what was implicit in the beginning has now come out of its hiddenness. In the course of the development, he says:

The whole situation has altogether altered. This, however, we must not regard as a mere accidental misfortune suffered by art from without owing to a distress of the times, the sense for the prosaic, lack of interest, etc.; on the contrary, it is the effect and the progress of art itself which, by bringing before our vision as an object its own indwelling material, at every step along this road makes its own contribution to freeing art from the content represented. What through art or thinking we have before our physical or spiritual eye as an object has lost all absolute interest for us if it has been put before us so completely that the content is exhausted, that everything is revealed, and nothing obscure or inward is left over any more. . . . The spirit only occupies itself with objects so long as there is something secret, not revealed (*ein Geheimes, Nichtoffenbares*), in them. This is the case so long as the material is identical with the substance of our own being. But if the essential world views implicit in the concept of art, and the range of the content belonging to them, are in every respect revealed by art, then art has got rid of this content which on every occasion was determinate for a particular people, a particular age, and the true need to resume it again is awakened only with the need to turn *against* the content that was alone valid hitherto; thus in Greece Aristophanes rose up against his present world, and Lucian against the whole of the Greek past.[27]

The subjectification of artistic origination gives the individual creator a new, more democratic freedom, in the sense of licensing him to take up any content as the occasion of the display of his own virtuosity. But this greater subjective freedom means for Hegel the loss of substantial grounding, and so in a real sense a loss of spiritual seriousness for art. Thus we have the paradox: the deeper subjective inwardness becomes, the more its nature as spirit is developed, the greater the danger of the *loss* of spiritual seriousness on the part of that subjectivity. If everything and anything can now be the content of art, nothing really shows itself as aesthetically absolute anymore, except perhaps the subjective virtuosity of the individual creator. His subjective originality replaces (let us call it) the transsubjective origin whose aesthetic self-mediation is historically effected by the three for-

27. VA 14, 234; HA I, 604–05; Hegel goes on to talk about humor and comedy in relation to the debunking power of subjectivity. See "Can Philosophy Laugh at Itself?" cited note 25. On Hegel's own harshness toward the subjectification of *Originalität*, see VA 13, 380–84; HA I, 294–98.

mations of art. Hegel, I believe, provides us with a hermeneutic narrative that claims to show *the necessity of that loss,* though his own vituperation against the shallowness of subjectivity in his own time shows him in no way to be reconciled with its spiritual bankruptcy.[28]

How does he escape this dilemma? Hegel's answer is to leap beyond the aesthetic, for it is the consummate form of the aesthetic that creates the dilemma that it itself cannot solve. If the language of leap is too Kierkegaardian, let us say he follows the thrust of the aesthetic in the direction of its own self-transcending; the aesthetic as romantic inwardness *itself* points to its own self-transcending. Only a more intensive inwardness and a more spiritual self-mediation will effect the solution. Ultimately only philosophy, as Hegel understands philosophy, can effect absolute self-mediation, in both form and content, though religion and art themselves contribute the absolute content but not the absolute form, since their forms are still burdened with an otherness not yet dialectically overcome.

In sum, then, the dialectical origin is driven by the quest to overreach all otherness, a quest that cannot be completed aesthetically. Yet the dialectical essence of that quest is very manifest aesthetically in Hegel's account of the progress from Symbolic, through Classical, to Romantic art. The Symbolic is the immediate, impoverished first; the Classical is the aesthetic middle; the Romantic is the end which entirely mediates the sense of beyond of the Symbolic, though it returns to a new sense of disproportion in inwardness, indeed it yields the aesthetic aporia just outlined. The aesthetic cannot complete the quest for the dialectical overreaching of all otherness; ultimately this Romantic disproportion can be overcome only by Hegel's philosophical concept as the articulation of spirit where inwardness is both the content and the form.

V

What can we conclude about this aesthetic self-mediation of otherness? The above aesthetic aporia is extremely significant, I believe, but one's response to it need not be solely the Hegelian intensification of dialectical self-mediation in religion and philosophy. My remarks have to be brief, though some of the fuller implications have been developed elsewhere.[29] The main point I will make is that, even if we grant

---

28. There is an analogous aporia in Hegel's ethical-political views in relation to the place of subjective freedom in the modern state. On this see article cited note 26.

29. In *Desire, Dialectic and Otherness: An Essay on Origins* (New Haven: Yale University

to Hegel the outcome of the aesthetic mediation (namely infinite inwardness), otherness is not in fact unambiguously overcome. Why? The issue of otherness reappears in an even more recalcitrant form *within* the context of inwardness. At the so-called end of art in Romantic art, inwardness as itself other and recalcitrant to dialectical encapsulation suggests a sense of origin that is in excess of dialectical self-mediation. What Hegel grants as the infinitude of Romantic inwardness suggests an inward otherness which, it is not clear, can ever be entirely mediated in a dialectical fashion.

Granting the rich complexity of Hegel's subordination of all otherness to dialectical self-mediation, the question is: Does the inward otherness resist total self-mediation? Is inwardness an otherness precisely because its infinitude points to a ground beyond encapsulation, its own ground? Is the enigma of this ground dialectically overcome, as Hegel believes, by either religious representation or the philosophical concept, if both the latter are also the issue of or derivative from this unmastered ground? One might multiply questions. Let me but cite Rimbaud's famous utterance: *Je c'est un autre*, I is an other. This is a post-Romantic echoing of Augustine's great exclamation, itself spoken in the context of religious inwardness (Romantic inwardness for Hegel): *grande profundum est ipse homo*. When inwardness is seen as an inward otherness, the self is always other to itself. One need not say that dialectical self-mediation breaks down *simpliciter*; rather, that its claims to encapsulate all otherness falter. Is the new *disproportion* of inwardness that Hegel sees in Romantic art ever dialectically overcome, or does it point to the transcendence of even the self-mediation of inwardness to dialectic? Is dialectic itself derivative of this original otherness which, as infinite, is never exhausted by its own issue? Such an origin as other may originate its own self-mediation, but it exceeds every one of its own mediations. Something remains dialectically unmastered, namely the originative ground of all dialectical self-masterings. In conclusion let me take my cue from Hegel's triad of absolute spirit and speak of the aesthetic other, the religious other, and the other of philosophical logos itself.

Aesthetically, a point of major interest is that Hegel does recognize

---

in this infinite inwardness what I called an inward otherness; certainly other in its resistance to aesthetic encapsulation. What develops in Romantic art is a certain *excess of subjectivity*, as I call it elsewhere.[30] Hegel tended to see the negative side of this excess. Romantic subjectivity becomes an inward restlessness that provides an aesthetic version of what he called the "bad infinite"—the inability to attain any standpoint of harmony or wholeness, a voraciously discontented subjectivity that flits from one aesthetic possibility to another. It is interesting that Kierkegaard and Hegel are in agreement here. Kierkegaard's figure for this dissatisfied excess of subjectivity that endlessly seeks ever-new satisfactions is Don Juan. Inward otherness, of course, can take this form of negative excess. But there can also be a positive expression of the "excess," the "more." I think Nietzsche was getting at something of this when he spoke of individuals who create out of an affirmative excess, out of plenty rather than lack or poverty. The negative side is a dissolving, ontologically unanchored selfhood; the positive side is the inward otherness that creates from out of an original plenitude.

My claim is that if we grant this latter sense of original plenitude, then the issue of art, origins, and otherness has to be thought of in ways that may be other to dialectical self-mediation. This is not to jettison the great power of dialectical mediation, as many of Hegel's antagonists claim to do, but to think through its limit more deeply. Can we say that art after Hegel sometimes vacillates between these two poles of excess or transcendence? One thinks of Nietzsche's distinction between the decadent and the tragic artist, the first creating from lack, the second from a rich surplus of will to power. One thinks of Picasso saying that a painting is a sum of destructions. Picasso himself might be seen as a unity of the two: great destroyer, great creator, mixing violent disgust with being with intrepid exploration of the labyrinth of the dark breast. One senses here something of the ancient duality of eros as a destroyer, eros as creator—*eros turranos, eros uranos.*

Hegel himself tends to turn away from any celebration of this inward otherness in the manner of some Romantics, because he wanted uncompromisingly to overcome all otherness. Any Romantic celebration of otherness struck him, one might say, as a "feminine" dwelling in enigmas that a more masculine logical thought would penetrate. But certainly one of the lessons of art after Hegel points toward the above-noted ambiguity in the "excess" of inwardness. Hegel clearly saw that this excess can degenerate into the "bad infinite"—the ex-

---

30. On Romantic and post-Romantic art and excessive subjectivity, see *Art and the Absolute*, 114–20.

cessive subjectivity that is despair of finding peace with being. But it can also be an excess subjectivity that is open to another sense of origin as the enigmatic ground of selfhood within self.[31] Indeed this sense of the excess of origin to dialectic is central to some post-Hegelian thinkers concerned with art's importance. These take a different message from art (with significant implications for the nature of philosophical thought) than Hegel does. Indeed, here begins exploration of the limits of "logocentrism," perhaps even its explosion from within.

Thus already, in breaking with subjective idealism, Schelling (as briefly noted before) seemed intent to preserve a sense of otherness to the imperialistic subject: the great artwork concretizes that otherness in a way that resists complete conceptualization. The original or primal identity of subject-object as realized in the great artwork manifests an *unconscious* as well as conscious side. And this duality of unconscious/conscious will never be entirely transmuted into an absolutely singular consciousness that lucidly incorporates the unconscious as other; for without the otherness of the unconscious, self-consciousness would itself not be possible. Similarly, Schopenhauer understood will as primal being, a dark origin in relation to which the deepest source of art is said to be on reason's other side. As original being, the will for Schopenhauer transcends the principle of sufficient reason and the subject-object split that obtains in the phenomenal realm. In so far as music is *the* metaphysical art for Schopenhauer, we are on the other side of any logicist determination of the character of primal being. So also for Nietzsche, the sense of the ultimate origin or original being is spoken of as will to power. This is sacrally or mythically named as Dionysus, whose irreducibility to the Apollonian logos signals its otherness. Heidegger points to the otherness of the origin, which withdraws from manifestation even as it makes all manifestation possible. Being in its primal plenitude is other to the subjectivism and will to power of the modern era, other to the putative "logocentric" mastery of the metaphysical tradition. Even Derridean *différance* might be seen as an inward otherness relative to the absolute self-presence of Husserl's transcendental ego considered as an absolute origin.[32]

---

31. Hegel's notion of true infinitude is always articulated in terms of self-mediation, while the "bad infinite" is the failure of dialectical self-mediation, failure to articulate a new whole. But one can make the case that there is a sense of infinitude that is not simply self-mediating and yet not the "bad infinite." On this see *Desire, Dialectic and Otherness*, chap. 7; also chap. 3, on what I call "equivocal desire" in relation to Hegel's "bad infinite."

32. See note 8 above; also my "Dialectic, Deconstruction and the Comedy of Failure,"

The issue of the religious other can only be mentioned. If we reraise the issue of inward otherness and ask if something about this infinity (Hegel's own term) resists the dialectical self-mediation he privileges, so we also have to ask whether there is an ambiguous relation between wholeness and infinity here. There is a matter here that concerns (among others) Levinas and Derrida: Athens and Jerusalem.[33] Does not Hegel always tip his hat toward wholeness because of dialectical self-mediation, hence tipping toward Greek circularity rather than the unmastered infinite whose otherness resists the Greek logos (see above on Jewish sublimity)? Admittedly Hegel is ambiguous, since infinite inwardness can never be adequately understood in terms of Greek circularity, understood as an *aesthetic* self-mediation. But he does imply that in the Christian religion there is a complete return to self in genuine inwardness, hence a spiritual, and not just sensuous, dialectical circularity, and that this inward dialectical circle is fully closed only in the philosophical *Begriff* in terms of form (itself absolutely inward) and content (always ultimately inward). In religion and philosophy, thus understood, does not dialectical self-mediation again predominate and appropriate all infinitude and transcendence? This is a complex variant of the question of divine otherness that has been put repeatedly to Hegel, in the accusation of "pantheism" in his own life, and trenchantly by Kierkegaard in relation to the mediation of the finite and the infinite. Indeed Kierkergaard's insistence on the *final hiddenness* of religious inwardness is relevant to the issue at stake vis-à-vis the inward otherness.[34]

Turning to the third issue, the question of the other to philosophical logos already emerges in what I have said. Let me add: if inward otherness, precisely as infinite, evidences a resistance to dialectical self-mediation, if the self in its inward otherness cannot be entirely self-mediated, then the issue need not be a return to any simple, that is, undialectical "either-or" between reason and the irrational, thought and nonthought. (One can be other than dialectical without being undialectical: Kierkegaard is a classic case.) The issue is not one of

to appear in proceedings of the Hegel-Hölderlin Conference, held Yale University, October 1987. I address there Derrida's interest in Bataille's laughter as purportedly exceeding the mastery of Hegelian dialectic.

33. On Athens and Jerusalem in relation to Levinas and Derrida and Hegel, see Derrida's "Violence and Metaphysics," in *Writing and Difference*, trans. A. Bass (Chicago: University of Chicago Press, 1978); see Richard Kearney's interviews with both Levinas and Derrida in *Dialogues with Contemporary Thinkers* (Manchester: Manchester University Press, 1984), chaps. 2 and 5.

34. See also what I call a "post-romantic symbol" in *Desire, Dialectic and Otherness*, 200–202, 238, 246; this also relates to Hegel's understanding of infinitude as a dialectically self-mediating whole and some of the consequences of this.

abandoning thought for deconstructive celebrations on the margins of philosophy, but of developing thought in a manner that does justice both to the power of dialectical self-mediation and to the necessity of openness to otherness at the limit of self-mediation. Thought must think not only itself but also its other, and not simply its other in a dialectical sense only.

So the question of art's beginning and end also brings us back to the question of the beginning of philosophical thought, as Nietzsche and Heidegger would agree. Wonder (*thaumazein*) is the pathos of the philosopher, Socrates says, and also philosophy's *archē*, as Aristotle reiterates. But if in fact otherness were entirely overcome by Hegel, this originating wonder would vanish. Hegel grants as much in the citation above (p. 227) on art and hiddenness. If we transpose Hegel's remark on art to thought, and if there is no hiddenness, then philosophical thought too loses interest in the matter. Here it is very relevant that ever since Descartes, *doubt,* not wonder, has been the beginning of philosophy. Doubt, as it were, is wonder's negative counterpart, and their difference mirrors philosophically the two senses of transcendence or excess distinguished above. Hegel wanted to overcome doubt through doubt itself, as the negative that negates itself, thus sharing Descartes' quest for certainty. But this again implies a certain subordination of otherness in that (in the *Phenomenology*) Hegel seeks the dialectical identity of truth and *self*-certainty. Hence his controversial claim that philosophy as love of wisdom (where ontological wonder is never put to rest, only deepened) at last becomes wisdom as science (*Wissenschaft*), where the negatively transcending power of doubt is affirmatively transformed into systematic knowledge.

By contrast, in Schelling, Schopenhauer, Nietzsche, and Heidegger, as indicated, I venture that the great artwork, in its otherness to the logical concept, offered (as it may also offer us) the philosophical occasion of such originating wonder—ontological admiration, appreciation of being. If wonder at the origin is entirely brought out of its initial hiddenness by art's dialectical development, it must cease to provide this challenge to philosophy, and philosophy itself, if it cannot be challenged by originating wonder coming from elsewhere or itself, must itself atrophy—at least in the traditional sense.

Is it then surprising that soon after the end of art is suggested by Hegel, we find talk of the end of philosophy? Or that where "wonder" survives, its astonishment is transmuted into intellectual curiosity about technical puzzles—as has happened with the analytical heirs of Hegel in twentieth-century thought. Alternatively, one might react against Hegel and reassert the power of otherness, in art and elsewhere. This is what happens in many of Hegel's continental heirs—perhaps most challengingly in Heidegger, who was extremely aware of the modern tendency toward the deformation of philosophical wonder into mathematicized, technicist virtuosity. The danger here (deconstruction risks this danger) is that in an excess of fear that Hegel's dialectical self-mediation encloses all otherness and exhausts *all possibilities* of philosophy, one claims to take a leap outside philosophy. But our alternatives are not the contraction of dialectic into analytical virtuosity or a deconstructive surpassing of dialectic into a nonphilosophical "outside."

Thus the origin/end of art cannot be separated from philosophy's quest for origins, including its own. Similarly the origin of philosophy itself, that is, its renewal of its own originating wonder, is itself at issue in how we think of the otherness of being and the ontological relatedness of the human being to that otherness. If there is a sense of the original otherness of being beyond dialectical self-mediation which art (and not only art) serves to unfold, then post-Hegelian philosophy can renew itself only by regaining contact with that otherness and thinking it through in terms other than Hegel's dialectical self-mediation. It will not do this in terms of the alternatives above, but only by thinking through the limit of Hegel's dialectical self-mediation.[35] Reflection on the ontological significance of art, and indeed on the richness of Hegel's own reflections on art, is indispensable to bringing philosophical thought to this limit. Ontological perplexity before this limiting otherness provokes philosophy's own need of ever-renewed beginning.

35. See *Desire, Dialectic and Otherness*; also my *Philosophy and Its Others: Ways of Being and Mind* (Albany: SUNY, 1990).

The Religion of Art

DANIEL O. DAHLSTROM

"Je poetischer, je wahrer."
NOVALIS

I

Whatever one might think of Feyerabend's philosophy of science, there is certainly much to be said for his claim that, in the twentieth century, science has in large measure finally fulfilled its Enlightenment mission and replaced religion as the accepted authority, source, and guardian of the truth. The rites of scientific method yield reliable, visible wonders even as they define new mysteries of force fields, neutrinos, and quarks. Legal, political, and economic decisions are considered recklessly irresponsible, indeed punitively liable, if they are not made under suitable consultation, not with clergymen, but with scientists. Research institutes are the bastions of a twentieth century monasticism; like the great cathedrals that once dwarfed European cities, a testimony to the collective religious will and sacrifice of generations, linear accelerators in our century cut through large swaths of the contemporary landscape (Stanford's two-mile accelerator in Palo Alto is a good example) inspiring another sort of social pride, piety, and fear.

Philosophers have, of course, repeatedly reminded us of the limits of science, and this reminder is a point of convergence even among quite different conceptions of science. Aristotle, for example, argues persuasively that, though the task of science consists in syllogistic demonstration, not everything is demonstrable. Moreover, while declaring primary, individual substances to be substances in the highest degree, underlying all species and genera, Aristotle points out that there can be no science of the individual.[1] Kant developed a rather different

---

1. *Posterior Analytics I*, chap. 3 (73a16–20); *Categories*, chap. 5 (2b15–16); *Metaphysics* Bk. E, chap. 2 (1026b25–26).

theory of science, based on the premise that a part of nature can become a subject of science only to the extent that mathematics is applicable to it.[2] That Kant recognized a world not confined to the parameters of natural science is well known. Yet even among natural phenomena Kant saw limitations for science. The inapplicability of mathematics to the phenomena of the inner sense—feelings, perceptions, dreams—makes it impossible, Kant thought, for empirical psychology ever to be a legitimate natural science.

Study of Aristotle and Kant is, of course, hardly required to recognize that science cannot replace religion or, at least, that science has certain limitations. Science is revered in the public domain, in the courts, and in the boardrooms, indeed wherever a premium is put on explaining how things in general come about. Yet we do not, and know we cannot, look to science to explain the dense and terminal phenomena of an individual human life. The uniqueness and contingency of events and emotions, the personal choices, fates, and responsibilities of individuals, relationships, families, and communities defy the logic of measurement and experiment. Human life is a spring of desire and hope, disappointment and despair, rushing in a current of willed and unwilled habits, to a quite definite, private end. Religion articulates a meaning for this personal odyssey, thus accomplishing what science, construed as the study of nature in its universal or mathematical features, cannot. The appreciation of that meaning accordingly demands the assent to something supernatural, something otherworldly. At the same time that meaning remains in force within historically and geographically defined traditions, by concretely defining rites of passage in terms of bonds sustaining the individual in a particular community.

Nevertheless, the Enlightenment's discrediting of religion did create a personal vacuum for many, a vacuum filled not by religious revival but by the arts. Science may indeed have usurped the role of religion in the public domain, but art has become the private tabernacle to which even religious souls find themselves retreating to celebrate and to mourn, to contemplate and to fantasize the mysteries of individual and social fates. Wackenroder's remark, "I compare the enjoyment of noble artworks to prayer," was prophetic.[3] We confess our sins and are purged—in the theater. High mass is sung to perfection—in the concert hall. Solemn altarpieces of Grünewald and Van Eyck beckon us to piety—in museums.

2. *Metaphysische Anfangsgründe der Naturwissenschaften,* Vorrede in *Kants Werke,* 5 (Berlin: de Gruyter, 1968), 470.

3. Wilhelm Heinrich Wackenroder and Ludwig Teick, *Herzensergießungen eines kunstliebenden Klosterbruders* (1797) (Stuttgart: Reclam, 1979), 72: "Ich vergleiche den Genuß der edleren Kunstwerke dem *Gebet.*"

That art acquires its own religious significance, that a religion of art is celebrated, not so much as part of, but rather in contrast to traditional religion, is itself part of a historical development characterized as the *Verbürgerlichung* of the arts. This term "Verbürgerlichung" is not easy to translate, but it refers broadly to the gradual detachment of the arts from the claims of the nobility and the Church, as part of the historical emergence of the social and political autonomy of the middle class, the *Bürger,* the bourgeoisie. This process should not, however, be interpreted in crude Marxist fashion, as though artists simply transferred allegiance (along with a shift in source of income) from *l'Ancien Regime* to the *tiers état.* To be sure, often enough the new forms and subjects of art are deliberate reflections of bourgeois values. The realism of Dutch painting, for example, is due not only to the abolition of religious art by the Reformed Church of Holland but also to the fact that artists had now to work, not for patrons, but for a thoroughly middle-class market. Lessing's *Miß Sara Sampson* (1754) is the first German *bürgerliches Trauerspiel*; Diderot's *Fils naturel* and *Père de famille* (1757) are bourgeois tragedies. Even Winckelmann, no friend of bourgeois tastes, who urged contemporary painters, sculptors, and architects to take neither Dutch nor Baroque masters but the idealized "noble simplicity" of the ancients as their model, recognized that this artistic perfection required the public spirit and political freedom enjoyed by the Athenians.[4]

Nevertheless, despite these examples, the "Verbürgerlichung" of the arts signifies not so much the hold of a newly autonomous bourgeoisie over the arts as the increasing autonomy of the arts and artists themselves—indeed, if anything, their hold over the bourgeoisie. That autonomy is relative, to be sure, as any commercial artist will testify. Yet in a culture determined by the mechanism of the market, painters and sculptors, musicians and actors increasingly come to think of themselves as professionals and even professional high priests; opera companies, art institutes, and societies for the performing arts are formed like so many latter-day religious orders; with all the enthusiasm once reserved for great cathedrals, architects compete to design museums, temples of civic pride. The different autonomy of artworks of earlier ages and different cultures as well as the truths they have to reveal, meanwhile, are re-discovered. Artworks, old and new, Romanesque churches and royal galleries become national treasures, im-

---

4. Johann Joachim Winckelmann, *Gedanken über die Nachahmung der griechischen Werke in der Malerei und Bildhauerkunst* (1756) (Stuttgart: Reclam, 1982); see Armand Nivelle, *Kust- und Dichtungstheorien zwischen Aufklärung und Klassik,* zweite, durchgesehene und ergänzte Auflage (Berlin: de Gruyter, 1971), 67f.

portant sources of financial equity and income through tourism. Modern technology's role in this development grows in tandem with the increasing autonomy of art, a curious (though, thanks to Heidegger, not wholly unexpected) reaffirmation of the original Greek sense of "techne." In our century the lure of the original is offset—pardon the pun—and yet, in a certain respect, even enhanced by the commonplace of copies, records, and slides. The sounds of a Wagner opera in Bayreuth are heard in a Texas country kitchen; in waiting rooms and offices a different reproduction of Franz Marc or Rubens announces a different week or month.

In the increasing autonomy enjoyed by the arts, the artist is able to see his or her activity as something having its own integrity, and the artwork is recognized as having its own essence and existence. Perhaps this historical development helps explain the misgivings felt toward traditional theories of art that construe art as akin to a shadow world, a mere imitation of something substantial. Artworks continue to be artworks even if no one in fact comes forth to appreciate their excellence. A work of art, as Paul Weiss has aptly characterized it, is "a self-sufficient, substantial reality, creatively produced, and possessing its own rationale."[5] The experience of art, moreover, is not something "accidental" and certainly not on the periphery of contemporary life. Art is no longer just our Sabbath, as nineteenth-century critics observed. The experience of the arts has become no less profoundly routine (with all the paradox of a routine profundity) than monks chanting the Divine Office.

Art thus comes into its own as a world of its own, with a promise, at least, beyond the normal headaches and worries, the profit motive and power struggles, that otherwise dominate the everyday world. The artworld is another world, an inverted world, if you will. But just because it is inverted, the world of art often becomes our conscience, a world in which truth can break down prejudice and unmask pretenses that cloud what is clear in obscurity or substitute cheap clarity for genuine ambiguity.

The artworld's self-conscious otherworldliness, even as it populates the world it confronts, explains its obsession with originality. The naturalistic works of Flaubert or Zola were no less controversially novel parables than *Paradise Lost* or, for that matter, Kafka's fragments. At the turn of this century artworks were cheekily canonized *Jugendstil*

---

5. Paul Weiss, *Nine Basic Arts* (Carbondale, Illinois: Southern Illinois University Press, 1961), 63; see also *The World of Art* (Carbondale and Edwardsville, Illinois: Southern Illinois University Press, 1961), 79.

and *l'art nouveau.* The romantic cult of the genius survives in the myth of the misunderstood artist, the aesthete as martyr.

The thesis that the arts develop as a relatively autonomous institution in the contemporary world, usurping in a certain measure the traditional role of religion and religious experience for the individual and the community, is neither novel nor uncontroversial. The refinement of the thesis, which can be traced to the German critic Friederich Theodor Vischer, later to Nietzsche, and most recently to Thomas Nipperdey, demands investigations proper to the history and sociology of the arts.[6] However, the thesis of art's *otherworldliness within the world* also sharpens certain traditional and contemporary philosophical questions about the identity of art. A philosophy of art must be able to explain the universal respect enjoyed by the arts, a respect that verges on a kind of religious piety. In what does this religion of art, this otherworldliness of art consist or, more prosaically, what makes an artwork art? Artworks, to be sure, require some human activity, but what then distinguishes them from mere artifacts or at least from other things produced by human deed? In what relation does the identity of art stand to the identity of philosophy itself? To the extent that there is a religion of art, does this phenomenon present another version of the ancient problem of reconciling aesthetic sensibilities, an artistic faith, if you will, with theoretical and practical reasoning?

II

The problem of explaining the nature of art and, in particular, its apparent discontinuity with reality, its otherworldliness, has dominated much contemporary philosophy of art. This very discontinuity seems to undermine traditional mimetic as well as deliberately counter-mimetic theories of art. A robust theory of art must be able to take into account the Baroque as well as the Classical, suprematism as well as naturalism, and, following Weiss, at least nine different, basic arts. There seems to be no way to identify a particular sort of content, realistic or idealized, the attributing of which to a particular object guarantees that that object is a work of art. Contemporary art or at least the contemporary artworld has, moreover, exacerbated the problem of a philosophy of art. Picasso's collages, Duchamp's ready-mades, and pop art, for those who take it seriously, make a farce of traditional

---

6. See the excellent article by Thomas Nipperdey, "Wie die Kunst autonom wurde: Das Bürgertum und die unbürgerliche Moderne, Erinnerung an das 19. Jahrhundert" in *Frankfurter Allgemeine Zeitung,* Samstag, 8. August 1987, Nummer 181.

art and art theories, by giving us artworks indiscernible from objects found on grocery shelves or in lavatories.

The response of several contemporary philosophers of art has been to abdicate the question of the identity of an artwork to the artworld.[7] With the help of Wittgenstein's analysis of 'games,' Morris Weitz persuaded many of his peers that subconcepts of art, such as tragedy, the novel, the opera, and even the concept of art itself are open concepts, specifying no necessary or sufficient conditions for something to be an instance of that concept. Weitz insists that there is no true theory of art, because there cannot be one. "Such a theory," Weitz reasons, "forecloses on the concept of art."[8] Given the very way the concept of art is wielded, the attempt to identify necessary or sufficient conditions for it is like trying to slam shut a revolving door. A theory of art, moreover, is not only impossible, but unnecessary. If we "look and see," we find that no set of definitive criteria, the stuff of essentialistic definitions, is required for intelligible discourse about art and arts and, indeed, new art forms.[9]

Weitz has been criticized for confusing classificatory and evaluational notions of art and, like Goodman, for restricting the properties of artworks to what meets the eye, in other words, for assuming that all aesthetic differences are perceptual differences.[10] His appeal to similarities (none of which need be necessary or sufficient) to determine whether something should be called an 'artwork' is contested on the grounds that it invites an infinite regress, failing to explain the original basis of the similarities, "nonsimilarity art," as Dickie puts it.[11] There are other properties of an artwork, not sensibly patent and not similar to the properties of other works, namely the work's historical

7. What follows is a cursory review of three *distinct* and leading responses (Weitz, Dickie, Danto) to the question of determining what it means to identify something as an artwork. For all their differences these responses invoke the linguistic practice, the theory, and/or history of a specific art world.

8. Morris Weitz, *The Opening Mind* (Chicago: University of Chicago Press, 1977), 50f; "The Role of Theory in Aesthetics" in *Journal of Aesthetics and Art Criticism* 15, 1 (1956): 27–35; "Wittgenstein's Aesthetics" in *Aesthetics: A Critical Anthology*, ed. Dickie and Sclafani (New York: St. Martin's Press, 1977).

9. While continuing to insist that art is an open concept, Weitz later advises that some concepts such as tragedy are, in contrast to a concept like art, "open-textured" concepts, that is to say, allowing for the possibility of the rejection of prevailing criteria.

10. Maurice Mandelbaum, "Family Resemblances and Generalization Concerning the Arts," in *Aesthetics: A Critical Anthology*, ed. Dickie, Sclafani, and Roblin (New York: St. Martin's Press, 1989); George Dickie, *Aesthetics: An Introduction* (Indianapolis: Bobbs-Merrill, 1971), 99–101; *The Art Circle* (New York, New York: Haven, 1984), 110; Arthur Danto, *The Transfiguration of the Commonplace* (Cambridge, Massachusetts: Harvard University Press, 1981), 43.

11. George Dickie, *The Art Circle*, 32f. See Weitz's telling responses to Mandelbaum's and Dickie's criticisms in *The Opening Mind*, 54–58 and 81–90.

and social context.[12] That something is an artwork, it was argued, is determined by these relationships. "To see something as art requires something that the eye cannot decry—an atmosphere of artistic theory, a knowledge of the history of art: an artworld."[13]

This thesis, originally drafted by Arthur Danto, was developed by George Dickie into an "institutional" theory of art. According to the initial version of this theory, there are actually two necessary conditions of artworks, artifactuality and institutionality. However, as the theory's name suggests, institutionality "wore the trousers." Consider, for example, the following remarks by Dickie: "A year or two ago The Field Museum of Natural History in Chicago exhibited some chimpanzee and gorilla paintings. In the case of these paintings we must say that they are not works of art. However, if they had been exhibited a few miles away at the Chicago Art Institute they would have been works of art—the paintings would have been art if the director of the Art Institute had, so to speak, gone out on a limb. It all depends on the institutional setting—the one setting is congenial to conferring the status of art and the other is not."[14] Dickie, who is also known for successfully debunking the idea that there is something like a specifically aesthetic attitude, insisted that a work need not actually be appreciated.[15] An artwork, good or bad, appreciated or not, is an artifact—not necessarily human!—enjoying the status of being a candidate for appreciation, conferred by someone representing the art world. Indeed, in an attempt to countenance Duchamp's ready-mades, Dickie originally considered artifactuality itself something that can be conferred.

As Weitz pointed out, this construal renders the condition of artifactuality otiose. In recent years Dickie has revised his theory in favor of the artifactuality condition. In his "new institutional theory of art," not only can artifactuality not be conferred,[16] but the status of being an artwork is not something conferred by an artworld at all, but rather something *achieved* by a creative use of a medium, against the back-

---

12. Dickie insists that artifactuality is a *necessary* condition, in contrast to Weitz who construes it only as an "unrejectable" criterion. See George Dickie, *Aesthetics: An Introduction,* 98; "The New Institutional Theory of Art" in *Aesthetics: A Critical Anthology* (1989), 197; *The Art Circle,* 6–7, 62f.

13. Arthur Danto, "The Artistic Enfranchisement of Real Objects: The Artworld" (1964) in *Aesthetics: A Critical Anthology* (1989), 177.

14. George Dickie, *Aesthetics: An Introduction,* 106.

15. He adds that, while someone cannot make a mistake in conferring the status of art, the individual may lose face, if in fact the work remains unappreciated.

16. "Readymades" are correspondingly construed "as the artifacts of artists as the result of a kind of minimal work on the part of those artists." See *The Art Circle,* 11 and 44–46.

ground of the art world. "A work of art is an artifact created to be presented to an artworld public."[17] Just as in the earlier version a work need not actually be appreciated, so in the revised version a work need not actually be presented.[18]

Dickie is undoubtedly correct to think that what makes something an artwork cannot lie simply in some sort of peculiarly aesthetic response.[19] This anti-aesthetic direction does not, however, mean that works of art are conceivable in absence of its devotees, connoisseurs, and publics. Accordingly, Dickie rightly insists that a theory of art— or, *pace* Weitz, even consideration of the conditions for normal use of the term "art"[20]—respect the "thick" network of relations informing the artwork, encompassing both artifactuality (the relation between artist and artwork)[21] and the intention of public presentability (the artist's intention of making something able to be presented to a public).[22]

However, what Dickie's institutional theory fails to explain is *why* an artifact should be considered a candidate for appreciation or, according to his revised theory, why creations of a certain kind are such that they can be presented to a specific public (the artworld). By virtue of what is the status achieved?[23] The notion of achievement seems to entail the possibility of failure, e.g., an artifact that cannot be presented to the artworld. *Either* this is a possibility and it is incumbent upon Dickie to explain why, *or* no artifact is unpresentable and the (revised) institutionality condition—together with talk of status and

17. *The Art Circle*, 80 and 12.

18. *The Art Circle*, 65–66 and 71–72.

19. The determination of that experience is notoriously difficult and, moreover, according to the intended, original sense of the term, an 'aesthetic' experience may be a response to nature as well as to a work of art and, in the latter case, a response to the nature or likeness to nature in the artwork.

20. Duchamp's *Fountain* may, indeed, be more than a "gesture" (Cohen's characterization), but at least to my linguistic intuitions, to my *Sprachgefühl* a chiefly honorific, courtesy, or parasitic sense of "art-*work*" is employed when it is applied to readymades or shells displayed as decoration. Some parasites can, of course, be exceedingly interesting and beautiful (think of the mistletoe!).

21. See, however, in this volume the criticism by John Brough that Dickie, in an attempt to countenance readymades, weakens this requirement, conflating it with mere utensility.

22. George Dickie, "The New Institutional Theory of Art," in *Aesthetics: A Critical Anthology* (1989), 201–2; *The Art Circle*, 77f. Dickie makes no reference to Heidegger, but, by not privileging artwork, artist, or art-world public in their mutual relations and thereby affirming the circularity of definitions of art, he repeats a claim running throughout Heidegger's 1935 address on art. See *Der Ursprung des Kunstwerkes* (Stuttgart: Reclam, 1986).

23. *The Art Circle*, 10: ". . . I want in this book to maintain that being a work of art is a status. The view of art as a status which I now wish to defend, however, conceives of this status not as being conferred but as being achieved in another way."

achievement—becomes otiose. In Dickie's defense, one might argue that he is concerned not with an evaluative, but with a "more basic, classificatory" theory of art, capable of explaining why even bad works of art are nonetheless entitled to the ascription.[24] Yet this line of defense is inadequate, since even a bad work of art is "an artifact of a kind to be presented to an artworld" and, hence, subject to some sort of canons of presentability. The distinction between classificatory and evaluative theories seems to break down inasmuch as the criterion of classification supposes a principle of evaluation. The passive infinitive construction (*"to be presented"*) built into the definition itself is, in traditional grammars, identified as a "model infinitive" or an "infinitive of purpose."[25] Given this construction, it is difficult to understand how the classificatory sense of "artwork" can be considered "more basic" and distinguishable from at least some minimal evaluatory sense.

The difficulty can be put in rather traditional terms. Not because something can be presented (appreciated) is it an artwork; rather, it can be presented (appreciated) because it is an artwork. Presentability (appreciability) is, in scholastic terms, an *accident* of artworks, allowing us to identify possible artworks, but not to differentiate them unmistakably from other artifacts. That, however, the artifact is intended for appreciation or presentation to the artworld public is, again in scholastic terms, a *proprium*, enabling us to distinguish artworks from other artifacts. However, this property is not the end of the analysis, but supposes some ground or reason (*differentia specifica*) by virtue of which an artifact is created for presentation to the artworld public.

The preceding formulation, however, is intended solely for purposes of illustration. It is not meant to suggest that there is some sort of timeless essence to art, identified by its specific difference within a genus. How such an essence could be known or, indeed, what precisely that could mean is exasperatingly obscure. There is no sufficient reason to think that the traditional classificatory (definitional) scheme of genus, species, and specific difference, controversial enough when applied to nature, should have any more application to artworks than does the form/content distinction, proper to implements. I am sympathetic both to Dickie's rejection of undefinable, primitive terms (thus, the inevitability of circularity in defining art) and to Weitz's respect for the perennially flexible character of the concept of art

---

24. *The Art Circle*, 8; 12–14; 43. Dickie addresses the subject of evaluation in *Evaluating Art* (Philadelphia: Temple University Press, 1989).

25. The modal infinitive indicates necessity or fitness, while the infinitive of purpose typically follows forms of the verb "make." The latter infinitive is frequently illustrated with Wilde's remark: "Women are made to be loved, not to be understood."

(thus, the failure of any *theory* of art). However, meaningful discourse about art takes place, at least for a time, because an artwork is *seen to succeed*. Against Dickie it must be emphasized that something like success or failure is implicit in his definition and needs to be accounted for (within his circular framework and without undermining the good art/bad art distinction). Such success or failure presents itself, like artifactuality, as, in Weitz's terms, an "unrejectable criterion."

In defense of Weitz and Dickie, it bears noting that neither is interested in illuminating what it is that constitutes the otherworldliness, the religion of art, described in the first section of this paper. Weitz's concern is to demonstrate that intelligible discourse about art need not presuppose some theoretical definition of art, and Dickie's theoretical aim is an exclusively classificatory definition of art. What I want to suggest is that meaningful discourse about art ('looking and seeing' the way we wield the term 'artwork') supposes, not simply criteria that are more than classificatory, but an experience of art's achievement. What is the achievement of art?[26]

One contemporary answer, which has much to recommend it, is offered by Arthur Danto in a work entitled *Transfiguration of the Commonplace*. What differentiates an artwork from an indiscernible counterpart and thus from non-artworks in general is "the fact that the artwork uses the way the nonartwork presents its content to make a point about how that content is presented."[27] The artwork does not simply present its subject, but is significant for the way it presents its subject. Built into the artwork is an intensional structure for which, as with intensional structures in general (e.g., quotations), there is no substitute for the work itself.[28] The artwork succeeds by enabling us,

---

26. What needs to be examined is the purpose and meaningfulness of the classificatory/evaluatory distinction together with the talk of criteria, be they necessary and sufficient or merely a disjunctive set, in regard to art. These *theoretical* devices themselves may sabotage the very attempt to understand art. In that case, not only would a *theory* of art be at odds with art or at least with our use of 'art,' as Weitz correctly observed; so, too, would the *theoretical* dismantling of the theorizing by recourse to disjunctive criteria. In any case, if an artifact is deemed (even when wrongly) a success, something able to be presented to the art world, it is not principally because some value or principle of classification, existing independently of the artwork, is invoked or applied.

27. Arthur Danto, *The Transfiguration of the Commonplace* (Cambridge, Massachusetts: Harvard University Press, 1983), 146. So taken is Danto by the problems posed by Duchamp's readymades that he considers the issue of discriminating between indiscernibles belonging to different (but not natural) kinds as a paradigm of a distinctively philosophical problem. See also Danto's "Philosophy as/and/of Literature" and "Philosophizing Literature" in *The Philosophical Disenfranchisement of Art* (New York: Columbia University Press, 1986), 151f. and 170–73.

28. *The Transfiguration of the Commonplace*, 176–89.

sometimes even forcing us, to see the world through the artist's sensibility. It is as though the artist not only *uses* but *mentions* some medium. This intensional structure is obviously more than meets, indeed, more than can meet the eye, since what meets the eye may have look-alikes that are not artworks (e.g., Duchamp's *Fountain* and one of Mott Works's urinals, both of 1917). In short, "Only in relationship to an interpretation is a material object an artwork, . . ."[29]

Extending his notion of basic actions to Schopenhauer's definition of style as "the physiognomy of the soul," Danto construes style as the artist's spontaneous ability of enabling us to see his way of seeing the world, thus at the same time permitting us a glimpse of the artist's soul from the outside. In contrast to a manner that might be learned or a fashion that might be discarded, style is a gift, indissociable from the artist's identity. The artwork itself, by this account, is always metaphorical and rhetorical, presenting *a* as *b* so as to cause us to take a certain attitude and have certain emotions toward *a*.[30] "To understand the artwork is to grasp the metaphor that is, I think, always there."[31] Understanding the metaphor and being suitably moved are, to be sure, historically conditioned by the knowledge and moral sensibility of artist and audience. Yet, whether appreciated or not, artworks thus express something about the content they represent, even when the perceivable content they represent is identical to the content of some nonartwork. *A,* the content or subject, retains its identity but is *transfigured.*

Ironically, just as Christ's Transfiguration prefigures his end (ἔξο-δος) and glorification (and ours if we are faithful),[32] so modern art's transfiguration of the commonplace signals the exodus of art from culture. What Danto calls "the end of art" does not mean the end of artmaking, but rather the end of the idea of art. With its readymades and Brillo boxes, art has turned to itself for its content and, in the process, become philosophy. Or, at least, according to Danto, this development has confirmed the Hegelian model of art's history culminating in art's absorption into the self-questioning and self-under-

29. "Appreciation and Interpretation" in *The Philosophical Disenfranchisement of Art,* 39.

30. "The Disenfranchisement of Art" and "Language, Art, Culture, Text" in *The Philosophical Disenfranchisement of Art,* 21 and 79.

31. *The Transfiguration of the Commonplace,* 172; see also "Philosophy as/and/of Literature" in *The Philosophical Disenfranchisement of Art,* 154–56 where Danto elaborates how the text becomes a metaphor for the reader.

32. See St. Anselm's comment on the Transfiguration: "suam suorumque glorificationem praemonstravit," cited by Arthur Michael Ramsey, *The Glory of God and the Transfiguration of Christ* (London: Longmans, 1949), 119. See also Thomas Aquinas, *Summa Theologiae,* Tertia Pars, quaestio 45.

standing proper to philosophy. On this view, Danto notes, art has a history (its advantage over the "all too thin" theory of art as expression) though not a history of representational progress (abandoned by painters themselves in the face of the novel technology of narrative cinema).[33]

Danto's use of the term *transfiguration* is intriguing, especially for the theme of the current essay, yet the metaphor limps in decisive respects. After all, Christ's Transfiguration (μετεμορφώθη) on the mountain was itself a change in his appearance, not his essence or nature (Matt. 17.2; Mark 9.2–3), while Danto's conception of artworks as transfigurations is designed to countenance artworks whose appearance at least may be no different from the appearance of counterparts that are not artworks. Danto speaks of transfiguring, not only in regard to the artworks themselves, but also in regard to the experience of art. But here, too, the notion of "transfiguration" is hardly apt. The greatest metaphors of art, Danto maintains, are those in which the spectator identifies with the character represented, thus seeing his or her life through the sensibility of the artist or at least through the lens provided by the artwork; in short, "where the artwork becomes a metaphor of life and life is transfigured."[34] In the experience of such great metaphors of art, however, insofar as that transference or identification takes place (and "you cannot altogether separate from your identity your beliefs about what that identity is"), the spectator or listener is, unlike Christ on the mountain, transformed and not merely transfigured.[35]

These breakdowns in Danto's appeal to the significance of "transfiguration"—his metaphor for art as metaphor—are telling, but secondary. Certainly the validity of his philosophy of art-as-metaphor does not turn on the use or abuse of the term "transfiguration."[36] Yet there is another and perhaps more telling ambiguity to Danto's pro-

33. "The End of Art" and "Art and Disturbation" in *The Philosophical Disenfranchisement of Art*, 86–99 and 117–18.

34. See note 31. Scripture scholars suggest that the term *metemorphōthē* does not appear in the third account of the Transfiguration (Luke 9:28–36) precisely because it suggests the pagan doctrine of gods changing into men.

35. In one sense, however, Danto's use of the "transfiguration"-metaphor might be pressed. The Transfiguration has been traditionally interpreted as prefiguring the glorification of Christ and his faithful (see note 32). Thus, those faithful who participate in the mystery of the Transfiguration are transformed.

36. Several aspects of Danto's splendid analyses, nevertheless, beg for clarification. His study thrives principally on examples drawn from the pictorial and literary arts, leaving a host of questions about the musical arts. Also requiring extensive emendation is the matter of the relation between expressive and aesthetic predicates. Above all, the role of the artist's creativity and intentions in the constitution of the artwork's identity is only tenuously sketched in some brief remarks about style.

vocatively rich reflections. At the conclusion of "The End of Art," Danto laments the pluralism ("... you can cut out paper dolls or do what you damned please. The age of pluralism is upon us. ...") that a postmodern world takes for happiness.[37] Art no longer exists, that is to say, art that makes a statement and a difference, since the (end)point of art, graphically demonstrated by the twentieth century, has been to fold over into philosophy. Just as there have always been servile arts, posthistorical artmaking will go on, but, like any true missionary, art has put itself out of a job.

This is pretty heady stuff, with implications vitiating the claims about the religion of art, advanced in the course of this paper. There can hardly be a genuine religion of art, if we have indeed come to an art-less age. Of course, if art gives way to philosophy, perhaps the proper inference is that a religion of art gives way to a religion of philosophy.

However, before jumping to such speculative conclusions, it is important to ask what the lamented pluralism of an artless age is and, perhaps more significantly, why Danto decries it. The age is not pluralist by virtue of the thinness of the theory of art-as-expression, since according to Danto the discontinuities of twentieth-century art have overtaken or, rather, deconstructed the aesthetics of Croce and Collingwood. Nor is it pluralist by virtue of the conceptual indeterminacy of 'art' (à la Weitz), given Danto's claim that "relationship to an interpretation" is a necessary condition for a material object's being an artwork.[38] Rather the pluralism Danto finds repugnant is the pluralism of an artless age "when one direction is as good as another," when it does not matter what form artmaking takes, since art has evolved to make itself its own content or subject-matter. Art no longer has a point, since its own evolution confirms that it was trying to be philosophy all along. Wistful nostalgia for the heady days of history-making art explains Danto's discomfort with posthistorical (postart) pluralism.

Elaborating this end of art in the course of essays the purported aim of which is to contest the political metaphysics that, since Plato,

37. "The End of Art" in *The Philosophical Disenfranchisement of Art*, 114–15; see also "Art, Evolution, and History" in *The Philosophical Disenfranchisement of Art*, 210 where Danto styles himself the "prophet" of the philosophers who can give us the philosophy that art has prepared us for.

38. "Appreciation and Interpretation" in *The Philosophical Disenfranchisement of Art*, 39. At the conclusion of "Art, Evolution, and History," however, Danto does suggest that the pluralism takes its stimulus "from the dizzying array of cases." Precisely in this situation the historical end of art makes a universal definition of art possible. Not, of course, that Danto offers one; he is, as he puts it, merely its prophet. See *The Philosophical Disenfranchisement of Art*, 209–10.

have contributed to the disenfranchising, the insubstantiating of art, is, to say the least, cheekily ironic.[39] Hegel's model of art's historical significance is hardly an anomaly to the warfare Danto otherwise sees being waged between philosophy and art. "*Aber die schöne Kunst ist nur eine Befreiungs-Stufe, nicht die höchste Befreiung selbst.*"[40] Indeed, if Danto's thesis holds, and work like Duchamp's confirms Hegel's vision, then philosophy has finally won, the enemy having apparently capitulated with the discovery, not only that its tactics are outmoded and its weaponry no match for philosophy, but that, after all, it shares with philosophy a common foe: the darkness of self-ignorance. Danto is, of course, not unaware of the irony of his discussion, yet he leaves it unaddressed, as though it were a brute and brutal fact that the prophet must cry out in the wilderness.[41]

If there is no sustainable alternative to Danto's thesis about the end of art, then I am wrong about the religion of art. Just as art replaces religion, the religious experience becoming an artistic experience, so philosophy replaces art and the thesis about the religion of art must be revised into a thesis about the religion of philosophy. Yet philosophy, even a postmodern, postart philosophy, can no more replace religion than can science, as noted at the beginning of this paper.[42] Moreover, there is a reasonable alternative to Danto's philosophy of art and art's history, an alternative capable of countenancing the developments of twentieth-century art without succumbing to its pluralism and without surrendering art to philosophy. This alternative, furthermore, sustains the thesis of the religion of art by explaining why art, as Kandinsky stressed, is "the mother of our feelings."[43]

---

39. "The Philosophical Disenfranchisement of Art" and "Philosophizing Literature" in *The Philosophical Disenfranchisement of Art*, 4f. and 169.

40. G. W. F. Hegel, *Enzyklopädie der philosophischen Wissenschaften im Grundrisse* (1830), ed. F. Nicolin and Otto Pöggeler (Hamburg: Meiner, 1969), no. 562, Zusatz, 445.

41. "The Philosophical Disenfranchisement of Art" in *The Philosophical Disenfranchisement of Art*, 16f.

42. Indeed, since Danto takes up Hegel's model, it is noteworthy that in the *Enzyklopädie* art and religion remain timelessly necessary forms of absolute spirit, that is to say, neither is eliminated or displaced by philosophy. To be sure, since philosophy is superior, the possibility of bad faith in the practice of art and religion may seem inevitable. What sort of Lutheran was or even could Hegel have been?

43. Kandinsky, *über das Geistige in der Kunst*, 10. Auflage, with an introduction by Max Bill (Bern: Benteli, 1952), 21: "Jedes Kunstwerk ist Kind seiner Zeit, oft ist es Mutter unserer Gefühle." Reflecting on "the mission for art projected by Kandinsky's essay on spirituality," Danto writes: "It was an era whose chief artistic product, I believe, was the manifesto. And if I may bite conjecturally the hand that feeds me, the thesis that art is a means, even *the* means, to the further evolution of humanity belongs to this stage of thought." See "Art, Evolution, and History" in *The Philosophical Disenfranchisement of Art*, 208.

III

What is striking about Danto's conception of art is its close affinity, at least in outline, with that of romantics and idealists. "Transfiguration of the commonplace" sounds like a gloss on Novalis's explanation of what it means to "romanticize": namely "to give a higher significance to the commonplace, an appearance of mystery to the ordinary, the dignity of the unknown to the familiar, the semblance of infinity to the finite."[44] Like the romantics, Danto concedes that the rhetorical intentions of the artist may be unconscious and that historicity informs the artwork, from the standpoint both of the artist and of the spectator. Danto's conception of style as the spontaneous externalization of the artist's soul, as already noted, is indebted to Schopenhauer. Most contemporary philosophers of art (Danto is no exception) follow the romantics and idealists in criticizing the mimetic theory of art, that is the view that art is to be conceived primarily as an imitation of nature's appearances.[45]

Yet lying at the center of the romantic conception of art, including its rejection of the mimetic theory, is a conception of the creativity of the artist in relation to the artwork, a dimension that Paul Weiss has repeatedly chastised contemporary philosophy of art for ignoring. Romantics criticize the mimetic theory as though an artwork contained nothing that might not be able to be encountered in nature as such, that is to say, the nature that is the object of theory, science, technology. Artworks embody precisely what cannot be so encountered, namely, the consciousness of the artist. The artwork takes the form of an object, to be sure, but only by virtue of the creativity of the artist. An artwork is thus above all an objectification of pure subjectivity or consciousness. Or, to put it differently: for both romantics and idealists the mimetic theory is decisively overcome only when art makes itself its object, a line of reasoning foreshadowing efforts by contemporary artists to put art itself in question.[46] Other similarities to Danto's view of style and to his account of an artwork as an attempt to cause us to see the world through the artist's sensibility are patent. But for the romantics and the idealists the result is more than a shift

44. "Romantisieren heißt, dem Gemeinen einen hohen Sinn, dem Gewöhnlichen ein geheimnisvolles Ansehen, dem Bekannten die Würde des Unbekannten, dem Endlichen einen unendlichen Schein geben." Cited in Fritz Martini, *Deutsche Literaturgeschichte*, 17th, expanded edition (Stuttgart: Kröner, 1977), 319.

45. For a concise statement of idealist aesthetics, see Dieter Henrich, "Kunst und Natur in der idealistischen Ästhetik" in *Nachahmung und Illusion*, ed. H. R. Jauß (München: Eidos, 1964), 128–34.

46. See Henrich, "Kunst und Natur," 130.

in one's point of view or course of action, and there is something else at work in addition to the artist's style and rhetorical skill. The creative unity of the subject and the object in the artwork is a theophany and, in a post-Enlightenment age, the event of a new religion of art, replacing traditional religion and, in a certain sense, even traditional philosophy.

Thus, the young Hegel in 1796 penned the following lines: "I am now convinced that the highest act of Reason, the one through which it encompasses all Ideas, is an aesthetic act, and that *truth and goodness only become sisters in beauty*—the philosopher must possess just as much aesthetic power as the poet. . . . Poetry gains thereby a higher dignity; she becomes at the end, once more, what she was in the beginning—the *teacher of mankind*; . . . Thus in the end enlightened and unenlightened must clasp hands, mythology must become philosophical in order to make the people rational, and philosophy must become mythological in order to make the philosophers sensible. . . . A higher spirit sent from heaven must found this new religion among us; it will be the last and greatest work of mankind."[47] This youthful outburst is certainly not to be identified in every respect with Hegel's mature views. There are even those who argue that these words were dictated to Hegel by Hölderlin or Schelling. Nevertheless, these remarks testify to an insight Hegel shared with many of his contemporaries and, in a certain sense, never relinquished: namely the primacy of an aesthetic way of knowing, at least in relation to the scientific rationality elaborated by the Enlightenment.[48] This insight in fact formally reverses Baumgarten's original characterization of "aesthetics" as the science of the subordinate or inferior cognitive faculties.[49] Moreover, aesthetics for Hegel, in contrast to Baumgarten and to Kant, is identical to philosophy of art, thus underlining the priority of art and the aesthetic. This view, not to be found in any of the mature works of Hegel, is formally adopted by Schelling at least during the year 1800. For Schelling aesthetic production is "the first principle of philosophy,"

47. See "Das älteste Systemprogramm des deutschen Idealismus (1796 oder 1797)" in G. W. F. Hegel, *Frühe Schriften, Werke* I (Frankfurt am Main: Suhrkamp, 1971), 234–36.

48. Cf. Fritz Martini, *Deutsche Literaturgeschichte* (Stuttgart: Kröner, 1977), 319: "Friedrich Schlegel bezeichnete als den Anfang der Poesie, 'den Gang und die Gesetze der vernünftig denkenden Vernunft aufzuheben und uns wieder in die schöne Verwirrung der Phantasie, in das ursprüngliche Chaos der menschlichen Natur zu versetzen.'"

49. It should be noted, however, that Baumgarten does not appear to have considered this science of the inferior cognitive faculties to be itself inferior to logic and the sciences of the higher cognitive faculties (see especially Baumgarten's *Aesthetica*, No. 1; *Metaphysica*, No. 533).

philosophy's "only true and eternal organon," "because it opens up to the philosopher as it were the all holy, where . . . there as it were burns in a single flame what is severed in nature and history."[50]

Proceeding from the premise that all knowing rests upon the agreement of something objective with something subjective, Schelling maintains that the chief task of philosophy is to explain this agreement, which is nothing short of truth itself. This agreement can be explained by beginning with the objective in general—the philosophy of nature—or with the subjective in general—transcendental philosophy. Transcendental philosophy divides in turn into two disciplines, theoretical and practical philosophy, explaining how our thoughts can correspond to things and how things can correspond to our thoughts or, better, our designs and willings. These two disciplines lead, however, to an impasse. Theoretical philosophy demands subjection to what is objective, practical philosophy, the subjection of the objective world to the demands of free subjects. "The contradiction must be resolved, if there is to be a philosophy at all," Schelling insists, adding that this "supreme task of transcendental philosophy" can be resolved neither in theoretical nor in practical philosophy, but in some "higher" philosophy. That higher philosophy is the philosophy of art. *Art alone* reveals the absolute, the identity between the activity producing the objective world and the activity expressing itself in human willing.[51] the youthful Schelling's philosophy of art thus stands as a monumental counterinstance to Danto's claim that philosophy historically has alternated between defusing art and "treating it as doing what philosophy itself does, only uncouthly."[52] For Schelling, philosophy does not disenfranchise art; it is rather art that enfranchises philosophy.

In order to see how Schelling comes to his conclusion it is necessary to review briefly the principle on which Schelling's argument in *System des transzendentalen Idealismus* rests. That principle is a postulate, the

50. F. W. J. Schelling, *System des transzendentalen Idealismus* (1800), with an introduction by Walter Schulz (Hamburg: Meiner, 1957), S. 297: "Wenn die ästhetische Anschauung nur die objektiv gewordene transzendentale ist, so versteht sich von selbst, daß die Kunst das einzige wahre und ewige Organon zugleich und Dokument der Philosophie sei, welches immer und fortwährend aufs neue beurkundet, was die Philosophie äußerlich nicht darstellen kann, nämlich das Bewußtlose im Handeln und Produzieren, und seine ursprüngliche Identität mit dem Bewußten. Die Kunst ist eben deswegen dem Philosophen das Höchste, weil sie ihm das Allerheiligste gleichsam öffnet, wo in ewiger und ursprünglicher Vereinigung gleichsam in Einer Flamme brennt, was in der Natur und Geschichte gesondert ist, und was im Leben und Handeln ebenso wie im Denken ewig sich fliehen muß."

51. *System des transzendentalen Idealismus*, 15–16.

52. "The Philosophical Disenfranchisement of Art" and "Philosophizing Literature" in *The Philosophical Disenfranchisement of Art*, 7, 16, and 165–66.

requirement to think of oneself thinking. This act of self-consciousness, which is supposed to be a pure consciousness not to be confused with any empirical consciousness, yields an absolute and immediate identity of myself as subject and object, form and content, consciousness and being. This self-consciousness is produced in the very act by which it is known. "The *I itself* is an object, which exists *because it knows of itself.*"[53] Self-consciousness in no sense exists prior to this act of thinking; it is no thing, no fact, and is objective only for itself. Indeed, there is no normal sense in which it would be appropriate to say that this self-consciousness exists. Because of its unusual character, and because it is no thing and yet is presupposed in knowing any thing, this principle can be known only in a way completely different from the common way of knowing, that is to say, from conceptual and judgmental ways of knowing. Self-consciousness requires an intellectual intuition.

Yet because it is not part of the objective world as such, the identity of subject and object in self-consciousness is only subjective. An intellectual intuition is a strictly private affair. As such it is hardly capable of explaining how we can to some extent know and influence things other than ourselves. The purely speculative solution to these first questions of philosophy is nominally given in the intellectual intuition of self-consciousness, but these questions are answered objectively only by art. "The universally recognized and indisputable object of the intellectual intuition is art itself. For the aesthetic intuition precisely is the intellectual intuition that has become objective. The artwork alone reflects me, what otherwise is reflected by nothing, that absolute identity, which even in the I has already severed itself."[54] As Danto has already ably shown, the idealist model of art-as-self-referential seems particularly well suited for understanding much of twentieth-century art. On the youthful Schelling's rendition, however, art cannot come to an end by becoming philosophy, since there is no philosophy without art. To paraphrase Kant, interpretations without intuitions are empty.

The artwork shares with other artifacts the fact that it is produced freely and consciously while at the same time, as with natural objects, there is something decisively unconscious about their genesis. This juxtaposition of nature and freedom with the conscious and the unconscious reworks conclusions reached by Kant. Nature proceeds unconsciously according to mechanical laws and at most the organic

---

53. *System des transzendentalen Idealismus,* 37.
54. *System des transzendentalen Idealismus,* 294–95.

products of nature must be construed as if they were based upon some conscious, purposive activity. Freedom is, on the other hand, a conscious, purposive activity, yet striving for a moral self-determination that remains an endless task, never completely achievable. In art, however, in the artwork as well as in the making, consciousness and unconsciousness, human freedom and the natural order, unite uniquely and inextricably.

What, furthermore, unites freedom and nature in art can be attributed neither to the individual nor to nature but, as Schelling notes, to "the freely bestowed favor of a higher nature": the absolute. This absolute is not known through arguments; nor is it something simply present in consciousness. The absolute reveals itself, and its revelation takes place in a fundamental way in art. For the artist or, more exactly, for the genius, the absolute is what fate is for us as moral agents, "an obscure, unknown power," completing and perfecting. "Just as the fated man carries out not what he wants or intends but what he must carry out by virtue of some incomprehensible fate, under whose influence he stands, so the artist, however deliberate he may be, nevertheless, in regard to what is really objective in his work, appears to stand under the influence of a power that separates him from all other men and forces him to articulate and to exhibit things that he does not fully see through and whose meaning is endless."[55] The absolute thus exhibits itself in the artwork as the overcoming of a contradiction, emotionally felt even when less than clearly understood by the artist.

IV

It is not possible here to elaborate further on Schelling's account of art. The account can only be suitably understood within the context of the grand project of German Idealism to solve the post-Kantian problem of epistemic and ethical scepticism by construing Kant's supreme transcendental principle of self-consciousness as an absolute ontological principle of nature and morality.[56] Certainly, the project strikes us today as exotic and, in the wake of the anti-Cartesian polemics of Heidegger and Wittgenstein, its appeal to consciousness or subjectivity perhaps even wrong headed. Schelling himself later mod-

55. *System des transzendentalen Idealismus*, 284; 286. At least in emphasis, Danto's account seems to overlook this necessity of looking beyond the intentionality or subjectivity (style) of the artist. (Is this due to a deeper reading of Sartre than of Heidegger?)

56. See, for example, "Verhältniß des Skepticismus zur Philosophie" in *Kritisches Journal der Philosophie* in G. W. F. Hegel, *Jenaer Kritische Schriften*, ed. Buchner and Pöggeler (Hamburg: Meiner, 1968), 235f.

ifies the bold claims he makes for art in relation to philosophy. Nevertheless, for all his speculative excess, Schelling gives us an insight into something missing in the careful analyses offered by much contemporary philosophy of art: the dynamics of that creativity that expresses itself in the artwork, that overcomes artist and public. Only appeal to some such creative power explains the religious character of art—for the artist and for the public—and only by explaining the religion of art can the identity of art be explained.

The emotional hold over the artist is the way the artist knows the creative power of something absolute. It is a distinctive kind of knowing, an emotional knowledge with a seductive clarity that heaves forward and shrinks back in the execution; knowledge neither by acquaintance nor by understanding, but knowledge through intimacy. Beyond the limits of science as defined by Aristotle and Kant, through intimacy the individual and the inner sense shed their opacity. But the condition of the possibility of intimacy is creativity. For all its spontaneity, intimate knowledge takes time and discipline, requires taking risks and taking care; if anything, it fuses style and manner; the artist lets himself or herself go, surrenders, but in devotion to the constraints of paint or clay, words or notes, attendant, waiting for the response only the medium can provide. To be sure, in this emotional surrender the artist forgets himself or herself, and it is appropriate, with Danto, to say that the artist's style is in a certain respect unconscious to the artist himself. Yet the intimacy just as surely heightens the artist's awareness of himself and his style, his groping toward a unity that is more than his individuality or his style, and creatively beckons him to paint or compose. This emotional knowledge is expressed in the artwork, but then it hardly suffices to say that it is an expression of the artist's subjectivity or style—any more than it would to say intimacy is a private accomplishment. It is not the artist, the artist's style or the artist's genius, that constitutes creativity; it is creativity that constitutes the artist.

When we are moved to draw or compose, sing or dance, we interrupt time in time, capturing for a time more or less successfully what moves us even as it moves on. When this happens, we are artists and not manufacturers or drones. There are, finally, no artworks without artists. Artworks themselves are our children, having our likenesses and genetic makeup, bearing the imprint of our styles, but also having their own fate, their own meaning, their own reality. They tell us about ourselves, about our finitude, and they reveal our dependence on a creative power transcending our dreams and deeds.

Contributors

John Barnett Brough is a professor in the Department of Philosophy at Georgetown University in Washington, D.C. He received his doctorate from Georgetown in 1970 and has been a member of the faculty there since 1966. He was awarded an NEH Research Fellowship in 1981. Most of Professor Brough's publications have dealt with themes in Husserlian phenomenology, particularly with issues involving time, the consciousness of time, perception, and aesthetics. His "Art and Artworld: Some Ideas for a Husserlian Aesthetic" appeared in *Edmund Husserl and the Phenomenological Tradition*, published by The Catholic University of America Press in 1988. He recently translated volume 10 in the *Husserliana* series, which is devoted to Husserl's writings on time-consciousness from 1893 to 1917.

Ted Cohen is a professor in the Department of Philosophy and a member of the Committee on General Studies in the Humanities and the Committee on Art & Design at the University of Chicago, a faculty he joined in 1967 after completing his graduate studies at Harvard University. In 1983 Professor Cohen received the Quantrell Award for Excellence in Undergraduate Teaching at the University of Chicago and, during 1986–87, he was the William R. Kenan, Jr., Distinguished Visiting Professor of the Humanities at The College of William and Mary. A co-editor and contributor to *Essays in Kant's Aesthetics* (1982), Professor Cohen is well known for frequently anthologized essays on taste, metaphor, and the possibility of art, as well as for more recent studies of jokes, photography, and sports.

William James Desmond is a professor of philosophy and chair of the Department of Philosophy at Loyola College, Baltimore, Maryland, where he joined the faculty in 1982, after completing his doctoral studies at Pennsylvania State University. His principal publications include: *Art and the Absolute: A Study of Hegel's Aesthetics* in 1986, *Desire, Dialectic and Otherness: An Essay on Origins* in 1987, and *Philosophy and its Others: Ways of Being and Mind* in 1990. Professor Desmond is currently serving as General Editor of the SUNY Series in Hegelian Studies.

Karsten Harries received his Ph.D. from Yale University in 1962. After teaching at Yale, the University of Texas, and the University of Bonn, he returned to Yale in 1966, where he is now Mellon Professor of Philosophy. A former Guggenheim fellow, he is the author of *The Meaning of Modern Art, The Bavarian Rococo Church, Between Faith and Aestheticism,* and *The Broken Frame: Three Lectures.* In addition he has written many articles and reviews, where Heidegger's thought, early modern philosophy, and the philosophy of architecture have been areas of special interest. He is currently at work on a book with the provisional title, *The Ethical Function of Architecture.*

Walter Hinderer has been a professor of German at Princeton University since 1978. Professor Hinderer, who received his Ph.D. at the University of Munich in 1960, was an Institute for Research in the Humanities Fellow, University of Wisconsin, in 1976–77, a Deutsche Akademische Austauschdienst Research Fellow in 1984, and a Fellow of the Institute for Advanced Study, Berlin, 1985–86. In addition to numerous articles, books authored by Professor Hinderer include: *Elemente der Literaturkritik* in 1976, *Büchner Kommentar zum dichterischen Werk* in 1977, *Geschichte der Politischen Lyrik in Deutschland* in 1978, *Der Mensch in der Geschichte: Versuch über Schillers Wallenstein* in 1980, *Über Deutsche Literatur und Rede* in 1981, and *Geschichte der Deutschen Lyrik vom Mittelalter bis zur Gegenwart* in 1982. He has also edited volumes on the plays of Schiller, Goethe, Kleist, and Brecht and is responsible for English editions of Kleist, Schiller, and Büchner.

Francis J. Kovach is professor emeritus of philosophy at the University of Oklahoma, where he joined the faculty in 1964. After predoctoral studies at the Pázmány Péter University, Budapest, Hungary, and one year of doctoral studies, he received his Ph.D. in philosophy *summa cum laude* from the Albertus Magnus University of Cologne, West Germany. Professor Kovach represented the American Council of Learned Societies with an award-winning essay at the Fifth International Congress of Aesthetics, in Amsterdam, 1964, and acted as chairman at the fourth plenary session of the Third International Scotistic Congress, in Vienna, 1970. An editorial consultant for *The New Scholasticism* and *The Journal of the History of Philosophy,* Professor Kovach is the author of numerous articles and three books, including *Scholastic Challenges to Some Mediaeval and Modern Ideas* in 1987.

Joseph Margolis received the Ph.D. in philosophy at Columbia University in 1953 and has been professor of philosophy at Temple University in Philadelphia since 1968. The recipient of awards from the Fulbright Commission, the National Institute for Mental Health, the center for Dewey Studies, and the National Endowment for the Humanities, Professor Margolis has also served as president of the American Society for Aesthetics. His principal publications include *Art and Philosophy* in 1980, *Culture and Cultural Entities* in 1984, *Philosophy of Psychology* in 1984, and a systematic three-volume work, *The Persistence of Reality* (1986, 1987, 1989), for which a fourth volume is pending.

Thomas Prufer is an associate professor at The Catholic University of America, Washington, D.C. He joined its faculty in 1960 after receiving his doctorate from the University of Munich. He has received a scholarship from the German Academic Exchange Program and the Harbison Award for Distinguished Teaching from the Danforth Foundation. He has published articles on Plato, Aristotle, Augustine, Hume, Husserl, and Heidegger.

Kenneth Schmitz is Professor Emeritus of Philosophy and Fellow of Trinity College in the University of Toronto, where he received his Ph.D. in philosophy in 1952. The recipient of Humboldt grants and a Canada Council Research Grant, Professor Schmitz has also been President of the Hegel Society of America, the Metaphysical Society of America, and the American Catholic Philosophical Association. His numerous publications have focussed on the philosophies of Kant and Hegel, the philosophy of religion, aesthetics, and philosophical issues in theology. His essay "Why Philosophy Must Have a History: Hegel's Proposal" appears in *Doing Philosophy Historically,* recently published by SUNY Press. In 1988 Professor Schmitz was awarded the Aquinas Medal by the University of Dallas.

Paul Weiss took up his current position as the Heffer Professor of Philosophy at The Catholic University of America in 1969, after becoming an emeritus professor at Yale University, an institution he joined in 1945. Dr. Weiss received his Ph.D. at Harvard University in 1929, having written his doctoral dissertation under Alfred North Whitehead. A former Guggenheim fellow, Dr. Weiss's first major work, *Reality,* appeared in 1938, while he was teaching at Bryn Mawr. *Modes of Being* appeared in 1958, followed by *The World of Art* and *Nine Basic Arts* in 1961. In addition to several works, including the eleven volume, philosophical/autobiographical journal, *Philosophy in Process,* begun in

1966, Professor Weiss's major publications since his arrival at The Catholic University of America include: *Beyond All Appearances* (1974), *Cinematics* (1975), *First Considerations* (1977), *You, I and the Others* (1981), *Privacy* (1983), *Toward a Perfected State* (1986), and the forthcoming *Creativity*.

Robert E. Wood is Graduate Dean, Director of the Institute of Philosophic Studies and Associate Professor of the Philosophy at the University of Dallas, Irving, Texas, where he has been teaching since 1979. He received his Ph.D. from Marquette University and has been the recipient of an NEH summer grant and a Fulbright travel grant. His principal publications include *Martin Buber's Ontology* in 1969 and *A Path Into Metaphysics: Phenomenological, Hermeneutical and Dialogical Studies* in 1990. Professor Wood has translated Stephen Strasser's *The Phenomenology of Feeling* and has recently assumed editorship of *The New Scholasticism*. He is currently working on a new book, *Approaches to Aesthetics*.

Paul Woodruff is Chair of the Department of Philosophy and Mary Helen Thompson Centennial Professor in the Humanities at The University of Texas at Austin, where he has taught since 1973. He studied at Merton College Oxford under a Marshall Scholarship, and received his Ph.D. from Princeton University. He is the author of *Plato: Hippias Major* and is the co-translator of a new edition of Plato's *Symposium*.